# Governance
# as social and political
# communication

# Governance as social and political communication

edited by
**Henrik P. Bang**

**Manchester University Press**
Manchester and New York
distributed exclusively in the USA by Palgrave

Published by Manchester University Press
Oxford Road, Manchester M13 9NR, UK
and Room 400, 175 Fifth Avenue, New York, NY 10010, USA
www.manchesteruniversitypress.co.uk

Distributed in the United States exclusively by
Palgrave Macmillan, 175 Fifth Avenue,
New York, NY 10010, USA

Distributed in Canada exclusively by
UBC Press, University of British Columbia, 2029 West Mall,
Vancouver, BC, Canada V6T 1Z2

British Library Cataloguing-in-Publication Data is available

Library of Congress Cataloging-in-Publication Data  is available
ISBN 978 0 7190 8094 4  paperback

First published by Manchester University Press in hardback 2003

This paperback edition first published 2010

Printed by Lightning Source

# Notes on the contributors

**Henrik P. Bang** was awarded his doctorate at the University of Copenhagen, where he is a senior lecturer in the Department of Political Science and Director of the Centre for Research on Democracy, Media and Steering (DEMES). He is also co-director of the state-sponsored Centre for Research on Media and Democracy in the Network Society (MODINET), at the Faculty of Humanities, University of Copenhagen, Amager. He specialises in and teaches governance theory, theories of deliberative democracy, democratic research and policy analysis. His most recent publications include *The Everyday Maker* as co-author (2000, 2001) and *Democracy from Below* as co-editor (2000).

**Mark Bevir** received his doctorate from the University of Oxford in 1989. He is now a member of the Department of Political Science at the University of California, Berkeley. His recent publications include *The Logic of the History of Ideas* (1999).

**Mitchell Dean** is Professor of Sociology and Dean of Arts and Social Sciences at Macquarie University, Sydney. Among his many works is *Governmentality: Power and Rule in Modern Society* (1999). His research interests are in security, sovereignty and the international order.

**Torben Bech Dyrberg**, MA, is political theorist and lecturer in the Department of Social Sciences at Roskilde University. His primary research interests are theories of power, democracy and political identification. His publications include *The Circular Structure of Power* (1997), articles and edited books on post-structuralist political and social theory as well as right-wing populism.

**John G. Gunnell** is Distinguished Professor of Political Science at the State University of New York, Albany. He specialises in the history and philosophy of political and social science, the history of political theory, and democratic theory. His recent work includes *The Descent of Political Theory* (1993) and *The Orders of Discourse* (1998). He is completing a book on the history of democratic theory in US political science, *Imagining and Imaging the American Polity*.

**Jens Hoff** is a senior lecturer in the Department of Political Science at the University of Copenhagen. He teaches and researches governance, democracy and information and communication technology. He was Director of the Centre for Research on Public Organisation and Management 1996–98 and Director of Studies at the Department of Political Science 1999–2000. He is chairman of a Europe-wide research network 'Government and Democracy in the Information Age' (COST Action A14). Most recently he has co-edited *Informationsteknologi, organisation og forandring* (1999), *Democratic Governance and New Technology* (2000) and *Demokrati fra neden* (2000) and co-authored *Internet og demokrati* (1999) and *Citizenship and Democracy in Scandinavia* (2001).

**Bob Jessop** is Professor of Sociology and Director of the Institute for Advanced Studies in Management and Social Sciences at Lancaster University. He is best known for his contributions to state theory, the regulation approach in political economy, the political economy of post-war Britain and theories of governance and governance failure. His publications include *The Capitalist State* (1982), *Nicos Poulantzas* (1985), *Thatcherism* (1988), *State Theory* (1990) and *The Future of the Capitalist State* (2002) as well as over 150 refereed journal articles and contributions to edited collections. He is researching the contradictions of the knowledge-based economy.

**Jan Kooiman** is professor emeritus of the Faculty of Business Administration at the Erasmus University in Rotterdam. He has been Secretary of the Labour Party in the Dutch Parliament, a deputy member of the Dutch Social and Economic Council for fifteen years, and has served on several government commissions. He is a Harkness Fellow of the Common Wealth Fund and Fellow of the Netherlands Institute for Advanced Study in the Social Sciences and Humanities. He has published on public decision making in the United States and the Netherlands, on Parliament in the Netherlands and in a European context, and on civil servants in a comparative perspective. Among recent publications are *Modern Governance* (1993), *Governance* (forthcoming) and (co-edited) *Creative Governance* (1999).

**Renate Mayntz** is professor emeritus of the Max Planck Institute for the Study of Societies, Cologne, which she established in 1985 and directed until her retirement in 1997. She has held positions at Columbia University, the New School for Social Research, New York, the University of Edinburgh, the Facultad Latino-Americana de Cienzias Sociales, Santiago de Chile, and Stanford University. She has published extensively on the subjects of macro-theory in the social sciences, policy analysis, technology research, organisations and research concerning public administration.

**Rod Rhodes** BSc, BLitt, is Professor of Political Science and Head of Program in the Research School of Social Sciences, Australian National University; Emeritus Professor of Politics at the University of Newcastle, UK; and Research Director of the Australia and New Zealand School of Government (ANZSOG). He is the author or editor of twenty books including recently *Transforming British Government Volume 1: Changing Institutions; Volume 2: Changing Roles and Relationships* (Macmillan, 2000); and (with Mark Bevir), *Interpreting British Governance* (Routledge, 2003). He has been editor of *Public Administration* since 1986. He is President of the Political Studies Association of the United Kingdom.

**Tracy B. Strong** is Professor of Political Science at the University of California, San Diego. He is the author of many articles and the author or editor of several books, including *Friedrich Nietzsche and the Politics of Transfiguration* (1975), *The Idea of Political Theory* (1990), *The Self and the Political Order* (1991), *Jean-Jacques Rousseau and the Politics of the Ordinary* (1994), (with Marcel Henaff) *Democracy and the Many* (2000) and (edited with Richard Madsen) *Ethical Pluralism in Contemporary Perspective* (forthcoming). From 1990 until 2000 he was editor of *Political Theory*.

**David L. Swartz** is visiting assistant professor at Boston University, where he teaches in the Department of Sociology and in the Social Sciences division of the core curriculum. He is the author of *Culture and Power* (1997) and book review editor of *Theory and Society*. Professor Swartz's research interests include the study of elites and stratification (particularly in the areas of non-profit organisations), education, culture, religion and social theory.

# Introduction

This book is the result of several years of ongoing discussions in various seminars and conferences staged in Copenhagen by the Centre for Research in Public Organisation and Management (COS). The Centre served for many years as both a national network for PhD education in governance research and a platform for interdisciplinary and multi-institutional research projects. It was run in collaboration by all political science departments in Denmark. COS has now changed into the Danish Postgraduate School of Political Science. The various special projects and PhD educational networks established around the study of governance in the 'old' COS have been handed over to my new Centre for Democracy and Media Studies (DEMES, www.demes.dk) in the Department of Political Science at the University of Copenhagen. DEMES is a part of a new 'joint venture' between the humanities and the social sciences in a nationwide research project, Media and Democracy in the Network Society (MODINET, www.modinet.dk). MODINET is sponsored by the Danish government and is located in the Department of Film and Media Studies at the University of Copenhagen.

The book is dedicated to all those who have been involved in the running of COS under my directorship, whether as students, researchers or employees, who through their various efforts have helped to lay the foundation of the theoretical perspective on governance presented here. The governance discussion at COS continues today at DEMES, which includes among other things a Nordic Governance Network of researchers from twelve Nordic universities. It is centred on two broad issues. (1) Can there be a history of governance as a conception of rule in modern society? (2) Can there be a theory of governance, as a set of approaches which can do something for the study of politics (process), policy (content) and polity (structure) substantially different from what could be done without them?

In this volume we are basically concerned with the theoretical dimension and will leave the more historical or genealogical discussion for a future volume. What is of special concern in this book is the question of how to approach the connection between steering and the practice of freedom in a high modern world, where everyday life is growing increasingly complex, dynamic and differentiated, and where the globalisation and localisation of power relations are putting increasing pressures on the state as the 'natural' centre of ruling the nation (Rhodes 1997; Bang *et al.* 2000; Heffen *et al.* 2000; Pierre 2000; Stoker 2000).

Broadly following Newman (2001: 24), one may summarise the literature on governance as involving:

1 A move away from hierarchy, competition and solidarity as alternative models for delivering services towards networks, teams and partnerships traversing the public, private and voluntary sectors.
2 A recognition of the blurring of boundaries between public and private, state and civil society, and national and international and thereby also of responsibilities for handling political, social and economic issues.
3 The recognition and incorporation of issue networks and policy networks into processes of governing.
4 The replacement of traditional modes of hierarchical control and command by 'governing at a distance'.
5 The development of more reflexive and responsive policy tools.
6 The role of government shifting to a focus on providing leadership, building partnerships, steering and co-ordinating, and providing system-wide integration and regulation.
7 The emergence of 'negotiated self-governance' in communities, cities and regions, based on new practices of co-ordinating activities through networks and partnerships.
8 The opening-up of decision-making to greater participation by the public.
9 Innovations in democratic practice as a response to the problem of the complexity and fragmentation of authority, and the challenges this presents to traditional democratic models.
10 A broadening of focus by government beyond institutional concerns to encompass the involvement of civil society in the process of governance.

All ten points may be said to involve a communicative turn of political analysis. However, they comprise only the multiple new ways in which 'the system' is entering into communicative relations with its members and environments to cope successfully with the vast increases in complexity, dynamics and difference in high modern society. However, in this book we suggest that governance has to be considered from the vantage points of lay people in a political community too. This will broaden the notion of governance still further to include how lay people and civil society create new identities and new forms of self- and co-governance which are put to use in expanding their own autonomy and common understandings as members of a political community.

# 1

# Governance as political communication

Henrik P. Bang

Many definitions of and approaches to governance will be presented in this book. I simply localise governance within the terrain of political authority as a communicative relationship, which is not merely or primarily hierarchical, and which can take effect in society only through the practical knowledgeabilities and capabilities of ordinary individuals (Easton 1953; Foucault 1994). A new realm of politics and democracy thus appears in the shape of an interactive politics of presence and becoming in which political power is as intrinsic to effectiveness, order, autonomy and solidarity as are meaning and norms (Andersen *et al.* 2000; Bang *et al.* 2000; Heffen *et al.* 2000).

Just as governance, as a communicative relationship, indicates that political power does not always hinder or constrain but can also facilitate or enable, so it simultaneously makes it obvious that there could be no freedom or equality in society outside the exercise of political power. In governance, therefore, empowering and ruling together with lay people and civil society in dialogical and co-operative relationships become a new criterion for success. In the same fashion governance can fertilise the ground for new, moral practices in society, where the exercise of political freedom is experienced by every individual, as an existential and ethical project linked with the pursuit of identity (Bauman 2001; Castells 1997; Hutton and Giddens 2001).

We need a conception of the political which renders it distinct that there can be no autonomy or solidarity in society without practices of political power (Rabinow 1994). Political power is everywhere in society, which means that freedom is always a freedom within relations of power. A practice void of political power would simultaneously be one void of the practice of freedom.

Hence the terrain of the political is not to be identified by the terrain of the modern centralised state. Hierarchy may be necessary to protect and develop the rights and liberties provided by a democratic regime, but it can never guarantee the practice of political freedom in an autonomous political community (Bang 1998). This requires another kind of authority, namely one that does not only command and say no! A more interactive, negotiable, dialogical and facilitative authority is here needed to help people in governing themselves.

We employ a notion of political society to suggest the possibility of abstracting from the whole of concrete interrelated societal activity an aspect which we can identify as political (Easton 1965a: 38). Political society is claimed to go far beyond the power of a group of institutions and mechanisms that ensures the subservience of the citizens of a given state (cf. Foucault 1990: 92). It identifies a function or web of interrelated activity in and through which values are allocated authoritatively for groups of people, populating certain fields or territories and/or sharing in the solving of their common concerns (Bang 1998; Easton 1953: 143).

The concept of political society does not link with any specific circumstances such as the state or government in their many irreducible, historical forms. Political society comprises all those processes of authoritative decision and action that go on within its domain or terrain, which frames the play of difference. It concerns every activity, however remotely related to differences and struggles over the making and implementing of decisions that require acceptance and recognition if they are to be settled or to reach a desired purpose or outcome. It cuts across the spheres of state and civil society, system and life world, national and international, and global and local. Political society is everywhere as a dimension of what is going on within any socially constructed domain.

### Epistemological and ontological presuppositions

By regarding political society as socially constructed, and societal theories as part of their own 'object', we are signalling that our common epistemological presupposition in this book is that order or unity in society is not naturally given but reflects a problem of self-reference (Luhmann 1995). That is to say, any social or theoretical order or unity is established from disorder and plurality; it can be established only 'autopoietically', from its own communicative vantage point or presupposition. 'There is no other possibility of seeing unity in plurality, of synthesising a multiplicity, of reducing complexity to unity and thereby regulating complexity' (Luhmann 1995: 483). Studying governance simply requires one to assume such an anti-essentialist epistemological stance. 'Autopoiesis is a recursive, therefore symmetrical, and therefore non-hierarchical occurrence. All regulation is itself regulated; all controls are themselves controlled' (ibid.). This is exactly what governance as social and political theory is all about. We believe that at the heart of governance analysis is the idea that knowledge and power are non-hierarchically intertwined qualities that emerge out of a recursive and interactive covering inside a given terrain, field, system or community.

Governance consequently breaks with the modern view of political authority as a hierarchical and uniform sovereign entity. Political authority is considered a distinct type of communicative relationship for articulating binding decisions and actions for a given field, terrain or group of people. Such communication can be hierarchical or bureaucratic in form, but it can also be negotiated and dialogical. What is important is that one is dealing with a communicated message, which is accepted and considered binding – for whatever reasons – by those to whom it is explicitly addressed (Easton 1953).

Where political authority was earlier associated with the rise of modern government as a centralised mode of imperative control between rulers and masses, political authority today also identifies the rise of new decentred forms of 'high modern' governance where self-reflexivity as self-reference is gaining an ever more prominent place. Political authority is no longer associated with relations of subordination and one-way control only but also with a set of flatly operating networks of political communication, where institutions and individuals are interlocked in multiple, reciprocal relations of autonomy and dependence. Governance here manifests the ability of institutions and individuals within any given political field, terrain or group to communicate about their environment and to use the perception and understanding of their difference from the environment in their internal communication.

Ontologically this means that, in our view, a political situation comes into being wherever or whenever a dispute or disagreement occurs over the allocation of valued things (material or immaterial) which cannot be solved or mediated by other means than by the timely and risky intervention of authority (Bang 1998). That is to say, a political situation can occur anywhere in society. It is not restricted to the terrain of the state, nor is it simply a feature of what the most influential 'political strata' say and do. The increasing dynamics, complexity and difference characterising high modern society produce ever more political situations across the conventional boundaries between state and civil society, public and private or national and international. These bind ever more political institutions and individuals together in shifting and multiple relations of authority relying on the capacity for self-reference.

Self-reference has since long been considered relevant to the workings of political institutions (March and Olsen 1989, 1995). However, it is only recently that the notion of self-reference has been extended politically to include 'ordinary individuals' and their construction of identity too (Benhabib 1996; Connolly 1999; Giddens 1990). The notion of 'the ordinary' has otherwise conventionally been enwrapped in collectivist terms as a 'product' of classes, communities, ideologies, groups, masses, etc. A good exponent of this change is Ulrich Beck's idea of what it means to *be* an individual living her or his life in a runaway world of ever more accelerating change and difference:

The choosing, deciding, shaping human being who aspires to be the author of his or her own life, the creator of an individual identity, is the central character of our time . . . Any attempt to create a new sense of social cohesion has to start from the recognition that individualism, diversity and scepticism are written into Western culture. (Beck 2001: 165)

### Strategy and tactics: distinguishing rationality from 'mere' reflexivity

In addition to Beck's notion of the new, more identity-seeking and sceptical individual in high modernity, I suggest in this book that we distinguish between whether this individual is acting strategically or tactically in her self-referential capacity. By strategic I refer to self-reference which has become rational. 'Rationality pertains only if the concept of difference is used self-referentially, that is, only if the unity of the difference is reflected' (Luhmann 1995: 474). Rationality presumes that one's orientation to differences must be checked for their conceptual self-reference and that one's conclusion contains a principled account of one's checking. This happens when individuals/institutions determine themselves through their difference from the environment and systematically programme this difference so that it can have operative significance and informational and connective value. Tactic, on the other hand, does not imply such programmatic activity, which is crucial to be able to control one's effects on the environment through control of oneself. Tactics do not give any principled account of phenomena but rather demonstrate through concrete interactions how things could have been done otherwise (Certeau 1984). Furthermore, tactics come into being not to acquire rational influence or control over others but more for the sake of reflecting on what is happening, of feeling engaged and of finding a space to exercise one's freedoms. A tactic manifests a fast and precise intervention, which can be transformed to a favourable situation, expanding one's possibilities of action (Shotter 1993).

It is important to note that the distinction between strategy and tactics is drawn within the conception of the political. This is done to avoid political analysis being trapped in the old opposition between the rational (strategic action) and the irrational (diffuse support or compliance), which tends to generate the expectation that the only alternative to a politics which is exercised calmly and rationally by elites is one which is exercised agitatedly and emotionally by the masses. Between these two poles is a large, rapidly growing reflexive terrain which is constituted by the everyday tactics of ordinary individuals. These may not be able to produce, tabulate and impose spaces upon the political, as do strategies in and through their contributions to direct decision and action. But tactics can influence strategic elite action indirectly by making new uses of, manipulating and diverting existing political spaces (Certeau 1984: 30).

Hence the notion of tactic makes it possible to avoid self-reflexive political action being identified only with a rationalised goal of attaining success or strategic influence over others. Although politics is indeed an arena for strategic struggle and negotiation between those who seek influence and success, it is also the ground of all those who, rather, participate tactically to feel politically alive and kicking and to make a concrete, immediate difference right where they are. I here follow the 'mature' Habermas, who recently seems to have substituted such a strategy–tactic distinction within the conception of political communication for his 'old' distinction between the state and apolitical civil society. As he highlights:

> the democratic procedure can lead to a rational will-formation only insofar as organized opinion-formation, which leads to accountable decisions within government bodies, remain permeable to the free-floating, values, issues, contributions, and arguments of a surrounding political communication that, as such, cannot be organized as a whole. (1996: 485)

Habermas still lacks a distinction between government and governance. Furthermore, his whole attempt to distinguish 'system' from 'life world' is fraught with ambiguities. Still it seems important to distinguish one's direct orientation towards the authoritative allocation of values as it is shaped by elites acting within the fields or terrains of the political regime from one's indirect one, which has to do with how one lives one's life as an ordinary political being in the political community. One can be in the political for strategic reasons, which require organisation and programmatic rationality to succeed in attaining one's plans or goals. This is how politics is mostly defined – as a struggle between rational actors for influence in the political regime. However, one can also participate as an ordinary member of the political community, to get involved in things, to exploit an existing institution or organisation, to practise one's own freedoms, to discuss new ideas, to give play to one's political imagination, etc. Such personal and communal activities unfold as tactics, which are self-referential but at the same time much more fluid, opaque, non-planned and impulsive than are strategies (Cavell 1979).

Drawing a line between strategy and tactics, it is thus possible to approach the political as comprising not only political authorities (formal or informal incumbents of authority roles) and a political regime (values, norms and structures of authority), but also a political community (a group of persons joined together in a political division of labour). From the vantage point of political authorities in a political regime, a political community reflects a 'world horizon that corresponds to the systems' internal horizon' (Luhmann 1995: 474). In the understanding of lay people in a political community, a political regime manifests such possibilities, limits or barriers which further or hinder one's engagement and practice of freedom. The important point about introducing the notion of tactic into the joint actions that go on in a political community is that it shows that such actions do not necessarily have to obey or result from the organising of what a given regime considers 'valid' decisions and actions and what political authorities choose to programme within this 'valid' conception. This is exactly what keeps the door open for something genuinely new to happen and also for continuous critiques from below of any going regime and mode of political organising. Distinct from political authorities, members of a political community are not programmed to produce and deliver. They may choose simply to 'consume' political products for their own personal reasons in a new, reflexive political culture (Clark and Hoffmann-Martinot 1998). But they may also engage in interaction oriented to articulating new ideals, values, images, identities, etc., which are intrinsically different from those that have been, and can be, systematically 'validated' by the regime (Certeau 1997).

Indeed, the direct decisions of political authorities do systematically articulate and organise the fields or terrains in which lay people operate in a political community. But through their joint actions lay people can acquire an autonomy which, as Certeau puts it, shows how their ordinary tactics 'circulate, come and go, overflow and drift over an imposed terrain, like the snowy waves of the sea slipping in and among the rocks and defiles of an established order' (1984: 34). Tactics gain their autonomy, as Habermas has always emphasised, by *not* being programmed to organise things in a systematic manner or to reach binding decisions (1996). They do not have to provide a systematic articulation of difference in order make themselves felt indirectly in the authoritative allocation of valued things (cf. Habermas 1996: 485).

## The problem of uncoupling

Both as a rhetoric and in its concrete exercise governance may be claimed to be above all a response to modernisation pressures for reorganising the state to deal with the massive increases in complexity, dynamics and difference that result from the ongoing globalising and localising of power and knowledge. Uncoupling between elites and lay people here becomes a central issue, because their coupling conventionally has been forged via the intimate connection between the state and the national community (Etzioni-Halevy 1997, 1999). The rise of the radical/extreme right, for example, seems to have much to do with the fact that when political elites go increasingly global to decide on boundary crossing rights, problems and solutions, it is easily felt in the political community as a desertion from the national conventions and values, underpinning the democratic traditions. Inversely, when political elites go more and more local to implement decisions in a democratically effective manner, reflexive individuals in the life world are politically habituated to estimate their rulers on their concrete capacity to connect and deliver rather than on whether they conform to some abstract democratic principles or political ideologies.

Uncoupling confronts the state with a double pressure for reconnecting with lay people both nationally and on the output side of political processes

(Bang and Dyrberg in chapter 12 of this volume). This places the state in a state of constant ambiguity. For how can it decide more globally and implement more locally in and through a representative democracy which is organised on a left–right axis, derives its legitimacy from the national political community and is geared to protect and expand free access to the exercise of influence on the input side of political processes? This book will not offer any final solutions to this dilemma of the nation state, resulting from the transference of sovereignty to higher and lower levels and from its transition from an input democracy to an output democracy. But it will provide some theoretical answers as to what politics is not under governance conditions, and thus what politics could be in the future under such conditions.

However, we are of the conviction that uncoupling undermines democratic effectiveness and legitimacy. Uncoupling draws attention away from how the strategic communication of elites, facilitating and moderating people's exercise of self- and co-governance is becoming an increasingly important key to securing free and open access to democratic processes. It furthermore ignores how acceptance and recognition of difference is becoming a *sine qua non* for both the regime's exercise of 'good governance' and our living democratically together in an 'overlapping consensus' in face of all disagreements and struggles over various 'comprehensive doctrines' (Rawls 1993).

Uncoupling is becoming more critical because the 'big' strategic politics, that goes on in the political regime, in recent decades has become increasingly uncoupled from the 'small tactics' which circulate as everyday communication about how one can live one's life in a political community (Bang *et al.* 2000). This problem is accelerating owing to the rapid increase in the self-referential capacities of both elites and lay people in high modernity. Political authorities and the political regime depend increasingly for their democratic effectiveness on listening to and learning from 'small' narratives or tactics which contain much potential information about how to persist and develop in a world of increasing complexity, dynamics and difference (Heffen *et al.* 2000). Lay people in the political community increasingly demand to be facilitated and moderated by political authorities and other 'experts' in the political regime in order for them to be able to contribute possible solutions to common concerns, interpreting and articulating new values, discovering new issues, etc. Yet, there is an accelerating tension between elites complaining about lay people being driven by emotions and populist forces and lay people accusing elites of ignoring their everyday problems and turning their back on the national community.

As already indicated, we consider the uncoupling problem from the perspectives of political authorities, political regime and lay people in the political community. The book discusses how this problem can be met by (1) *political authorities* paying increasing attention to the ways political decision and action are socially constructed, that is, how demands, issues, outputs and outcomes are formed within the framework of particular strategic and tactical narratives, beliefs, actions and assumptions; (2) *political regimes* offering new access points for exercising influence and setting new limits on the democratic imagination for what is to be included in and excluded from the exercise of 'good governance'; (3) *political communities* interlocking ideas and practices in multiple new ways, thereby constructing new divisions of political labour, new political identities and new narratives and commonalities.

These developments do not only imply that civil society loses its innocence as the bearer of all that is good, collectivist and harmonious. They also make it obvious that political power can no longer be labelled as a uniform and coercive power claiming command and control over all subjects within its territory. Politicising individuals in civil society by empowering them for the sake of getting them more actively involved in the political rule of the social is today articulated positively as 'good governance'. It is considered a necessary means to survive and develop as an organisation in face of rapidly accelerating change.

Appeals to the forging of partnerships and teams operating across old boundaries is becoming a new systems rhetoric, which more and more systems managers, administrators and other professionals, if not party politicians, consider imperative for acquiring success (Bang 2001; Catt 1999; Heffen *et al.* 2000; Johnson *et al.* 1998). An underlying assumption here is that democracy can no longer be sustained and developed only by means of the abstract ideas, goals, rules, rights and liberties of representative government (Klijn and Koppenjan 2000). It increasingly relies on its development as a life politics of choice and becoming (Connolly 1999; Giddens 1991; Hutton and Giddens 2001) connecting the exercise of political authority directly with lay people, as a facilitator and moderator of the practice of freedom (Bang 2000; Klijn and Teisman 2000).

In our view, therefore:

1 Governance analysis must move beyond its initial interest in state steering and co-ordination to 'configurations beyond hierarchies and networks' (chapter 2), 'thick descriptions' (chapter 4), 'governing as interaction' (chapter 5) and 'bottom-up institutionalism' (chapter 3), all of which point in the direction of governance as political communication between system and life world.

2 Governance must connect with more macro-sociological views of 'meta-governance' (chapter 6), 'governmentality' (chapter 7) and 'symbolic power' (chapter 8), in order to complement the decentred view of authority with one that allows for its recentring as regime and community governance. Complexity in hypermodern society has grown to a degree where political authorities (at whatever level) can no longer act for the whole and control that whole directly. Connecting with citizens, enabling them to partake in the system's governing processes on their own terms,

but with a commitment to fulfil its need for effectiveness, wholeness and coherence, is becoming a new steering imperative.

3 Governance must be tied to a *micropolitics of becoming and presence*, showing how important practical dilemmas, traditions and political contests are for the study of governance (chapter 11); how politics, however defined, is only a historically contingent genus of practice, and democracy is only a species of that practice (chapter 9); how thinking without hierarchy or without a banister means that thinking must be action and can no longer be separate from activity (chapter 10); and how having a sense of difference and common destiny means recognising and accepting the equal value of everybody making up the political capital of everyday life (chapter 12).

## A scheme of analysis for studying political communication

The understanding of governance as political communication seems roomy enough for showing that all the chapters of this book have grown out of the same conceptual terrain. This allows a recontextualisation of political decision and action grounded in negotiated and dialogical authority. Hence one can pursue an approach to governance which is both decentred and holistic, challenging mainstream trends, which for many years have been those of theories at the micro- and the meso-level, such as public choice theory and the new institutionalism (March and Olsen 1989; Peters 1999). In these theories, governing is made a matter of actors versus structures, whereas in our framework we speak of governing as a matter of connecting individuals and institutions within the holistic conception of political society.

### Political authority as a communicative connecting mechanism

The crux of the matter in our framework, I suggest, is the communicative power-knowledge of authority. Authority may be loosely defined as a type of political communication, which occurs (1) when B receives an explicitly communicated message from A that is intended to get B to do or refrain from doing something; (2) when B then accepts to carry out A's message; and (3) when B's grounds for acceptance are his or her practical recognition that a political communication received in this way must or ought to be carried out without evaluating the merits of the proposed conduct in the light of one's own standards of judgement (cf. Easton 1955: 28–9). Political authority thus allows the specialisation of political discourse as strategic communication on the part of A. At the same time it conditions A to pay regard to B's non-specialised considerations of how to act tactically upon the message and thereby to B's transformative capacity as an ordinary member of the political community.

By separating state from civil society, modern social analysis concealed the political nature of the life world, as a community for engaging in solving

common concerns, as well as the communicative nature of political authority acting within the limits of the political regime. Political authority is not
only, or even primarily, a distant and subjugating Leviathan but a communicative connecting mechanism, enabling and conditioning even the
most democratic vision of a political society in which political authorities
and citizens in the political community co-operate democratically in their
mutual acceptance and recognition of their differences (Botwinick and
Connolly 2001).

Authority is not just a toolkit in the hands of A, nor does it link with a
universal norm or abstract liberty which unfolds itself behind the backs of
A and B. Authority makes A's rational exercise of her or his power directly
dependent on B's self-reflexive *doing and refraining*. Authority in this way
conditions A and B to co-operate minimally, at least, across system and
life world in a political division of labour. Political authority is thus governing both at close range and as a distant power. Members of a political
community are chronically and logically involved in the structuration of
the political regime via their communicative relationship with political
authorities. Analysing governance from the point of view of system and
life world therefore means recognising the irreducibility of political authorities, political regime and political community as constituents of political
society.

*Political authorities* refer to the occupants of positions of authority in
society whose roles may be more or less formalised. Positions of authority
can express a variety of different roles from the global role as the President
of the United States to the local role as an elder in a nomadic band and it
can be occupied by a variety of different identities, from the most cruel to
the most benign politician, administrator, judge, councillor or whatever. At
times, authorities may be occupants of highly specialised roles, as in modern
political systems; but in many less specialised societies, where the life world
is more prominent than the system, occupants may not perform a specifically political role (Easton 1965b: 212). In any case, however, they may be
said to conform to the following criteria. They must engage in the daily
affairs of a political system; they must be recognised by most members of
society as having the responsibility for these matters; and their actions must
be accepted as binding most of the time by most of the relevant members,
as long as they act within the limits of their role (*ibid.*).

Part I, about governance theory and analysis in political science, has a
common point of observation at this level. It deals with the co-ordinating
capacities of political authorities, but at the same time extends this original systems approach to governance to comprise new examinations of
what is required to exercise one's authority position communicatively and
democratically in co-operation with civil society and individuals. Mayntz
describes in chapter 2 how 'the modern state has in fact become more "co-
operative", networks have proliferated, and European integration is a new
phenomenon;' In chapter 3 Hoff shows how:

access to a network (and thereby influence and political power) seem to depend not only on resources and thereby power-dependency, but also on acceptance in the sense of both accepting the dominant discourse of the network, and of being accepted as an equal and worthy partner by the other actors in the network.

In chapter 4 Bevir and Rhodes 'open the door to an understanding of how several actors have constructed the meaning, and so nature, of recent government changes. Simple solutions such as joining-up or holistic governance may have an appealing elegance. Governments will always seek simplicity – but they should distrust it;' and finally in chapter 5 Kooiman illuminates how 'only by speaking about action and action potential of governing in a broader overview can activation for governance get its proper place in the systematic thinking about governance'.

*The political regime* refers to 'the general matrix of regularised expectations within the limits of which political actions are usually considered authoritative, regardless of how or where these expectations may be expressed' (Easton 1965b: 193–4). It consists of values (goals and principles), norms and structure of authority. The values serve as broad limits with regard to what can be taken for granted in the guidance of day-to-day policy without violating deep feelings or important segments of the political community. The norms specify the kinds of procedures that are expected and acceptable in the processing and implementing of demands. The structures of authority designate the formal and informal patterns in which power is distributed and organised with regard to the authoritative making and implementing of decisions (1965b: 193). A specific regime at any moment in time will be the product of the accommodation among the pressures for new goals, rules or structures stimulated by social change and the limits imposed by existing conventions and practices (1965b: 194).

Part II, which deals with more sociological analyses of meta-governance, governmentality and symbolic violence, shifts the emphasis from political authorities to the regime level, examining how the regime changes in reponse to changes in state sovereignty and power. In chapter 6 Jessop points at the play of 'three general principles of governance in the face of complexity: these are the principles of requisite reflexivity, requisite variety and requisite irony. Since reflexivity and variety are relatively familiar principles, if not always fully integrated into the analysis of governance, I have paid most attention to the role of a 'romantic' public irony in dealing with the problems posed by the likelihood of governance failure' – in the sense that participants must recognise the likelihood of failure but proceed as if success were possible; Dean in chapter 7 stresses the need to link sovereignty and governmentality, to show how:

the problem with the thesis of culture governance is not its falsity. It is its truth that requires our contestation. That contestation might require us to think about how we are asked to constitute ourselves today and how we might think

differently about that request. It might require us to think of the consequences
of the entry of cultural governance and its valorisation of the arts of existence
as a specifically political problem.

In chapter 8 Swartz links the development towards culture governance with:

> Bourdieu's language of 'distinction', 'struggle' and 'domination'. Bourdieu has
> little to say about modes of co-operation; his fundamental concern is modes
> of domination. So while one finds in Bourdieu elements that echo concerns
> of the growing governance literature, the general tone of Bourdieu's conflict
> sociology is quite different from much governance thinking. Still, the impulse
> to expand democratic processes and to find new ways of doing so are shared
> by all.

*The political community* concerns that aspect of society that consists of
lay people seen as a group of self-reflexive individuals who are drawn
together by the fact that they participate in a common political structure
and set of processes – however tight or loose their ties with these structures
and processes may be. It does not matter whether people form a community in the sociological sense of a group of members who have a sense of
community or a set of common traditions. A political community may well
have different – even antagonistic – cultures and traditions or it may comprise entirely separate nationalities (Easton 1965b: 177). But regardless of
the degree of political cohesion in society, as long as people are part of the
same political society they cannot escape being linked by a common division of political labour. Furthermore, however high the actual degree of
oppression in a political community, the participation of people in authority relations will show how they practise their freedom to provide themselves with a political identity in relation to both political authorities and
one another.

The notion of political community may be the reason why Rousseau
holds that authority is 'one and single, and cannot be divided without being
destroyed' (1987: 153). In saying that a political community is identified
by co-operation or participation in an authority relationship of some kind
one is simultaneously problematising the heart of the original liberalist
project underlying most doctrines of representative democracy, which was
the goal of freeing the polity from religious control and freeing civil society
and individuals from unjustified political interference (Held 1996: 74).
Political democracy is no longer merely a problem of emancipation from
domination but an active relationship enabling one to exercise one's
freedom in practice (however minimally). Civil society and citizens are not
simply a permanent thorn in the side of political authorities; nor are they
only innocent victims of an arbitrary 'will to power' (Held 1996; Keane
1988). Every citizen, however marginalised s/he might appear to be, must
be thought of as bearing *some* responsibility for why things are as they are
– or happen as they do – in political society. Thus we should not presup-
pose that 'citizens who live together under democratic conditions *must be*

obliged to submit themselves to a highly centralised authority, without the rational domination of which they would fall into confusion and disorder' (Keane 1988: 237). If the citizens fall into confusion and disorder, the logic of the authority relationship is that the system, and even the whole of society, will do so as well.

Part III is about democracy and the politics of becoming. It sets out the terrain of the political community from the point of view of ordinary individuals, their conventions and their everyday tactics. In chapter 11 Bevir encourages us to treat governance as an opportunity to redefine democracy. He prompts us to search for 'patterns of devolution, participation, control and accountability that better reflect our capacity for agency, the contingency of our identities, the importance of moral conduct as well as moral rules, and an aspiration to an open community'. In chapter 9 Gunnell stresses how:

> conventionality entails that the relationship between theory and practice should also be a democratic relationship, since there are no hierarchical grounds on which it can be based. The question of how second-order discourses can at once recognise conventionality and seek critical purchase is predicated on the false premise that there is some general answer. As long as political theory holds on to an image of even 'privileged marginality' as its home, it will find that, in fact, 'there is no place like home' and that its commitment to democracy is ultimately fraught with paradox.

In chapter 10 Strong encourages us to accept that such paradox is intrinsic to a politics of becoming, which:

> both introduces contingency in any conception of justice (there may be a first word, but there is never a last) and makes impossible the 'core–periphery' conception of just political society so dear to the hearts of liberals. It also introduces a whole new set of questions and problems for a truly democratic theory for our modern, postmodern, Western times.

Bang and Dyrberg conclude likewise in chapter 12 that:

> another take on the challenges facing democracy is needed so as to make both elites and non-elites realise that political freedom and equality come from their mutual recognition and acceptance of the differences they make to the political constitution of society both as elites and as non-elites.

Hence, adopting a $3 \times 2$ dimensional approach to a holistic *and* decentred view of political rule and engagement, one can bring political authority back in as a communicative power that operates through the conventional practices of ordinary individuals in a political community. In addition one can simultaneously show how political authority, as distinct from the universal reason in modern thinking, can function as the very contingent necessity that enables practices of freedom in political society and thereby the free play of all the particularities of living together in a political division of labour.

Political authority thus opens for a new (tentative) definition of governance as networks of political communication, expressing the reflexive self-ordering of social relations by individuals and groups, co-operating and exercising their self-rule in terms of their reciprocal interdependence, deliberation and sense of common destiny and on the basis of continuing consultation, dialogue and resource sharing. Governance implies a variety of recursive practices oriented to both the creation of identity and the enhancement of the governing faculties of individuals and groups to produce effective and relevant outcomes through the processes and projects in which they are interacting.

This definition is put to use in my final chapter, where, having summarised the main theoretical points put forth in the book, I suggest that a new rule and a new citizen are beginning to take shape in the communicative relationship of authority, namely the *culture governor* and the *everyday maker* respectively. The culture governor occurs in a political system where the truth is beginning to take effect that only some but never all causes that are necessary for producing specific outcomes can be employed under the control of the system (cf. Luhmann 1995: 20). Culture governors are thus aware of the growing significance and relevance of listening to and learning from the small narratives which circulate in a political community and in the culture more generally in order to sustain some control over outcomes. Culture governors recognise that rule in all kinds of organisation must increasingly operate through self-governing capacities and thus needs to act upon, reform and utilise individual and collective identities so that they might be amenable to such rule (cf. chapter 7). Culture governors are profoundly anti-bureaucratic and individual in their orientation. They are aware that national and transnational processes of institutional change in political systems rely increasingly on more local and microscopic changes in choice, subjectivity and identity. Culture governors pursue a new politics and public management, advocating, facilitating, guiding and moderating the spread of new forms of democracy from below as well as new ways of holding leadership and management more directly accountable to people so that their conventional wisdoms and sovereignty can be immediately expressed.

In culture governance, just as civil society loses its innocence as the bearer of all that is good, collectivistic and harmonious, so political power is no longer victimised as a uniform and coercive power claiming command and control over all subjects within its territory. Politicising individuals in civil society by involving them in the rule of expert systems, whether as employees, customers, users or citizens, is articulated positively as a necessary means to survive and develop as an organisation.

Everyday makers are of intrinsic interest to culture governors because they are made of the very 'stuff' that the system needs to survive and develop. Everyday makers are strong, self-reliant and capable individuals. They conceive of politics and policy as the concrete and direct handling of diversity, difference and dispute concerning life political problems; they consider commonality as the handling of common concerns (political community) more than the pursuit of the common good (social community); and they accept and recognise 'the fact of pluralism' (Bang and Soerensen 2001c; Rawls 1993) as the basis of both the input politics of representative government and the output politics of various governance networks and projects operating in their locality. However, everyday makers are not easily controlled, either directly or indirectly. They have chosen to live their lives on the borderline between a political system and its environment, fluctuating back and forth, sometimes taking part in the system's strategic activities, sometimes escaping and circumventing them to pursue their own small tactics in their various life worlds. In the light of conventional notions of citizenship everyday makers easily appear unresponsive in solving common concerns, fighting for equality and solidarity and obeying public reason. Yet they possess a critical potential for democracy, precisely because they do not consider themselves in opposition to the system and yet insist on their right to be 'ordinary individuals' who are not, and should not, be programmed to engage in the organising and programming of the system's politics and policy.

In spite of, perhaps even because of, their lesser organisational complexity, their non-rational self-reflexivity and weaker capacity for controlling outcomes, everyday makers might turn out to be the exemplar of new democratic critiques. Everyday makers warn us not to hand over the whole of democratic discourse to the strategic communication of and between autopoeitic systems, just because such systems speak and act in the name of all conventional concepts of citizenship and civil association – engaging, learning, reflecting, connecting, participating, exercising self-governance, etc. After all, it still makes a difference to democracy that there are spaces in political society where one can feel engaged in politics and policy, dream up new alternatives, talk about and deliberate on the performance of political elites and regimes, etc., without being pre-programmed to engage in a kind of strategic communication which values influence and success above all else.

## References

Andersen, J. G., Torpe, L., and Andersen, J. (2000), *Hvad folket magter* (Copenhagen: Jurist- & Økonomforbundets Forlag).
Andersen, P., ed. (2001), *Bydelsrådet: gjorde det en forskel?* (Copenhagen: Indre Nørrebro Bydels råd).
Bang, H. P. (1998), 'David Easton's postmodern images', *Political Theory* 26 (3): 281–316.
Bang, H. P. (2000), 'Dansk republikanisme på en skillevej', in H. P Bang, A. D. Hansen and J. Hoff (eds), *Demokrati fra neden. Casestudier fra en dansk kommune* (Copenhagen: Jurist- & Økonomforbundets Forlag), pp. 275–307.

Bang, H. P. (2001), 'Kulturstyring gennem borgerinddragelse', in P. Andersen (ed.), *Bydelsrådet: gjorde det en forskel?* (Copenhagen: Indre Nørrebro Bydels råd), pp. 133–45.

Bang, H. P., and Dyrberg, T. B. (2001), 'Governance, self-representation and the democratic imagination', in M. Saward (ed.), *Democratic Innovation: Deliberation, Representation and Association* (London: Routledge), pp. 141–61.

Bang, H. P., and Sørensen, E. (2001), 'The everyday maker: building political rather than social capital', in P. Dekker and E. M. Uslaner (eds), *Social Capital and Participation in Everyday Life* (London: Routledge), pp. 148–62.

Bang, H. P., Hansen, A. D., and Hoff, J., eds (2000), *Demokrati fra neden. Casestudier fra en dansk kommune* (Copenhagen: Jurist- & Økonomforbundets Forlag).

Bauman, Z. (2001), *Community: Seeking Safety in an Insecure World* (Cambridge: Polity Press).

Beck, U. (2001), 'Living your own life in a runaway world: individualisation, globalisation and politics', in W. Hutton and A. Giddens (eds), *On the Edge* (London: Vintage), pp. 164–75.

Benhabib, S., ed. (1996), *Democracy and Difference* (Princeton NJ: Princeton University Press).

Botwinick, A., and Connolly, W. E., eds (2001), *Democracy and Vision* (Princeton NJ: Princeton University Press).

Castells, M. (1997), *The Power of Identity* (Oxford: Blackwell).

Catt, H. (1999), *Democracy in Practice* (London: Routledge).

Cavell, Stanley (1979), *The Claim of Reason* (Oxford: Oxford University Press).

Certeau, M. de (1984), *The Practice of Everyday Life* (Berkeley CA: University of California Press).

Certeau, M. de (1997), *The Capture of Speech* (Minneapolis MN: University of Minnesota Press).

Clark, T. N., and Hoffmann-Martinot, V., eds (1999), *The New Political Culture* (Boulder CO: Westview Press).

Connolly, W. E. (1999), *Why I am not a Secularist* (Minneapolis MN: University of Minnesota Press).

Dekker, P., and Uslaner, E. M., eds (2001), *Social Capital and Participation in Everyday Life* (London: Routledge).

Easton, D. (1953), *The Political System* (Chicago: University of Chicago Press).

Easton, D. (1955), 'A Theoretical Approach to Authority', Technical Report 17 (Stanford CA: Office of Naval Studies, Stanford University).

Easton, D. (1965a), *A Framework for Political Analysis* (New York: Prentice Hall).

Easton, D. (1965b), *A Systems Analysis of Political Life* (New York: Wiley).

Etzioni-Halevy, E. (1999), 'Elites, inequality and the quality of democracy in ultramodern society', *International Review of Sociology – Revue internationale de sociologie* 9 (2): 239–50.

Etzioni-Halevy, E., ed. (1997), *Classes and Elites in Democracy and Democratization: A Collection of Readings* (New York and London: Garland).

Foucault, M. (1990), *The History of Sexuality: An Introduction* (London: Vintage Books).

Foucault, M. (1994), *Power*, ed. J. D. Faubion (New York: Free Press).

Giddens, A. (1990), *The Consequences of Modernity* (Cambridge: Polity Press).

Giddens, A. (1991), *Modernity and Self-identity* (Cambridge: Polity Press).

Habermas, J. (1989), *The Theory of Communicative Action* II (Cambridge: Polity Press).

Habermas, J. (1996), *Between Facts and Norms* (Cambridge MA: MIT Press).

Heffen, O. van, Kickert, W. J. M., and Thomassen, J. J. A., eds (2000), *Governance in Modern Societies* (Dordrecht: Kluwer).

Held, D. (1996), *Models of Democracy*, 2nd edn (Cambridge: Polity Press).

Hutton, W., and Giddens, A., eds (2001), *On the Edge* (London: Vintage).

Johnson, T. J., Hays, C. E., and Hays, S. P., ed. (1998), *Engaging the Public* (New York: Rowman & Littlefield).

Keane, J. (1988), *Democracy and Civil Society* (London: Verso).

Klijn, E-H., and Koppenjan, J. F. M. (2000), 'Interactive decision making and representative democracy: institutional collisions and solutions', in O. van Heffen, W. J. M. Kickert and J. J. A. Thomassen (eds), *Governance in Modern Societies* (Dordrecht: Kluwer), pp. 109–33.

Klijn, E-H., and Teisman, G. R. (2000), 'Managing public–private partnerships', in O. van Heffen, W. J. M. Kickert and J. J. A. Thomassen (eds), *Governance in Modern Societies* (Dordrecht: Kluwer), pp. 329–48.

Luhmann, N. (1984, 1995), *Social Systems* (Stanford CA: Stanford University Press).

March, J. G., and Olsen, J. P. (1989), *Rediscovering Institutions: The Organizational Basis of Politics* (New York: Free Press).

March, J. G., and Olsen, J. P. (1995), *Democratic Governance* (New York: Free Press).

Newman, J. (2001), *Modernising Governance. New Labour, Policy and Society.* (London: Sage).

Peters, B. G. (1999), *Institutional Theory in Political Science: The New Institutionalism* (London: Pinter).

Pierre, J., ed. (2000), *Debating Governance: Authority, Steering and Democracy* (Oxford: Oxford University Press).

Rawls, J. (1993), *Political Liberalism* (New York: Columbia University Press).

Rousseau, J.-J. (1987), *The Basic Political Writings* (Indianapolis IN: Hackett).

Shotter, J. (1993), *Cultural Politics of Everyday Life* (Buckingham: Open University Press).

Stoker, G., ed. (1999), *The New Management of British Local Governance* (London: Macmillan).

# Part I
Governance theory and analysis
in political science

# 2
# New challenges to governance theory

Renate Mayntz

## Definitions of governance and the purpose of this chapter

The subject of this chapter is the development, and the successive modifications, of governance theory, a theory that began by being concerned with
the steering actions of political authorities as they deliberately attempt to
shape socio-economic structures and processes. In Germany this goes by the
name of *Steuerungstheorie* (Mayntz 1987). The English term 'governance'
has long been equated with 'governing', the process aspect of government,
thus complementing the institutional perspective of government studies.
In other words, governance was used roughly as a synonym of *politische
Steuerung*.

Recently, however, the term 'governance' has been used in two other
ways, both distinct from political guidance or steering. To distinguish these
different meanings is important not only in order to avoid misunderstand-
ings, but also because a change in semantics usually reflects a change in
perception, whether this in turn reflects changes in reality or not.

For one thing, 'governance' is now often used to indicate a new mode
of governing that is distinct from the hierarchical control model, a more
co-operative mode where state and non-state actors participate in mixed
public/private networks. Governance as an alternative to hierarchical
control has been studied on the level of national (and sub-national) and
of European policy making, and in international relations. Kooiman
(1993) and Rhodes (1997) illustrate the first, Bulmer (1994) the second,
and Rosenau and Czempiel (1992) the third of these strands. It is hard to
say where exactly this particular meaning of the term originated. In the
March 1998 issue of the *International Social Science Journal*, entirely
devoted to 'governance' in the sense of non-hierarchical modes of co-
ordination (UNESCO 1998), the concept is traced to a 1989 World
Bank report, i.e. the international context. In any case it is clear that
attempts at collective problem solving outside existing hierarchical frameworks, such as we can observe on the European and the international

levels, have contributed significantly to this shift in the meaning of the term governance.

The second 'new' meaning of the term 'governance' is much more general, and has a different genealogy. Here governance means the different modes of co-ordinating individual actions, or basic forms of social order. This use of the term seems to have grown out of transaction cost economics, more specifically Oliver Williamson's analysis of market and hierarchy as alternative forms of economic organisation (e.g. Williamson 1979). Williamson's typology was quickly extended to include other forms of social order such as clans, associations, and – most important – networks (e.g. Hollingsworth and Lindberg 1985; Powell 1990). It was in fact the 'discovery' of forms of co-ordination not only different from hierarchy, but also different from the pure market form, that led to the generalisation of the term 'governance' to cover all forms of social co-ordination – not only in the economy, but also in other sectors. In this way, the attention paid to forms of 'modern governance' (governance in the second meaning of the term) triggered another semantic shift. The third meaning of governance now includes the two more narrow understandings of the term as sub-types.

In what follows I first sketch the evolution of the theory of political governance in the narrow sense of steering (*Steuerungstheorie*). I then trace successive paradigm shifts, or modifications of this theoretical frame. Finally I discuss the most recent, and as yet only partly met, challenges to the theory. To avoid the disappointment that arises from mistaken expectations, a few disclaimers are in order. It is not the purpose of this chapter to make a substantive contribution to governance theory, to challenge one of its premises or to introduce new theorems. My intention is rather to reflect on the development of a certain body of political theory, a development in which I have actively participated over more than twenty years. In reconstructing this theoretical development it will not be possible to spell out in detail the content of the literature I shall refer to, nor shall I attempt to document the unfolding of governance theory by extensive references.[1] An account of the development of governance theory can serve to put seemingly separate fields of research into a broader context, but it also does more: It raises an important issue about the nature of theory development in political science. Does this development follow an internal cognitive dynamic, or is it simply a reflection of changes in political reality or in problem perception, as Dryzek and Leonard (1988) have argued? The answer to this question will indicate whether political science is cumulative, building step by step a more inclusive theory, or is meandering from topic to topic, following the shift in subjective definitions of what is salient.

## The development of the core paradigm of political governance

The modern theory of political governance (*Steuerungstheorie*) emerged after World War II at a time when governments aspired explicitly to steer their nations' social and economic development in the direction of defined goals.[2] The first paradigm of the theory evolved in three successive phases:

1 In the late 1960s it began with a – largely prescriptive – theory of *planning* (how to steer).
2 In the 1970s, with the planning euphoria waning, *policy development* became the object of empirical analyses; this directed attention to context factors influencing policy development, in particular executive organisation; different policy instruments were discussed, in particular the role of law.
3 Finally, in the second half of the 1970s, *policy implementation* became a new research focus.

The first paradigm of a theory of political governance was thus concerned with policy development and policy implementation, and it adopted a top-down, or legislators', perspective.

This theory carried in itself the seeds of its own transformation. Implementation research called attention to the fact of widespread policy failure, and proved that such failure was the consequence not only of cognitive mistakes in planning or of shortcomings on the part of implementation agencies, but of having neglected the recalcitrance of the target groups of public policy and their ability to resist or subvert the achievement of policy goals. This recognition led to a first, important enlargement of the initial paradigm. Had it so far concentrated on the *subject* of political steering, government and its ability or inability to steer, it now included also the structure and behavioural dispositions of the *object* of political control. In German, this meant to shift the focus from *Steuerungsfähigkeit* to *Steuerbarkeit*, i.e. governability. In a second step it was recognised that governability varies considerably between policy fields (or sectors). For instance, policy fields consisting of a specific category of individuals (e.g. youth) or households (e.g. single-parent households) call for a different policy approach from policy fields dominated by a few big organisations. Thus the top-down perspective of the initial paradigm (policy making and implementation) was extended by the inclusion of bottom-up processes of selective compliance with policy measures by their target groups, processes which are in turn conditioned by the structure of a given regulatory field. This expansion of the analytical perspective taught us much about the conditions of policy effectiveness.

However, the research that followed, and elaborated, this enlarged paradigm undermined what had so far been the basis of the model of political governance, i.e. the assumption that the state, even if it meets with resistance from target groups, is the control centre of society. The disappointment of the belief in the existence of an effective political control centre then directed attention to alternative forms of societal governance. In two separate lines of discussion, market principles and horizontal self-organisation were debated as alternatives to hierarchical political control. This ushered in another extension of the paradigm.

Market principles were first prominently discussed as a more effective alternative to regulation in American environmental policy. At about this time, market principles became the backbone of the political ideology of neo-liberalism and Thatcherism, promoting deregulation and privatisation as means to stimulate economic growth and to increase economic efficiency. Political scientists analysed the emergence and the policy consequences of this 'neo-conservatism', using the analytical framework of policy analysis (e.g. Döhler 1990). More recently the demise of state socialism strengthened the belief in the ordering power of the market. Meanwhile, however, attention turned to the potential contradictions between market principles (or capitalism) and democracy (e.g. Kitschelt 1985; Dunn 1990; Katz 1997), an issue that so far has not been part of governance theory. The development of governance theory, even of governance theory applied specifically to economic organisation, focused instead on the second alternative to hierarchical control, i.e. co-operative and horizontal forms of societal self-regulation and of policy development. In other words, attention turned to governance in the second of the three senses distinguished above.

At the centre of this new line of discussion were different kinds of negotiating systems. Along the way, traditional forms of what might generally be called societal self-regulation also received new attention, in particular local self-government and the so-called 'third sector' of private, non-profit service organisations, but this is not what is usually meant by 'modern gov-

---

**The governance paradigm and its extensions**

| | |
|---|---|
| *Basic paradigm* | Policy development (by government) + policy implementation (by public agencies) |
| *First extension* | Include bottom-up perspective: sectoral structure and target group behaviour |
| *Second extension* | Include policy development and implementation in public/private networks and self-regulating societal systems |
| *Third extension* | Include effect of European policy upon domestic sectoral structures and policy making |
| *Fourth extension* | Include European level of policy making |
| *Fifth extension* | Include political input processes at European and national level |

ernance'. The two major types of negotiating systems are neo-corporatist arrangements, or more generally mixed public/private policy networks, and systems of societal self-regulation in which the state does not directly participate, such as the institutionalised wage bargaining system between capital and labour (*Tarifsystem*) or the self-government of the German public health system, in which the organisations of health fund physicians and of public hospitals bargain with health fund representatives about fees. Another form of societal self-regulation are the so-called private interest governments (Streeck and Schmitter 1985). Here opposing interests are not represented by independent organisations, but are internalised within regulatory regimes that subject the activities of private agents to a self-imposed discipline; the German technical standardisation agency DIN is a case in point (Voelzkow 1996).

By the mid-1980s the theoretical discussion was dominated by the terms 'decentralisation', 'co-operation' and 'network'. This was quite in line with the spirit of the times, which was set against all manifestations of hierarchical authority, whether by parents, teachers or the state. However, it was quickly realised that the problem-solving capacity of public/private networks and of societal self-regulation may be limited. Networks typically emerge where power is dispersed among the agents in a policy field, but where co-operation is necessary for the sake of effectiveness. As the various public and/or private agents in a policy field typically have different interests, this poses the problem of how to agree on an effective solution without shifting the costs this implies on to outsiders (Scharpf 1993). The discussion of this issue within the framework of governance theory is an elaboration, rather than a further extension, of the theoretical paradigm as it had evolved by now.

A second important line of elaboration started from the observation that, from the viewpoint of the original, top-down conception of political governance, the negotiation of political with societal actors in policy networks or neo-corporatist structures and the delegation of regulatory functions to institutions of local or sectoral self-government indicate a loss of steering capacity. The state appeared weak, 'semi-sovereign' (Katzenstein 1987) – a perspective consonant with modern systems theory and with concepts of postmodernism, both of which are characterised by viewing society as centreless, or polycentric (e.g. Willke 1987). However, empirical political science research has made it clear that what we are dealing with is not so much a loss of state control as a change in its form. Societal self-regulation takes place, after all, within an institutional framework that is underwritten by the state. The state not only legitimises, but has often helped to establish various forms of self-government. Where state actors participate in policy networks, they are a very special and privileged kind of participant; they retain crucial means of intervention, and this holds even where decision making has been devolved to institutions of societal self-government. In particular, the state retains the right of legal ratification, the right to authoritative decision where societal actors do not come to a conclusion (e.g. in negotiations about technical standards), and the right to intervene by legislative or executive action where a self-governing system such as the German health system fails to meet regulatory expectations. Thus hierarchical control and societal self-regulation are not mutually exclusive. They are different ordering principles which are often combined, and their combination, self-regulation 'in the shadow of hierarchy', can be more effective than either of the 'pure' governance forms (Mayntz and Scharpf 1995).

### Challenges to governance theory: Europeanisation and globalisation

Having arrived at this point, the basic frame of a theory of political governance seems complete. But meanwhile new problems have arisen, notably the crisis of the welfare state that is connected with European integration and economic globalisation. In the light of Europeanisation and globalisation, certain accepted and apparently unproblematic features of the previously sketched theory of governance appear suddenly as deficits, deficits which can trigger a new phase in theory development by challenging governance theory to extend its analytical frame once more. The deficits in question are:

1 The concentration on the single nation state (even where international comparisons are made).
2 The selective concern with domestic politics – a point closely linked with the first.
3 The concentration on policy effectiveness, on the output and outcome of policy processes, neglecting the input side of policy formation and the relationship between both.

The theory of political governance has so far dealt with political systems that have a clear identity, a clear boundary, and a defined membership which implies specific rights and duties. This kind of approach is incapable of dealing with the problems raised by European integration, and especially with the problems raised by globalisation.

The formation of the European Union has established a new, transnational governance structure. The European Union is decidedly more than a regime, a contractual frame or a negotiating arena, but it is as clearly not a federal state; it can best be described as a complex multi-level system whose dynamics cannot well be understood in the conceptual frame developed for the analysis of political governance in nation states. Private interest governments, for instance, are still largely of a national scope. The tripartite configurations, or triangles, that at the national level link political parties, interest groups and government agencies, or the neo-corporatist arrangements linking the state, employers and organised labour, are not structurally replicated at the European level. There are no true European political parties, organised labour is only weakly represented, and the representation of industry is even more diverse and complex than at the national level. New categories are needed for the analysis of European policy making and implementation.[3]

For a theory of political governance, European integration has two consequences: (1) it raises new problems of governance on the national level, and (2) it requires the extension of governance theory to a supranational level.

1 The shift of powers to the European level requires us to study the effect of European directives upon various sectors of the national economy (agriculture, foodstuffs, the banking and insurance sector, energy, railways, road transport, etc.). This is in fact being done (e.g. Schneider 1988; Lütz 1998). In this way the previous paradigm is extended once again, this time by adding an important *external* factor of policy formation and implementation. European policy decisions affect the conditions of effective domestic policy resting in the structure of the regulatory field, and at the same time restrict the freedom of national policy choice. This results in a loss – this time a genuine loss – of control for national governments (Scharpf 1997). But this loss does not only follow from the shift of legislative and regulatory competence's from the national to the European level; it also follows from European market integration, the gradual dissolution of national economic boundaries. The consequences for national economies are intensified competition and increasing mobility of production capital and of finance capital. This creates new problems for national tax regimes and tax policy, national economic policy and, last but not least, the national welfare state, problems that have in fact all become prominent topics in political science research.[4]

2 We can also observe the growth of a field called 'European policy making' (e.g. Héritier *et al.* 1996; Richardson 1996). What is not yet clear is whether, in the long run, this will become a separate field of study or remain a genuine extension of existing governance theory. The latter requires that such studies are not undertaken in a comparative perspective of policy sectors, but focus on the connection between different levels of policy making. In other words, the object of study would be not what happens in Brussels (or between Brussels and Strasbourg) but the mutual interdependence of national and European policy processes in a multi-level system.

Concern with European policy making also calls attention to the third blind spot of the national governance paradigm mentioned above. It is a peculiarity of European policy making that democratic elements are largely lacking, or at least weakly developed. As Scharpf (1999) demonstrates, rule making by the European Commission is based on technical expertise wherever action goes beyond the implementation of the common interest of all member states. Where national interests diverge, which is generally the case with decisions having redistributive consequences, technical expertise alone cannot legitimise intervention. Where redistributive decisions require full consensus, the result will simply be deadlock. Decisions with redistributive effects are tolerated only within stable communities ('we' groups) and only if they have been arrived at by democratic procedures. The European Union meets neither of these conditions: It is not a socially integrated system, and it lacks a Europe-wide democratic decision process.

The debate about a European democracy deficit makes us aware that what is clearly lacking in European policy making – a fully developed and well functioning democratic input process – has apparently been taken for granted at the national level, an assumption that permitted neglect of the political input process in the analysis of national policy making.[5] In retrospect it is indeed surprising how long democracy theory and the theory of (national) political governance have remained isolated from each other. When governance theory came to focus on horizontal co-operation and policy formation within networks, it was recognised that this raises the problem of democratic accountability, because the private actors in policy networks typically lack democratic legitimacy. Horizontal co-operation and negotiation in networks can be no substitute for democracy, even though, in view of the difficulty of representing very specific interests within a system of general elections, the development of policy networks that include representatives of opposing socio-political interests is sometimes seen as a more practicable modern form of interest representation. Voelzkow (1996) is one author who has explicitly dealt with the tension between these two different forms of interest representation. If this tension is not recognised there is the danger that a governance theory highlighting horizontal co-operation and societal self-regulation will lead inadvertently to a renaissance of old corporatist models (see Bowen 1971). But to recognise the existence of a problem of accountability where policy-making occurs in mixed public/private networks is not the same as trying to include the input part of the policy process explicitly into the theoretical paradigm of political governance. This challenge has not been met so far, and it is indeed a question whether the integration of democracy theory and governance theory as we know it would over-extend the latter. Still, it might be worth pursuing this path of theory development a few steps further.

While political science has responded, at least partly, to the challenges which Europeanisation poses to governance theory, this does not equally hold for the challenges connected with globalisation. Globalisation is in fact a much more serious challenge to any theory of political governance. At the European level it is, in principle, still possible to talk of a *policy process* with its input and output aspects. This is no longer possible at the global level, where there exists no identifiable steering subject, and no institutionalised framework containing the object of steering. What is, often rather vaguely, referred to by 'globalisation' has not resulted in the formation of a new higher-order system, a truly transnational system with its own identity, boundary and membership roles. This of course raises the question whether the structures and processes generated by globalisation can still be a subject for the theory of governance. This question can be answered affirmatively if, and only if, we speak of governance in the widest sense as basic modes of co-ordination, because only in that case is the concept not tied to the existence of some sort of a political control structure.

Globalisation is usually taken to refer to two interrelated processes (e.g. Stykow and Wiesenthal 1996):

1 Expanding *communication*, both transport and information exchange, and growing personal mobility (migration!), meaning that the formation of social groups becomes increasingly independent of geographical location.

2 The emergence of *global markets* for capital, goods and services, as a consequence of liberalisation, deregulation and the growing ease of communication.

As in the case of European integration, these processes raise both (1) new problems for a theory of national political governance, and (2) issues of transnational governance different from European integration.

1 Though national governments have themselves spurred the process of globalisation through policies of liberalisation and deregulation, they are now forced to consider how to respond to the challenges it raises. There are basically three different strategies. One strategy is unilateral adaptation; the possible measures are similar to those that are being discussed in relation to the European common market, which means that this issue is already being covered in contemporary research. A second strategy is protectionism and isolationism; at the most, this adds a new policy problem to the catalogue of domestic policies already dealt with by policy studies. A third strategy would be efforts to ward off specific impacts (e.g. illegal immigration) by international co-ordination. At this point we are leaving the national level of analysis and must turn to the issue of transnational governance.

2 Problems of international co-ordination beyond the European context have already been the subject of study for some time by scholars of international relations (e.g. Krasner 1983). This sub-discipline of political science evolved quite separate from (national) governance theory. In international relations, the actors and negotiating partners are states that stand in a relationship of strategic interdependence. This is the reason why there exists an obvious affinity between international relations and game theory. The international relations approach assumes that nation states are the most important actors on the global scene. This perspective is misleading if we take a closer look at the governance issues that present themselves at the global level.

Globalisation does not simply mean that economic and non-economic relations become increasingly transnational. There is more *movement* across national boundaries – movement of goods, services, capital, information, scientific knowledge and, last buy not least, of people. This results in new, often one-sided dependences, but only partly in new transnational *relationships*. Unbridled competition, for instance, is increasing, though it does not affect all branches of all national economies in the same way. New transnational markets are less well regulated and hence tend more toward atomism and anarchy than has been true of market relationships contained within nation states. This also means an increase in uncontrolled negative externalities, ecological as well as social and economic. There is a growing disjunction between increasingly unbounded and far-flung economic and communication networks, on the one hand, and bounded political systems on the other, a disjunction between problem structures and regulatory structures that might cope with these problems. In response to this situation, conscious efforts have been made, and continue to be made, to institute transnational regulatory structures. The United Nations is, of course, the most inclusive of such structures, a conglomerate of sub-organisations and special organs ranging from a simple forum (UN Conference on the Environment and Sustainable Development, UNCED) to corporate actors such as the World Bank, with UNESCO, ILO, WHO and WTO possibly somewhere in between (Rittberger *et al.* 1997).

To investigate the emergence and functioning of transnational regulatory structures *beyond* the European Union is certainly a fascinating agenda for a theory of political governance. But that is not where the challenge ends. Globalisation poses yet another theoretical problem: the problem of the coexistence of many different types of structures and processes, i.e. different governance modes. Market models and the non-linear dynamics of ecological systems seem best able to deal with the aggregate outcomes of a fragmented, but interdependent, global economy. In the structurally diffuse context created by globalisation, specific events or changes often cannot be causally attributed to the behaviour of identifiable actors. Situations of recognised strategic interdependence that can guide the choice between alternatives are rare. In the global market, most agents play, as it were, most of the time 'against nature'. At the same time, however, the transnational scene is not devoid of structure. The new regulatory structures have already been mentioned. There are, furthermore, many kinds of international as well as transnational organisations – the large multinational corporations, transnational professional associations, interest organisations and scientific organisations. Finally there exist transnational epistemic communities and social movements, incipient social groups without a clear geographical reference. Together, these various transnational groupings, regimes and organisations, with their often fluid boundaries and cross-cutting domains, their mutual and one-sided dependences, form a structure of such complexity that it seems to defy all our analytical efforts: What confronts us here is truly Habermas's *neue Unübersichtlichkeit* (Habermas 1985). Only if we enlarge the governance perspective to include *all* the different modes of social ordering, *all* the different types of actor configurations beyond hierarchies and networks, their combinations and particularly *their interactions*, might we be able to address the issues created by transnationalisation and globalisation. Should such a theory emerge, it would have to be a governance theory of a very different kind from the one we started with in this account.

What is an obvious theoretical problem on the global level alerts us to the existence of an analytical dimension that also applies at the national level. Governance studies at the national level have typically used an approach that has come to be called actor-centred institutionalism (Mayntz and Scharpf 1995; Scharpf 1997), i.e. they are concerned with actors acting and interacting within institutional frameworks. The actors whose decisions (and non-decisions) are studied to explain policy outcomes are normally corporate actors: agencies, organisations, associations (represented, of course, by individuals). Simple 'populations', collections of many individuals responding to given stimuli in the same way, normally play a role only as target groups of some policy. Aggregate effects arising from the unco-ordinated actions of many individuals appear only as parameters in policy analyses, not as a process to be explained *within* the theoretical framework of governance. Only in exceptional cases do we find an analysis of the *interplay* between steering attempts on the part of corporate actors and processes of collective behaviour that evolve first for reasons of their own, but may then motivate, and later on also react to, political intervention. In sectoral studies of the transformation processes in East Germany there are some analyses of this kind (e.g. Wasem 1997). But in general the fact that processes following different logics – collective behaviour, market exchange, bargaining, negotiation, and authoritative intervention – coexist and are causally interrelated has not been a topic in (national) governance theory.

Whether this can be called a deficit of governance theory in particular is, however, an open question. Parallel to what has been argued for a global governance theory, it may well be that to extend the paradigm to include *pari passu*, i.e. on an equal footing, all the distinguishable forms of co-ordination, or social ordering, would *over*extend it, making it lose the necessary amount of selective attention that is a prerequisite of theory building – for human minds at least. In any case we would no longer be dealing with a theory of political governance, but with a much more comprehensive theory of social dynamics, i.e. not with an extended, but with a completely new, theoretical paradigm.

## Conclusion

In this chapter I have traced through several stages the development of a body of theory concerned with the forms and problems of social and political guidance. In retrospect, this development looks like the successive unfolding of a cognitive agenda, driven step by step by awareness of blind spots and of deficits in explanatory power *vis-à-vis* observable reality. There have been some interesting bifurcations in the process, e.g. when governance theory concentrated on horizontal co-operation rather than the market as an alternative to hierarchical authority, and there are still blind spots in the theory to which it has not reacted. But, up to now, this has been a cumulative cognitive process that did not follow the developmental logic of political science described by Dryzek and Leonard (1988), who argued that the objects of political science are historically contingent, wherefore political scientists must continually begin to develop new and different analytical frames and substantive theories that cannot build upon each other. At least in the case of governance theory (which is not, of course, all there is to political science) we find instead a successive extension of the initial framework, not its suppression and exchange for a new one, i.e. not a paradigm shift in the radical Kuhnian sense (Kuhn 1962). In this development, changes in political reality have played an important role, influencing the direction in which the paradigm was being extended. The modern state has in fact become more 'co-operative', networks have proliferated, and European integration is a new phenomenon. These observable real changes were challenges that could be accommodated by extending the paradigm. But with globalisation, there may well have come the point where a further extension of the paradigm would be dysfunctional, and we may witness the emergence of an altogether new field.

### Notes

1  For such a documentation see Mayntz (1996) and the literature cited there.
2  For a more detailed description of the theory development summarised in this section see again Mayntz (1996).
3  This does not mean that the European Union is a *sui generis* case that can only be analysed in a framework uniquely tailored to it alone; for this discussion see Hix (1998).
4  The present research programme of the Max Planck Institute for the Study of Societies in Cologne is nearly entirely devoted to these problems.
5  An early exception is Scharpf (1974).

### References

Bowen, R. H. (1971, 1947), *German Theories of the Corporative State* (New York: Russell).
Bulmer, S. (1994), 'The governance of the European Union: a New Institutionalist approach', *Journal of Public Policy* 13: 351–80.
Döhler, M. (1990), *Gesundheitspolitik nach der 'Wende'. Policy-Netzwerke und ordnungspolitischer Strategiewechsel in Grossbritannien, den USA und der Bundesrepublik Deutschland* (Berlin: Sigma).
Dryzek, J. S., and Leonard, S. T. (1988), 'History and discipline in political science', *American Political Science Review* 82 (4): 1245–60.
Dunn, J. (1990), 'Capitalism, socialism and democracy: compatabilities and contradictions', in *The Economic Limits to Modern Politics* (Cambridge: Cambridge University Press), pp. 195–220.
Habermas, J. (1985), *Die neue Unübersichtlichkeit. Kleine politische Schriften* V, Neue Folge 321 (Frankfurt: Suhrkamp).

Héritier, A., Knill, C., and Mingers, S. (1996), *Ringing the Changes in Europe: Regulatory Competition and Redefinition of the State. Britain, France, Germany* (Berlin and New York: de Gruyter).

Hix, S. (1998), 'The study of the European Union' II, 'The "new governance" agenda and its rival', *Journal of European Public Policy* 5 (1): 38–65.

Hollingsworth, J. R., and Lindberg, L. N. (1985), 'The governance of the American economy: the role of markets, clans, hierarchies, and associate behavior', in W. Streeck and P. Schmitter (eds), *Private Interest Government: Beyond Market and State* (London: Sage), pp. 221–54.

Katz, C. (1997), 'Private property versus markets: democratic and communitarian critiques of capitalism', *American Political Science Review* 91: 277–89.

Katzenstein, P. J. (1987), *Policy and Politics in West Germany: The Growth of a Semisovereign State* (Philadelphia: Temple University Press).

Kitschelt, H. (1985), 'Materiale Politisierung der Produktion. Gesellschaftliche Herausforderung und institutionelle Innovationen in Fortgeschrittenen kapitalistischen Demokratien', *Zeitschrift für Soziologie* 14: 188–208.

Kooiman, J., ed. (1993), *Modern Governance: New Government–Society Interactions* (London: Sage).

Krasner, S. D., ed. (1983), *International Regimes* (Ithaca NY: Cornell University Press).

Kuhn, T. S. (1962), *The Structure of Scientific Revolutions* (Chicago: University of Chicago Press).

Lütz, S. (1998), 'The revival of the nation state? Stock exchange regulation in an era of globalized financial markets', *Journal of European Public Policy* 5 (1): 153–68.

Mayntz, R. (1996), 'Politische Steuerung. Aufstieg, Niedergang und Transformation einer Theorie', in K. von Beyme and C. Offe (eds), *Politische Theorien in der Ära der Transformation* (Opladen: Westdeutscher Verlag), pp. 148–68.

Mayntz, R., and Scharpf, F. (1987) 'Politische Steuerung und gesellschaftliche Steuerungsprobleme. Anmerkungen zu einem theoretischen Paradigma', in *Jahrbuch für Staats- und Verwaltungswissenschaft* 1, 89–110.

Mayntz, R., and Scharpf, F. W., eds (1995), *Gesellschaftliche Selbstregelung und politische Steuerung* (Frankfurt: Campus).

Powell, W. W. (1990), 'Neither market nor hierarchy: network forms of organization', *Research in Organizational Behavior* 12: 295–336.

Rhodes, R. A. W. (1997), *Understanding Governance: Policy Networks, Governance, Reflexivity and Accountability* (Buckingham: Open University Press).

Rittberger, V., Mogler, M., and Zangl, B. (1997), *Vereinte Nationen und Weltordnung. Zivilisierung der internationalen Politik?* (Opladen: Leske & Budrich).

Rosenau, J. N., and Czempiel, E-O., eds (1992), *Governance without Government: Order and Change in World Politics* (Cambridge: Cambridge University Press).

Scharpf, F. W. (1974), *Politische Durchsetzbarkeit innerer Reformen im pluralistisch-demokratischen Gemeinwesen der Bundesrepublik* (Göttingen: Schwartz).

Scharpf, F. W. (1993), 'Co-ordination in hierarchies and networks', in F. W. Scharpf (ed.), *Games in Hierarchies and Networks: Analytical and Empirical Approaches to the Study of Governance Institution* (Frankfurt: Campus), pp. 125–65.

Scharpf, F. W. (1997), *Games Real Actors Play. Actor-centered Institutionalism in Policy Research* (Boulder CO: Westview Press).

Scharpf, F. W. (1997), *Globalisierung als Beschränkung der Handlungsmöglichkeiten nationalstaatlicher Politik*. MPIfG discussion paper 97/1 (Cologne: Max Planck Institut für Gesellschaftsforschung).

Scharpf, F. W. (1999), *Governing in Europe: Effective and Democratic?* (Oxford: Oxford University Press).

Schneider, V. (1988), *Politiknetzwerke der Chemikalienkontrolle. Eine Analyse einer transnationalen Politikentwicklung* (Berlin: de Gruyter).

Streeck, W., and Schmitter, P., eds (1985), *Private Interest Government. Beyond Market and State* (London: Sage).

Stykow, P., and Wiesenthal, H., eds (1996), *Globalisierung ökonomischen Handelns und ihre Folgen für politische Steuerung. Forschungsberichte der AG Transformationsprozesse in den neuen Bundesländern* (Berlin: Humboldt University).

UNESCO (1998), 'Governance', *International Social Science Journal*, March.

Voelzkow, H. (1996), *Private Regierungen in der Techniksteuerung. Eine sozialwissenschaftliche Analyse der technischen Normung* (Frankfurt: Campus).

Wasem, J. (1997), *Vom staatlichen zum kassenärztlichen System. Eine Untersuchung des Transformationsprozesses der ambulanten ärztlichen Versorgung in Ostdeutschland* (Frankfurt: Campus).

Williamson, O. E. (1979), 'Transaction-cost economics: the governance of contractual relations', *Journal of Law and Economics* 22: 233–61.

Willke, H. (1987), 'Entzauberung des Staates. Grundlinien einer systemtheoretischen Argumentation', *Jahrbuch für Staats- und Verwaltungswissenschaft* 1: 285–308.

# 3

# A constructivist bottom-up approach to governance: the need for increased theoretical and methodological awareness in research

Jens Hoff

The purpose of this chapter is firstly to problematise a number of assumptions that are very often taken for granted in research on policy networks/ governance. Secondly, the chapter will, through this problematisation, develop a new methodological approach to policy networks/governance, which, for the lack of a better name, we call a 'constructivist bottom-up approach'. Thirdly, the chapter will show – through a concrete case study – the usefulness and added value of this approach.

There are three assumptions in particular which are often taken for granted in governance theory, but which, on the basis of both theoretical considerations and empirical evidence, we find it highly relevant to question. The first assumption is that policy networks exists (in modern Western countries) on such a massive scale as to warrant talking about a shift from 'government' to 'governance' when characterising the overall mode of political steering in society. The second assumption is that interdependence or power dependence is (always) the 'explanatory motor' (Rhodes 1997: 9) in policy networks. The third assumption is that when studying policy networks/governance the natural point of observation is 'the managerial perspective'; the perspective of the civil servant or the government politician, which means that the main analytical concern becomes that of how to create coherence, consensus and integration around certain policies and/or across policy fields (see, for example, Kickert *et al.* 1997).

In questioning these assumptions we develop a new methodological framework for studying policy networks, which draws upon institutionalist and social constructivist theories, and which, in its empirical dimension, relies on a bottom-up method. This methodology was originally developed in relation to a project on 'Democracy from Below', one of five subprojects under a major project on 'Democracy and Institutional Development' supported by the Danish Social Science Research Council.[1] The methodology as well as the case study presented here is described in more detail in Bang *et al.* (2000). However, this chapter spells out more clearly the differences between this approach and most other approaches to policy networks/governance. The case study, of industrial policy in a region of Denmark, will then show how this new 'anti-essentialist' methodology produces an understanding of the dynamics of a policy network, which would not have been possible within, for example, an 'interdependence perspective'. The case study will also demonstrate how the use of our methodology serves to highlight two issues which are all too often downplayed in policy network theory. (1) Inclusion/exclusion of the network. How does the mechanism of inclusion/exclusion work? And to what extent can the construction of a network therefore be seen as a power strategy? (2) The relation of the network to formal (democratically elected or controlled) political institutions. This directs attention towards the democratic aspects (threats and possibilities) of policy networks.

## Questioning assumptions in governance theory

There have been a great many attempts at defining the term 'governance' (see, for example, Kooiman 1993: 2; Rhodes 1997: 53; Jessop 1998; Stoker 1998: 18). However, very roughly it seems possible to distinguish between a perspective which is basically descriptive and a perspective which is basically analytical; trying to define governance as an ideal typical form of political steering (see also Mayntz in chapter 2). The descriptive approach uses the term governance as a 'fishing net' concept, a way to characterise a number of policy networks which some similar traits. A typical example of this approach is Rhodes (1997), who states, 'Governance refers to self-organising, interorganisational networks', and lists the following shared characteristics of 'governance' [institutions – J. H.]:

1 Interdependence between organisations. Governance is broader than government, covering non-state actors. Changing the boundaries of the state meant the boundaries between public, private and voluntary sectors became shifting and opaque.
2 Continuing interactions between network members caused by the need to exchange resources and negotiate shared purposes.
3 Game-like interactions rooted in trust and regulated by rules of the game negotiated and agreed by network participants.
4 A significant degree of autonomy from the state. Networks are not accountable to the state; they are self-organising. Although the state does not occupy a sovereign position, it can indirectly and imperfectly steer networks.

From the context it is quite clear that this is a list of characteristics based on Rhodes's analyses of different concrete policy networks, and also a list which has gradually been expanded and refined as (new) cross-boundary, interorganisational networks have popped up and come under scrutiny.

In chapter 2 Renate Mayntz traces the analytical perspective back to transaction cost economics, and Williamson's (1979) analysis of market and hierarchy as alternative forms of economic organisation – an analysis which was extended by heterarchy, or networks, as yet another type of social co-ordination. However, there has also been a parallel organisation theory and/or political science approach to the discussion about mechanisms of social co-ordination stretching from the neo-institutionalist perspective of Rokkan (1969), and the neo-corporatist perspective of Schmitter and Lembruch (1979) via Heclo (1978) to parts of the 'modern' or 1990s debate about policy networks.[2] A newer example of this type of approach is Jessop (1998). Jessop sees government (hierarchy), market and governance as ideal typical forms of steering (co-ordination), and describes the differences between them on the basis of five criteria. Government, for example, is characterised by a rationality of substance (*raison d'état*), steering is evaluated on the basis of its effectiveness, the typical individual in the model is 'homo hierarchicus' (as described by Weber), the time and space horizon is the nation state, and the model's criterion for failure is lack of goal attainment. In contrast, governance is characterised by a reflexive rationality, steering is evaluated on the basis of its ability to produce consensus and gain acceptance, the typical individual is 'homo politicus', the time and space horizon is variable (it crosses the borders between local, national and global), and the model's criterion for failure is lack of consensus and coherence.

Even though one might not agree completely with the five criteria Jessop sets up for defining the different types of social co-ordination/steering, I argue that there are a number of advantages in defining governance as an ideal typical type of social co-ordination/steering.

Firstly, seeing governance as an ideal type of social co-ordination makes the distinction between governance and policy networks clear. Thus governance is a macro-level (analytical) concept while policy network is better seen as a meso-level (empirical) concept. The difference between the two concepts might be characterised in statements like 'political steering (social co-ordination) through networks can be characterised as governance' or, maybe better, that 'steering through policy networks can be characterised as governance', the point being that the actual policy process taking place in and through the network can be characterised by its closeness/distance to the ideal type (or to ideal types of 'market' and 'hierarchy').

Secondly, if we use governance as a 'fishing net' concept, which is gradually being expanded as new types of policy networks emerge, we run the risk of over-extending the concept. If the term 'governance' is used to characterise all new types of social co-ordination, whether based on any combination of collective behaviour, market exchange, bargaining, negotiation, authoritative intervention, etc., it becomes very difficult to understand what governance is not (see also Mayntz in chapter 2). Staying with the metaphor, we can say that just expanding the 'fishing net' every time a new type of 'fish' pops up is neither theory development (testing and revising different assumptions about the world) nor (theoretically informed) analysis, but a kind of ad-hocism, similar to what Rhodes has called 'butterfly collecting'.[3]

We are now in a position to tackle the first of the three 'taken for granted' assumptions about governance mentioned at the beginning. The first assumption was that there has been a shift from 'government' to 'governance' when characterising the overall mode of political steering in modern Western countries. The way this claim is normally substantiated is by pointing to the expansion of (policy) networks at all levels – local, national, global – and between and across these levels. However, according to the definition of governance used here this is a necessary but not a sufficient condition. What is needed is a closer look at these networks in order to analyse the extent to which the types of steering they practise qualify as 'governance'. Such an analysis cannot be done from 'above', but must be performed from below in a concrete empirical fashion. Thus using the concept of governance puts certain demands on both research design and research method – questions to be pursued in the following sections of this chapter.

One of the most well established and generally approved assumptions in governance theory is that interdependence or power dependence is the *raison d'être* for, or the 'explanatory motor' in, policy networks. A good example of this way of thinking is Kickert *et al.* (1997), who write: 'Interdependency is the key word in the network approach. Actors in networks are interdependent because they cannot attain their goals by themselves, but need the resources of other actors to do so' (1997: 6), and they sharpen the position further: 'Networks develop and exist because of the interdependency between actors' (1997: 31). And indeed, in almost all the concrete cases we can think of it is possible, either *ex ante* or *ex post*, to construct the exchange of some kind of resources as the motivating factor behind the establishment of the network.

However, this assumption seems to be highly dependent on the idea that policy networks are self-organised. Thus it is hard to imagine organisational actors interacting regularly, thereby constituting a network, unless 'there is something in it for everyone'. To assume that policy networks are always, or even most of the time, self-organised, i.e. created on a completely voluntary basis, is, however, highly questionable. In Scandinavia, for example (but also in Germany and the Netherlands), a great many policy networks are created on the initiative of public authorities of one kind or another; either directly or, as we shall see in the case study below, in an indirect fashion, where a municipality creates the conditions for the establishment of a policy network (see also Bogason 2000). One could of course take the position that these networks are not 'real' policy networks, but that would be closing one's eyes to the fact that these networks are policy-formulating, often policy-implementing, and generally live up to all other criteria for such networks, as depicted by, for example, Rhodes (above) or Marin and Mayntz (1991).[4]

What I am saying, in other words, is that there might be other reasons for the development and existence of networks than interdependence between actors. They might, for example, develop out of need to reach a common understanding concerning a certain policy problem, or because of the need to pool resources in order to implement policy in a certain field. One could of course argue that someone (a public authority?) must need 'the common understanding concerning the policy problem' or 'the pooling of resources', and that these examples therefore also constitute interdependences. However, the point here is that these interdependences are not internal or endogenous in the network, but rather brought about by outside pressure or intervention. This relates back to the question of the self-organised character of the network. Thus, if we relativise or give up the claim that policy networks must (always) be self-organised, we also have to allow for the existence of other mechanisms than interdependence as the 'explanatory motor' in policy networks.

What we have to do therefore is to give up the 'essentialist' or mono-causal approach to policy networks. Instead we must build our approach to the study of policy networks/governance on an 'anti-essentialist' foundation, which allows for the possibility that there might be different reasons for the establishing of networks in different policy fields, and which leaves the question about why networks develop and exist as a matter of empirical investigation. Methodologically this means (again) that policy networks must be studied 'from below', and that the emphasis must be on their formative period and their mode of functioning. What is called for is a contextual and process-oriented type of analysis which, so to speak, 'tells the history of the network'.[5] This must be a narrative type of analysis, but not in the sense of the individual stories of the actors in the network. What is called for is rather a type of 'institutional narrative', a concept developed further below.

The third assumption to be questioned here is that when studying policy networks/governance the 'natural' point of observation is 'the managerial perspective', i.e. the perspective of the civil servant or the government politician. By questioning this assumption I am not saying that it is not a legitimate or necessary perspective. Indeed, politicians and civil servants should certainly be concerned with how public policy is formulated and implemented in a more and more functionally differentiated (polycentric), glocalised and informatised society. Thus concerns with meta-governance, culture governance, etc., are an important part of governance theory and should be explored. What I am questioning is the fact that a 'managerial' or a 'top-down' perspective has – implicitly or explicitly – more or less become the taken-for-granted perspective in governance theory. This probably has to do with the fact that the discussion of governance and policy networks has in particular taken place within the discipline of public administration, a discipline with strong ties between researchers and practitioners. This means that researchers are often concerned with solving concrete problems or giving concrete advice to policy makers or public administration – a practice which serves to keep up the societal relevance of the discipline, but which can also, as in this case, limit the vision or approach to policy networks/governance too much.

For these reasons it is – even though it might seem a truism – necessary to stress the point that policy networks can also legitimately be seen from other perspectives; for example, from the non-government or non-public actor's point of view or from the citizen's point of view. Also, researchers might ground their research into policy networks in other problematics than just the question of steering/management (at different levels). Thus it might be just as relevant to approach policy networks/governance from a democratic[6] or from a power-oriented perspective.

Advocating the possibility of using other, or maybe even a multitude of, perspectives in the analysis of policy networks is not the same thing as advocating a 'multi-actor' perspective (a rational choice/New Public Management approach). In line with what has been said above, I rather advocate an institutional approach which is neither actor nor structure-oriented, but which tries to account for the interplay of actors and network in order to understand the possible outcomes of the network in terms of policies, democracy and power. It is to theoretical considerations concerning this institutional approach that we now turn.

## Policy networks as political institutions

Seeing policy networks as political institutions is not an entirely new idea (see also Mayntz and Scharpf 1995; Blom-Hansen 1996). However, as the kinds of institutionalism I advocate here have a more sociological orientation than most other types of institutionalisms used in policy network analysis, a brief explanation is warranted.

Political institutions are often described as structural determinants, for example, as social rules or sanctions (see, for example, Peters 1999). Their primary task is to create and preserve order. Rational choice institutionalism, for example, holds the opinion that political institutions emerge owing to the existence of a collective efficiency problem or dilemma in connecting opposing preferences in a rational decision. Normative institutionalism sees the emergence of political institutions as a result of a societal need to ensure social harmony, consensus and integration. (Note the similarity between these conceptions and the 'interdependence as motor' argument above.)

What is characteristic of these approaches is that they see political institutions as something which emerges or is disrupted when there is conflict, and which consolidates and develops when there is order. Thus political and social stability is made a prerequisite for viable political institutions. As soon as the social or political stability is threatened or undermined, new political institutions have to be designed to re-establish order.

In our view this is a misconception of political institutions. They should rather be seen as 'islands of order' (or continuity) in a 'sea of disorder'. Our first statement concerning political institutions is therefore that, if one wants to see political institutional order as contingent with different degrees of transformation and stability, one should not tie the analysis of institutions to essentialist approaches. Our second statement is that political institutions are not just institutions of the state or of a given political regime. They are not necessarily connected with rationality, hierarchy and steering from above under the authoritative rule of a given regime. They can also establish themselves in voluntary or third-sector environments at 'the bottom' of the political culture. In saying this, we are not denying the points that the 'old' institutionalisms are making; namely that political institutions help society and its actors to decide who has, and who can get access to, which decision situations, how information and communication are structured in terms of regime roles and positions, which authoritative actions can be taken in which sequences, and how individual acts are aggregated and integrated in collective decisions (March and Olsen 1989; Peters 1999). What we are saying is merely that political institutions are tied not only to questions about how to get access to the political regime, but also to how one is accepted in the political culture (Bourdieu 1998).

Thus, in looking at political institutions, we start from the fundamental assumption that they can be equated neither with (an aggregation of) rational actors nor with social structures. Instead we see political institutions (and thus policy networks) as regularised practices. In order for a regularised practice to become a political institution, it has to become sedimented and to have or get a relatively permanent and recursive character.

Such regularised practices have structures, which not only regulate but which are also constructed by individual and collective behaviour and action (Giddens 1979). Political institutions cannot therefore be seen as 'conceived' by social structures or political actors. They create structures, which are created by and create actors. They cannot be tied to any pre-given goals or preferences, because such goals and preferences are articulated and actualised in and by political institutions in a certain (temporal, spatial) situation. Thus political institutions are created in political decision and implementation processes, which runs through all of society, and which could always have been different. In these processes one finds a great many situations with their own logics of appropriateness, and sets of rules for how things are 'usually' done. Political situations can therefore be a part of the authoritative way in which an institution articulates and implements politics and policies here and now. But they can also just be 'floating around' in the political culture as a sign of something new, which has not yet been authorised, or as old stories, which are no longer a part of valid (authoritative) visions, ideals, discourses and strategies.

It is precisely the fact that political institutions are created in a transformation process, which can be seen from a great number of positions, which makes it possible to talk about them as 'sources of order and stability in an interactive world, which otherwise seem quite chaotic' (March and Olsen 1989: 53).

Even though this is so, we think it mistaken to tie (political) institutions to an opposition between order and disorder, conservation and renewal, stability and change, integration and conflict or static versus dynamic. All these conditions are always simultaneously present in varying degrees in a political situation and thus in the institution; for example, what looks like renewal from one point of view can look like conservation ('doing what we always do in this situation') from another. Therefore, institutional change cannot just be explained as the result of a rational choice from without (exogenously) or an exogenous social need. It must also, and maybe in particular, be explained endogenously as a result of the interplay between the institution and individuals/actors in the situation.

Another way to express this is that a political institution will always put certain constraints on the participating individuals/actors, but all the energy, information and communication which is to be found in a political institution cannot be submitted to the ruling actors or structures. There will always be deposits of unbound energy, information and communication floating around in and between the different layers of the institution in the form of forgotten routines, latent possibilities, new or excluded habits, etc. They make 'holes' or 'cracks' in any structural design in any institution; thereby making it possible to talk about institutions as being in constant state of change with a change rhythm which can vary from ultra-low to ultra-high.

These 'holes' or 'cracks' constitute arenas for the restructuring of the institution. Even the most disintegrated, non-confident and ineffective actor has an arsenal of rules and resources, which can challenge an institutional hegemony (Giddens 1979). It is self-evident that the more accepted actors are in the political culture, the easier access they will have to the political regime, and the easier it will be for them to articulate their own arenas and specify their own social environment. In so doing they are forcing other actors to submit to them. In this way the question of power and control becomes intimately tied to the investigation of how institutions constitute, regulate and normalise themselves and their environment through their interpretations and actions in a world dominated by continuing disorder, strife and disagreement (March and Olsen 1989).

It also seems self-evident that an institution with its authoritative interpretation can and will have an effect on the understanding which the actors have of themselves, the institution and the environment. The rules and resources connected with a given institutional hegemony will (probably depending on the centrality of the institution for the actor) form the intentions and wishes of the actors by affecting the way in which they interact in a situation and connect themselves with their environment.

Thus actors 'carrying' an institution are all the time confronted with the fact that they have to make risky choices about what to do, when and how, in fundamentally ambiguous situations. They would not be able to fill out and take on their roles and positions in the institution unless they had both the power and the freedom to actively interpret and articulate themselves in the situation by drawing upon their experiences with and feelings about their many-sided identities and overlapping memberships (of different institutions). Even though all (political) decision and implementation processes are of course affected by rational consideration about the consequences of the decisions, it is still the logics of appropriateness and comparison of cases (in terms of commonalties and differences) which make such considerations possible: 'The process maintains consistency in action primarily through the creation of typologies of similarity [identities – J.H.], rather than through a derivation of action from stable interests or wants' (March and Olsen 1989: 26).

Summing up, we can say that seeing policy networks as political institutions implies the following:

1 Regularised practices must be the point of departure when discovering and analysing policy networks.
2 Because politics is an activity which can take place everywhere in society, policy networks are not necessarily connected with steering 'from above'.
3 Policy networks cannot be tied to any pre-given goals or preferences, because such goals and preferences are always context-dependent.
4 Change in a network cannot just be explained by exogenous factors, but must also, and maybe in particular, be explained by the interplay between the network and its actors.
5 The network will be important for the identity of the involved actors, and will to a great extent form their intentions and goals when acting as part of the network in concrete situations.
6 The question of power must be a central part of an investigation of how policy networks constitute, regulate and normalise themselves.

From the exposition above it should be clear that the institutional approach to policy networks developed fits very well with the criticism of the three assumptions in the first part of this chapter. Firstly, it is anti-essentialist or constructivist in the sense that it does not tie networks to any pre-given goals or preferences but sees them as dependent on the concrete political situation, and as it stresses the endogenous character of both change and the identity formation of the involved actors. Secondly, an analysis of regularised practices and endogenously formed preferences and identities in concrete political situations is possible only with a bottom-up research strategy, which is therefore what this institutional approach calls for. Finally, as this approach is neither structure nor actor-oriented, but oriented to understanding the creation, development and functioning of a given policy network, it must tell this story as an institutional narrative. Thus we have now established, if in rudimentary fashion, a new theoretical and methodological foundation for the analysis of concrete policy networks. Let us see if the approach makes a difference in a concrete analysis.

## Case study: industrial policy in a Danish region

In accordance with our anti-essentialist and bottom-up approach we did not take the established field of (government initiated) industrial policy as our point of departure for the study of possible policy networks. Instead we took, as recommended in the bottom-up literature (see, for example, Elmore 1980, Bogason and Sørensen 1998), a point of departure in a self-defined policy problem related to the field, which we choose to be the local supply and demand for labour power in the municipality of Skanderborg in Jutland.

Apart from the more general arguments for this kind of approach put forward above, there are two more specific reasons for choosing this approach. Firstly, because it is a way of trying to avoid 'system bias' in the analysis, in the sense of taking certain organisational set-ups for given. Secondly, because it is a way of creating 'openness' towards the way in which the policy field is institutionalised. Thus what we were interested in investigating was whether this institutionalisation took the form of a policy network(s), and, if this was the case, how such a network(s) was created, and what kinds of practices were giving it a permanent character. Also, we were interested in the relation between the network and the local formal political institutions.

At the outset it was clear to us that there are a lot of factors which influence the local supply and demand for labour power which are outside the scope of local/regional industrial policy: the global economic situation, technological development, national taxation and environmental policies, etc. These factors have a big; maybe by far the biggest, effect on local supply and demand for labour power. However, what we were interested in studying were the conscious attempts made locally to affect this supply and demand. It is clear that a single firm can affect supply and demand by hiring and firing employees. However, our focus was the political dimension of this policy, by which we understand the way in which a number of businesses or actors jointly try to affect the supply and demand for labour power either as a unity, on behalf of a community or with reference to a community (the municipality, the region).

By framing our research question this way, it turned out that we came to touch upon three formal municipal policy fields which dealt with different aspects of supply and demand for labour: local/regional industrial policy, local labour market policy and local social policy.[7] We found a policy network related to local industrial policy (see below) and a network related to the local labour market and social policy. In order to simplify the analysis, we shall deal here only with the industrial policy network.[8]

In trying to trace the eventual existence of a policy network concerned with local industrial policy, our point of departure was (interviews with) different firms about their possible collaboration concerning business growth and employment, and their possible collaboration with local public authorities concerning these issues. We quickly realised that the businesses studied were not, in general, particularly oriented towards the municipality as such, but towards an environment that could be either global, national or regional, depending on the production and markets of the firm in question. In so far as the businesses in the municipality oriented themselves to their locality it was first of all towards the region; i.e. towards co-operation with other businesses and public authorities in the east of Jutland. As we shall see below, there is a nice 'match' between this orientation and the possibilities of co-operation offered by public or semi-public organisations in the region.

In a description of the development of local industrial policy the Ministry of Trade and Industry (Erhvervsministeriet 1995: 22) describes the policy as having taken place in three phases. The first phase (1958–80) is not relevant in this context. In the second (1980–90), described as the 'growth phase', the official (government) goal of regional industrial policy was changed from creating (more or less) uniform industrial development to creating equal conditions for growth in all regions. The Ministry became more active in trying to induce the regions and municipalities to pursue a regional industrial policy, and to this end industrial boards were established in many municipalities. In Skanderborg an industrial board was established in 1984.[9] The phase from 1990 to the present has been called the 'co-ordination phase', as a number of municipalities have tried to co-ordinate their efforts in formally organised regional co-operation. The municipality of Skanderborg participates in several such co-operations: the 'Corridor', which is a co-operation between seven municipalities in the East Jutland region, the 'ten municipality co-operation', which is a co-operation between ten municipalities in the county of Aarhus (the second largest city in Denmark), and finally in the so-called 'five-city co-operation', which is a co-operation between the five largest cities in the East Jutland region.[10]

These regional co-operations provide different services to businesses in the area, and create opportunities for businesses to meet. This creates contacts between different firms, which are maintained and used actively. The co-operation between different firms (brought about by regional co-operations and municipal industrial boards) concerns common marketing campaigns, sharing experience concerning exports and new technology, different courses and meetings, etc. Exchange of experiences typically takes place between firms in the same line of business, or by bigger, well established firms advising smaller firms. Our research shows that the businesses in the region feel a need to co-operate, but also that such co-operation would probably not take place unless mediated by the regional co-operations. The need to co-operate (and thus a feeling of mutual dependence) seem to be brought about by three factors: (1) to be able to face increased global and European competition, (2) to reduce uncertainty on the regional/local market, and (3) to improve the opportunities for political influence. In the municipality of Skanderborg, but also in the region in general, businesses experience benevolence and flexibility in their relations with politicians and administrators, and they experience few obstacles in relation to decision makers as the mayor or the head of the municipal administration. However, it is clear that in the municipality of Skanderborg the municipal board (elected politicians) consciously tries to steer local industrial policy. This steering is not done through rule making, but through the attitude that business is met with, and through the platforms provided for interaction and dialogue between different businesses (i.e. the municipal industrial boards and the regional co-operations), and between business and political and administrative decision makers.

Summing up concerning the existence of a policy network around local/regional industrial policy, the reasons for its establishment and its content, we can say that we found a well developed policy network around the platforms provided by the industrial board(s) and the regional co-operations. These semi-public institutions have served as catalysts for the creation of the network – which consists of important elements of business in the region, the mayors and administrative heads of the involved municipalities, parts of the municipal administrations and the heads of the industrial boards and regional co-operations. Businesses have joined the network in order to be able to perform better in international, national and regional markets and in order to have direct access to central local political and administrative decision makers. Thus, in terms of politics and policies, the value of the network is, that it provides a forum for the creation and exchange of ideas concerning economic and employment growth in the region, and thereby for the formulation of a common local industrial policy (see below).

One of the surprises in our analysis was that the local trade unions seemed to be excluded from the policy making in the network. This was surprising as the unions play an important role in other policy networks concerned with economic growth and employment – for example, the local labour market policy network we analysed. Also, it was particularly surprising as the unions (LO) are actually represented on the local industrial board (see note 9). The way we discovered this exclusion was by looking at a number of decision-making processes (and other events) where we found that the union was either excluded or not listened to.

Taking a closer look at the possible reasons for this exclusion, we found that the most likely one was the existence of a certain local discourse, of which the unions were not a part. The discourse presents the local industrial policy as a locally oriented general policy, in which the crucial concepts are 'growth' and 'quality of life'. The unions cannot or do not want to inscribe themselves in the local 'common destiny' which is articulated through this discourse. This because the unions represent another type of community: a community based on rights and duties of a universal (or at least national) character.

A thorough understanding of the creation and exact functioning of this discourse demands a historical account which the format here does not allow. Very briefly we can say that the municipality of Skanderborg experienced a severe recession in the 1970s and 1980s. The town itself lost its status as the seat of the county council, unemployment soared and motorcycle gangs ravaged the town. The industrial council, the mayor and some local businesses decided to do something about it, and in early 1991 they established three working groups consisting of a broad array of organisations, interest groups and concerned citizens, who drew up a plan for a new industrial policy for the municipality. This plan launched the industrial policy as a common project for the whole municipality with the aim of creating a 'feeling of commonality' around the municipality – the municipality as more than an organisation or a locality, but rather as a 'common destiny'. The main points in this plan were a coupling of the concepts of 'growth' and 'quality of life', and seeing the one as a condition of the other.[11]

The appeal of this discourse seems to have worked. Businesses demonstrate social engagement; local sports clubs 'advertise' the municipality and are sponsored by local business, etc. However, the unions do not inscribe themselves in this discourse, and are thereby excluded – or maybe they exclude themselves – from the local industrial policy network. Seeing themselves more as traditional organisations for the defence of wage-earner interests, they find it hard to accept the idea of a 'common destiny'. The unions are not 'local patriots' in the way local businesses portray themselves. Their loyalty is rather towards their historically hard-won rights of a universal charter. Hence they do not possess the 'ticket' to the municipal 'common destiny', and are excluded from most decision-making forums in the local industrial policy network.

The aim of this case study has been to demonstrate the usefulness and added value of our anti-essentialist bottom-up approach. We think this is most amply demonstrated by the case of the exclusion of the unions. Thus, in an interdependence approach to policy networks, one would expect exclusion to take place on the grounds of resources (you are excluded from a network if you are unable to contribute anything of value to the other partners).[12] However, our approach opened the possibility of detecting other reasons for exclusion, for example the lack of consent to common goals and values in a network. This was particularly noteworthy, as the part excluded was an actor who is normally, in a Danish context, regarded as big, strong and resourceful.

A point with our approach is also that it should be possible to ground the analysis of policy networks in other perspectives than a steering/man-

---

**The municipal 'discourse of communality'**

Skanderborg as a 'common destiny'
- Economic growth
- Quality of life


**The local industrial policy network**

*Why collaboration?*
- Global competition
- Reduction of uncertainty
- Possibility of political influence

*Content of collaboration*
- Exchange of experience
- Courses, meetings, etc., concerning exports, marketing, technology, in order to create business growth

*The actors*
- Local businesses
- Local industrial board
- Regional co-operation
- Mayor
- Central local politicians
- Representatives of municipal administration

---

agement perspective, for example a democracy or a power perspective. It is not possible to develop these perspectives in full here, only to hint at how such perspectives can be brought to bear on policy networks in a fruitful way.

In more conventional governance theory the problem of democracy in relation to (the spread of and possible dominance of) policy networks is discussed under the heading of 'accountability'. The networks should be democratically accountable, and if they are not, this is seen as a problem. The question of accountability is important, but does not by any means exhaust the range of democracy issues raised by policy networks. A possible way to approach the issue (used in, for example, Bang *et al.* (2000) is through looking at all the democratic procedural norms existing under the 'government' mode of steering, the newer set of norms created by 'governance' (see March and Olsen 1995), and then at how concrete policy networks match these sets of norms. The norms in question are: (under 'government') equality of access to influence, public debate concerning political decisions, the political authority's ability to act, the political authority's responsibility and accountability, the bureaucracy's responsibility and accountability, citizens' participation and political responsibility, and (under 'governance') the development of democratic identities of citizens and other political actors, the development of the capacity for appropriate political action among citizens and other political actors, the development of relevant political narratives, and the development of an adaptive political system which includes possibilities of democratic learning and experiment.

In analysing a number of different policy networks in the municipality of Skanderborg, among them the industrial policy network, we concentrated particularly on the question of equality of access to influence, and the question of the development of the capacity for appropriate political action among the members (and non-members) of the networks. The question of equality of access to influence is parallel to the discussion about inclusion in and exclusion from policy networks. Our analysis of different networks showed that most of them were, with some variation, in principle 'open' and 'inclusive'. However, many actors are not included, or are *de facto* excluded, owing to lack of resources, lack of 'cultural capital' or, as we saw in the case of the trade unions, dissent from the common goals and values of the network.

Concerning the question of the development of the capacity for appropriate political action, we found that members of networks were generally 'empowered' in the sense that members of policy networks (naturally) get an opportunity to participate in setting the political agenda, and/or implementing policies, but also that actors as a general rule see an increase in their political self-confidence, and acquire a number of competences, such as political know-how, organisational talent and the ability to create meaning, coherence and direction in their work in the network. The actors excluded from the networks naturally do not get these opportunities or acquire such a capacity, and are thus 'disempowered'.

What is rather obvious, judging from the case of Skanderborg, is therefore, that politics in (local) societies dominated by many policy networks tend to acquire an elite character. Whether this conclusion holds at a general level should be investigated further. But if it is true that the growth of policy networks entails a strengthening of the elite character of politics, this represents a tremendous challenge both to democracy and to governance theory.

We have not taken equal pains to develop a power perspective on governance. However, if one accepts the possibility of policy networks being grounded in, or constituting, a certain discourse, or sees the creation of discourse within a policy field as one possible 'explanatory motor' for the establishment of policy networks, it is not difficult to establish a link with a power perspective. Thus, for Foucault (1977, 1978) as well as for Laclau and Mouffe (1985), discourses are also expressions of power. As discourses are never closed entities there will always be different opportunities for action when different actors are trying to constitute or 'close' a certain discourse. These types of decision are expressions of power, which always include the repression of other possible decisions (Laclau 1990: 34). Thus power can be seen as the setting and construction of (a set of) differences which constitute a 'field' in which certain actors can pursue their goals. Power is the creation of a demarcation line between a discourse and its surroundings, and the way in which this demarcation is made self-evident in the discourse. Translated into the language of traditional governance theory this means that the inclusion/exclusion of actors (and their goals, ideas, etc.) is an expression of power or represents a power strategy, even though it might be non-intentional and impossible to pin to any single (set of) actors.

As with the democracy perspective, a power perspective has until now not really been used in policy network analysis or governance theory. However, it seems of crucial importance to analyse how the increasing dominance of policy networks in the political world affects societal power relations. A further development of such a perspective therefore seems highly relevant.

## Conclusion

In this chapter, through a questioning of three 'taken for granted' assumptions in governance theory, and through using an institutionalist perspective on policy networks inspired in particular by the works of March and Olsen and Giddens, we have argued for the necessity of an anti-essentialist or constructivist bottom-up approach to governance. The difference between this approach and most other approaches to the study of governance and policy networks is that:

1 Its point of departure is in the actual practices of the network.
2 These networks, albeit formed around politics and/or policies, are not necessarily:
  (a) Tied to any pre-given societal 'needs' or actor goals or preferences.
  (b) Connected with steering from a single centre.
3 It stresses the endogenous character of both network change and the identity formation of the involved actors (including goals, preferences).
4 It sees problems of democracy or power as possible starting points for an analysis of governance on an equal footing with problems of management, steering and effectiveness.

Furthermore, as an analysis of actual (regularised) practices and endogenously formed preferences and identities in concrete political situations is called for with this approach, it must be coupled with a bottom-up research strategy, able to produce an understanding of the creation, development and functioning of a given policy network, and formulating this in what we have called an institutional narrative; an example of which is given in our case study.

Using this approach in a case study of industrial policy in a region of Denmark, we found that it had a number of advantages in relation to other approaches to policy networks. Firstly, it made it possible to understand on what grounds the actors in the policy network were dependent on each other, and the crucial role played by semi-public intermediary institutions in the creation and development of the network. Secondly, and more important, it showed that approval of a certain municipal discourse on 'growth and quality of life' was a condition of inclusion in the network, and that non-acceptance of this discourse could be a reason for exclusion. Hence, judging from this case, access to a network (and thereby influence and political power) seems to depend not only on resources and thereby power dependence, but also on acceptance in the sense of both accepting the dominant discourse of the network and of being accepted as an equal and worthy partner by the other actors in the network. Thus using an anti-essentialist approach opened our eyes to the fact that other factors than resource interdependence can play a role in constituting a policy network.

Finally, we also gave examples of how our approach makes it possible to ground the analysis of policy networks in other perspectives than just political steering or public management. We showed how elements of democratic theory can be integrated in policy network analysis, thereby shedding new light on questions like inclusion in and exclusion from networks, and the empowering or disempowering character of network politics. We also took some preliminary steps in sketching how a power perspective on policy networks can be developed, and demonstrated how policy networks can be seen as power strategies.

It is my belief that if governance theory is to develop, and to be able to 'make a difference', not only for politicians, civil servants and other elites and sub-elites, but also for 'ordinary citizens' as laymen and non-experts, these new perspectives must be developed theoretically and investigated empirically.

## Notes

1 The project ran from 1996 to 2000, and received a grant of Dkr 7.6 million. Publications from the sub-project 'Democracy from Below' include Sørensen and Torfing (2000), Christensen (2000), Andersen *et al.* (2000) and Bang *et al.* (2000).

2 A good starting point for the 'modern' discussion is Marin and Mayntz (1991) and the special issue *Policy Networks* of *European Journal of Political Research*, 21 (1–2), 1992.

3 Marin and Mayntz (1991) put forward a similar warning: 'it is important to keep apart matters of conceptual clarification which must be settled by definition (i.e. the choice of properties included in a minimal definition of [in this case:

policy networks]) from empirical issues, i.e. the question what structures meeting the criteria which define policy networks actually look like'.

4  In summing up the defining dimensions along which policy networks may vary, Marin and Mayntz write: '[they are] anchored in policy sectors, requiring collective action, composed of corporate actors, structured as interorganizational relations, predominantly informal and horizontal (but not without asymmetric interdependences which means power relations), functionally defined by the formulation and implementation of policy; without stable or central hegemonic actors, involving not too many participants; and characterised by strategic interaction and a predominance of antagonistic co-operation or mixed-motive games' (1991: 18).

5  Kenis and Schneider (1991: 38) are on to the same point: 'In sum, policy analysis could restrict its research object not only to processes *within* a given and established institutional order, but also have to integrate the *problematique* of how an institutional order emerges in a highly decentralised and interdependent world'.

6  As was the case in the 'Democracy from Below' project referred to above.

7  We also looked at local educational policies, but found that this factor had only a very marginal importance for the local supply of labour. For this reason it was left out of the further analysis.

8  For a more detailed, in-depth analysis see Hoff and Melgaard (2000).

9  The industrial board is a typical example of a semi-public, cross-border institution. Its executive board consists of members from both labour market organisations and the municipality (the mayor and the director of the municipal administration), and it is financed by both public and private funds. In its first phase the funding was almost entirely public, but today the board is funded primarily by the participating firms through a yearly membership fee.

10  The 'Corridor' has its own independent secretariat. It has a steering committee consisting of the mayors of the municipalities involved and the heads of the municipal administrations. This is an indication of the high political priority which this area is given.

11  'The industrial policy of the municipality of Skanderborg shall produce a dynamic and thriving business development with the purpose of enhancing the quality of life of the citizens.' (From the industrial policy plan, 1991.)

12  Thus we also found that a number of small businesses were excluded from the network precisely because they did not possess any resources of value to the other actors in the network.

## References

Andersen, J. G., Torpe, L., and Andersen, J. (2000), *Hvad folket magter* (Copenhagen: Jurist- & Økonomforbundets Forlag).

Bang, H. P., Hansen, A. D., and Hoff, J., eds (2000), *Demokrati fra neden. Casestudier fra en dansk kommune* (Copenhagen: Jurist- & Økonomforbundets Forlag).

Blom-Hansen, J. (1996), 'A "New Institutional" Perspective on Policy Networks', working paper, Department of Political Science, University of Aarhus.

Bogason, P. (2000), *Public Policy and local Governance: Institutions in Postmodern Society* (Cheltenham: Edward Elgar).

Bogason, P., and Sørensen, E., eds (1998), *Samfundsforskning bottom-up: teori og metode* (Roskilde: Roskilde Universitetsforlag).

Bourdieu, P. (1998), *Practical Reason* (Stanford CA: Stanford University Press).

Christensen, B. (2000), *Fortællinger fra Indre Nørrebro* (Copenhagen: Jurist- & Økonomforbundets Forlag).

Elmore, R. F. (1980), 'Backward mapping: implementation, research and policy decisions', in W. Williams (ed.), *Studying Implementation* (Chatham NJ: Chatham House), pp. 18–35.

Erhvervsministeriet (1995), *Regionalpolitisk redegørelse 1995*. Copenhagen: Erhvervsministeriet.

*European Journal of Political Research* (1992) 21 (1–2), special issue *Policy Networks*.

Foucault, M. (1977), *Discipline and Punish* (Harmondsworth: Penguin).

Foucault, M. (1978), *The History of Sexuality: An Introduction* (Harmondsworth: Penguin).

Giddens, A. (1979), *Central Problems in Social Theory* (London: Macmillan).

Heclo, H. (1978), 'Issue networks and the executive establishment', in A. King (ed.), *The New American Political System* (Washington DC: American Enterprise Institute), pp. 87–124.

Hoff, J., and Melgaard, M. (2000), 'Erhvervspolitik som helhedspolitik. Politiknetværker og skæbnefællesskab i den lokale sociale økonomi', in H. P. Bang, A. D. Hansen and J. Hoff (eds), *Demokrati fra neden. Casestudier fra en dansk kommune* (Copenhagen: Jurist- & Økonomforbundets Forlag), pp. 165–93.

Jessop, B. (1998), 'The rise of governance and the risks of failure: the case of economic development', *International Social Science Journal* 50 (1): 29–46.

Kenis, P., and Schneider, V. (1991), 'Policy networks and policy analysis: scrutinizing a new analytical toolbox', in B. Marin and R. Mayntz (eds), *Policy Networks: Empirical Evidence and Theoretical Considerations* (Frankfurt: Campus), pp. 25–59.

Kickert, W. J. M., Klijn, E-H., and Koppenjan, J. F. M., eds (1997), *Managing Complex Networks. Strategies for the Public Sector* (London: Sage).

Kooiman, J., ed. (1993), *Modern Governance: New Government–Society Interactions* (London: Sage).

Laclau, E. (1990), *New Reflections on the Revolution of our Time* (London: Verso).

Laclau, E., and Mouffe, C. (1985), *Hegemony and Socialist Strategy: Towards a Radical Democratic Politics* (London: Verso).

March, J. G., and Olsen, J. P. (1989), *Rediscovering Institutions: The Organizational Basis of Politics* (New York: Free Press).

March, J. G., and Olsen, J. P. (1995), *Democratic Governance* (New York: Free Press).

Marin, B., and Mayntz, R. (1991a), 'Introduction: studying policy networks', in B. Marin and R. Mayntz (eds), *Policy Networks: Empirical Evidence and Theoretical Considerations* (Frankfurt: Campus), pp. 11–23.

Marin, B., and Mayntz, R., eds (1991b), *Policy Networks: Empirical Evidence and Theoretical Considerations* (Frankfurt: Campus).

Mayntz, R., and Scharpf, F. (1995), 'Politische Steuerung und gesellschaftliche Steuerungsprobleme. Anmerkungen zu einem theoretischen Paradigma', *Jahrbuch für Staats- und Verwaltungswissenschaft* 1: 89–110.

Peters, B. G. (1999), *Institutional Theory in Political Science: The New Institutionalism* (London: Pinter).

Rhodes, R. A. W. (1997), *Understanding Governance. Policy Networks, Governance, Reflexivity and Accountability* (Buckingham: Open University Press).

Rhodes, R. A. W. (2000), 'Governance and public administration', in J. Pierre (ed.), *Debating Governance: Authority, Steering and Democracy* (Oxford: Oxford University Press).

Rokkan, S. (1969), 'Norway: numerical democracy and corporate pluralism', in R. A. Dahl (ed.), *Political Oppositions in Western Democracies* (New Haven CT: Yale University Press), pp. 70–115.

Schmitter, P. C., and Lembruch, G., eds (1979), *Trends towards Corporatist Intermediation* (Beverly Hills CA: Sage).

Sørensen, E., and Torfing, J. (2000), *Skanderborg på landkortet* (Copenhagen: Jurist- & Økonomforbundets Forlag).

Stoker, G. (1998), 'Governance as theory: five propositions', *International Social Science Journal* 50: 17–27.

Williamson, O. E. (1979), 'Transaction-cost economics: the governance of contractual relations', *Journal of Law and Economics*, 22: 233–61.

# 4

# Decentring British governance: from bureaucracy to networks

Mark Bevir and R. A. W. Rhodes

British government has shifted, according to many political scientists, from the government of a unitary state to governance in and by networks (Rhodes 1997, 2000a; Stoker 1999, 2000a). Yet the difficulties surrounding the term 'governance' are considerable. It can refer to a new process of governing, or a changed condition of ordered rule, or the new method by which society is governed (cf. Finer 1970: 3–4). One colleague described it as a 'weasel' word – slippery and elusive, used to obscure, not to shed light. In this chapter we trace and illustrate its several meanings. However, as authors we do not seek to dictate what approaches and words mean. We have no wish to wear such a mantle of linguistic omniscience. We do not believe that our account should be privileged because, as political scientists, we have a means of deciding which accounts are true, which are false. Rather we provide an account of how elite political and administrative actors understand the term. In effect, we seek to replace current positivist accounts of British governance in and by networks with a decentred analysis that focuses on the various British political traditions and their several interpretations (and on decentred analysis see Bevir and Rhodes 2000).

Governance signals how the informal authority of networks supplements and supplants the formal authority of government. The governance literature explores the limits of the state and seeks to develop a more diverse view of state authority and its exercise. Broadly conceived, the concept of governance explores the changing boundary between state and civil society. This broader notion of governance in Britain exercises historians of the twentieth century. José Harris (1990: 66–7) argues that one of the 'tacit understandings' about political community at the beginning of the twentieth century was 'a belief among politicians of all complexions that the relationship between government and society was essentially a limited one'. Civil society was 'the highest sphere of human existence', while the state was 'an institution of secondary importance'. The corporate life of society 'was expressed through voluntary associations and the local community'. She argues that these beliefs had 'enormous tenacity' (1990: 69). Between the wars, they were sustained not just by professional civil servants, who favoured a return to more limited government, but also by the public, who 'resumed their Victorian habits of voluntary action and self-help' (1990: 77). However, the Second World War led Britain to develop 'a far more powerful centralised wartime state than any of her more metaphysical-minded, state-exalting continental enemies' (1990: 91). It also fuelled a reformist mood, which led to a 'profound break with some of the major conventions of the previous hundred years' (1990: 96). 'Promises, programmes and planning' became the new norm (1990: 97). Harris concludes that, by the 1950s, 'the common constitutional culture based on tacit acceptance of common history and unspoken assumptions about the nature of political behaviour which had been so pervasive earlier in the century had virtually ceased to exist' (1990: 111). We should not write the history of the twentieth century as a battle between collectivism and the free market, because they 'advanced in tandem at the expense of other more traditional social arrangements such as philanthropy, the family and the local community' (1990: 113). 'The ethos of voluntarism was . . . subtly transformed over the course of the twentieth century':

> They [voluntary associations] were the very sinews of autonomous 'civil society', supported by the state only through a general framework of law. This unpretentious and invisible private collectivism continued in some spheres throughout the period, largely falling through the meshes of the history of government. In many voluntary organisations, however, such autonomy progressively dwindled: they became increasingly the agents and clients of the state, holders of state licences, beneficiaries of state tax concessions, recipients of and competitors for state financial aid – or simply pressure groups urging government to change its policies on some deserving cause. The boundary between public and private spheres became more confused than in the late nineteenth century. (1990: 114)

Harris is describing the spread of organisational networks tied to the state. These networks are common both to the days of centralised planning and giant corporations and to the days of governmental minimalism and neo-liberal economics.

Rodney Lowe and Neil Rollings (2000: 101) similarly argue the balance between state and civil society, 'between government and governance', was disrupted by two contradictions. First, British government had a limited or minimalist role in practice but unlimited power in theory. Although there were no constitutional checks on the powers of government, 'public compliance depended on their non-use'. Second, the state was supposed to be neutral between classes but it was partial whenever it intervened on controversial economic and social issues. Britain enjoyed 'an exceptional degree of continuity and order', but this was 'an achievement of governance broadly defined, rather than government' (2000: 105). The crisis of the 1950s saw the breakdown of this broader governance as the government responded to perceptions of relative decline by pursuing a policy of modernisation though centralisation. The history of British government during the twentieth century appears as a shifting balance between government and governance.

We try to ground recent changes in the boundaries between state and civil society in an analysis of patterns of government or the mechanisms for authoritatively allocating resources and for exercising control and co-ordination. In other words, we focus on hierarchies, markets and networks. Bureaucracy remains the prime example of hierarchy or co-ordination by administrative order. Despite all the recent changes, it is still a major way of delivering services in British government; for example, the Benefits Agency remains a large bureaucracy. Privatisation, marketing testing and the purchaser–provider split are examples of government using market or quasi-market ways of delivering services. Price competition is deemed the key to efficient and better-quality services. Competition and markets are now a fixed part of the landscape of British government. It is less widely recognised that British government now works through networks characterised by trust and mutual adjustment to provide welfare services. The shifts from hierarchy to markets and then to networks involved changing the boundaries between state and civil society (and for a more detailed account see Rhodes 2000a). Indeed, the Conservative government explicitly defended its use of market mechanisms as a way of redefining the boundaries of the state, while New Labour is almost equally explicit about its use of networks.

We also ground our analysis of patterns of government in specific public-sector reforms. Policies such as contracting out are the specific means that brought about the change from hierarchy to markets. Thus, while we focus on governance, the study of the several rounds of public-sector reform during the 1980s and 1990s is vital to an understanding of governance. Nonetheless, we do not use the examples of the civil service or public management reform for their own sake. Rather, we treat them as instances of reforms of patterns of government and, therefore, of changes in the boundaries between state and civil society.

## Narratives of governance

There are four main constructions of British governance: intermediate institutions, networks of communities, reinventing the constitution, and joined-up government (see table 4.1). For each construction we outline the relevant tradition and give examples of associated narratives. Our choice of traditions is conventional (see, for example, Barker 1994). Equally, the table and our examples are not comprehensive. We are illustrating an argument, not documenting each narrative.

A decentred account should provide thick descriptions of governance using the accounts or texts of participants, not academic commentaries. Of course, there is often no clear-cut distinction between academic commen-

**Table 4.1** *Narratives of governance*

| | *Tradition* | | |
|---|---|---|---|
| *Tory* | *Liberal* | *Whig* | *Socialist* |
| *Narrative of reform* | | | |
| Preserving traditional authority | Restoring markets and combating state overload | Evolutionary change | The bureaucratic state |
| *Narrative of governance* | | | |
| Wrecked intermediate institutions | Building networks of communities | Reinventing the constitution | Joined-up government |
| *Practitioner examples* | | | |
| Gilmour (1992) | Willetts (1992) | Bancroft (1983) | Mandelson and Liddle (1996) |
| *Official report* | | | |
| Anderson (1946) | Efficiency Unit (1988) | Cm 2627 (1994) | Cm 4310 (1999) |

tators and elite actors. So, for example, Lord Crowther Hunt was both a member of the Fulton Committee on Civil Service Reform and a Fellow of Exeter College, Oxford University. Subsequently he became a political adviser to the Prime Minister, Harold Wilson, who he advised on implementing the recommendations of the Fulton committee. Individuals can be academics, authors of official documents and political actors all at once or at different times in their lives. Also, there is a shared language about 'the system'. Tivey (1988: 3) deploys the concept of 'the image' to denote 'a set of assumptions about "the system" . . . and how it works'. Each image contains 'operative concepts' or 'operative ideals': 'the views of the authors are taken', moreover, 'to be of some influence; what they have said has to some extent become operative'. Indeed, these images 'have gained currency among those who study politics, and diluted and distorted they have reached the practitioners' (Tivey 1988: 1; see also Beer 1965: xiii, 404). In this chapter all our examples, our shared images, are drawn from politicians and civil servants in this broad sense and from official sources.

## The Tory tradition

The Tory tradition is elusive and relentlessly inconsistent (Honderich 1991). All too often its proponents define it more by what it isn't than by what it is. Gilmour (1978: 121–43) argues the Conservative Party is not averse to change (1978: 121), not a pressure group (1978: 130), and not ideological

(1978: 132). More positively, 'the fundamental concern of Toryism is the preservation of the nation's unity, of the national institutions, of political and civil liberty' (1978: 143). Blake (1985: chapter 11 and postscript) argues Conservatives are against centralisation, equality and internal splits but, to leaven the mix, they are for the national interest. Gamble (1988: 170–1) describes the British state as the Tory state with the defining characteristics of racial and national superiority, a deferential attitude to authority, secrecy surrounding the practice of high politics, an anti-egalitarian ethos and a status hierarchy.

Some strands recur in the Tory tradition. For example, Michael Oakeshott (1962, 1975) provides the philosophical underpinnings for several raconteurs of Tory narratives. Ian Gilmour (1978: 92–100, 1992: 272–3) adopts Oakeshott's distinction between the state as a civil and an enterprise association. An enterprise association is 'human beings joined in pursuing some common substantive interest, in seeking the satisfaction of some common want or in promoting some common substantive interest'. Persons in a civil association 'are not joined in any undertaking to promote a common interest . . . but in recognition of non-instrumental rules indifferent to any interest', that is, a set of common rules and a common government in pursuing their diverse purposes (Gilmour 1978: 98; see also Mount 1992: 74–5; Willetts 1992: 72–3). So a free society has 'no preconceived purpose, but finds its guide in a principle of continuity . . . and in a principle of consensus' (Gilmour 1978: 97). The Tory tradition favours civil association and accepts the state as an enterprise association only 'when individuals are able to contract out of it when it suits them' (Gilmour 1992: 272). Nonetheless Gilmour (1978: 236) accepts that some state intervention will often be expedient, practical politics, essential to preserving the legitimacy of the state. For all its hedging about the role of the state, the Tory tradition upholds its authority. People are self-interested and hierarchy is necessary to keep order. Scruton (1984: 111) makes the point forcefully: 'the state has the authority, the responsibility, and the despotism of parenthood' (see also Gamble 1988: 170). Strong leaders wield that authority to uphold national unity, to correct social and economic ills and to build popular consent.

Inspired by the Tory tradition, Gilmour (1992: 198–224), a former Cabinet Minister (1979–81), portrays the public-sector reforms of the 1980s as a 'series of tactical battles' that wrecked Britain's intermediate institutions, such as the monarchy, the Church, the civil service, the judiciary, the British Broadcasting Corporation (BBC) and local government. These 'barriers between state and citizen', he argues, were torn down in the drive to create an enterprise culture and a free-market state. Gilmour values the pluralism of intermediate institutions and wants to return to moderation in the exercise of power. Similarly, on civil service reform, Gilmour (1992: 185) regrets that civil servants abandoned their principal function of drawing 'attention from long experience to the flaws of instant panaceas' and decided that 'the way to live with ideology was to appear to share it'.

So they 'executed ordained error without demur'. They neither retarded nor palliated. They did not resist reforms with a vigour nourished by a proper confidence in the old values of the British constitution.

There was never a neat divide in the Conservative Party between the paternal statism of the High Tories and economic liberalism but during the 1980s and 1990s the former was a submerged tradition. Official reports did not articulate the High Tory reverence for the old values. Of course there are many examples from earlier in the post-war period. A favourite example is the Anderson committee: because its truths were so self evident, it was never deemed necessary to publish the committee's report. It began work in November 1942 as a Cabinet committee enquiring into the fitness of the machinery of government for the extended role of the state after the war. Its status as a Cabinet committee ensured that the review lay in the hands of Ministers and civil servants rather than outsiders. In effect, the committee carried out a 'survey for practitioners by practitioners' (Lee 1977: 18). Anderson submitted his report to the Prime Minister in May 1945. It was never published (but see Anderson 1946). The following passage captures the tone of the exercise.

> The Ministerial Committee was paralleled by a small official committee of three senior civil servants chosen by Anderson himself for their special qualities of judgement. This collated the views of people who were referred to as 'great and wise men' and gave ministers the benefit of their advice in confidence. (PRO/T222/71:OM 290/01, cited in Chapman and Greenaway 1980: 129)

The following passage similarly captures the tone and scope of the review's conclusions:

> While I emphasise the departmental responsibility of ministers as a necessary and vital principle, I at the same time stress the importance, as a practical matter, of adequate machinery for making a reality of collective responsibility. As a means to this end, I would rely on the institution . . . of a permanent but flexible system of cabinet committees. (Anderson 1946: 156)

As Lee (1977: 151) concludes, the Anderson committee was a 'special mixture of ambiguity in definition and ambivalence in discussion'. Turbulent times produced not a radical review, but a return to the eternal verities of the insiders of British government. The committee sought to perpetuate such Tory themes and symbols as the generalist civil servant acting as Platonic guardian of an imagined, national good.

### The liberal tradition

For liberals such as Norman Tebbitt, former Secretary of State for Trade and Industry and former chair of the Conservative Party, Gilmore's belief that intermediate institutions such as local government were a check and balance on Westminster is 'an entirely new and quite false constitutional theory'. No matter that Enoch Powell, former Cabinet Minister, former Conservative and lifelong parliamentary romantic, could say that 'a hatred of bureaucracy' was a common and continuing feature of Conservatism. Until Margaret Thatcher's election there was, at least to the more ardent neo-liberals, little difference between, say, Edward Heath and the Fabian reforming agenda – both were technocratic and problem-solving. The Thatcher reforms had twin roots in the economic liberalism of the Institute of Economic Affairs (see Niskanen *et al.* 1973) and concern about bureaucratic inefficiency (see Chapman 1978). In her own words, Margaret Thatcher (1993: 48) 'preferred disorderly resistance to decline rather than comfortable accommodation to it' and the civil service would not be insulated from her reforming zeal. Thus began the era of corporate management, agencification and most notably marketisation. The key question became 'What public services must we keep?' The policies of privatisation and contracting-out redrew the boundary between the public and private sectors. 'Reformism gave way to revolution' as the government sought to create 'the minimalist state'. Some claim the changes wrought were as great as those of the Northcote–Trevelyan era.

'New Conservatism' revived the liberal tradition by stressing freedom, applying the principles of freedom to the economy and accepting the welfare state on sound Conservative grounds. Thus David Willetts (1992), Conservative MP and junior minister under both Margaret Thatcher and John Major, finds the roots of the New Conservatism in the One Nation Group's (1954) arguments against government intervention and in such philosophers as Friedrich Hayek and Michael Oakeshott. For Willetts (1992: chapter 6) Adam Smith's 'system of natural liberty' provides the intellectual justification for free markets. Markets tap 'two fundamental human instincts'; the instinct to better oneself and the instinct to exchange. These instincts, when 'protected by a legal order which ensures contracts are kept and property is respected', are 'the source of the wealth of nations'. Big government cannot deliver prosperity, undermines markets and erodes communities. But 'rampant individualism without the ties of duty, loyalty and affiliation is only checked by powerful and intrusive government'. So Conservatism stands between collectivism and individualism and 'Conservative thought at its best conveys the mutual dependence between the community and the free market. Each is enriched by the other' (Willetts 1992: 182). The Conservative Party's achievement is to reconcile Toryism and individualism. This achievement also belongs to Thatcher. Thatcherism is not the antithesis of conservatism because 'it too recognises there is more to life than free markets'; it too sought to reconcile 'economic calculation with our moral obligations to our fellow citizens' (1992: 47). It restores markets to their allegedly rightful place in Conservatism: it 'is within the mainstream of conservative philosophy' (1992: 54).

State intervention stultifies. Competition improves performance: 'free markets are . . . the route to prosperity' (1992: 136). Bureaucracy was the problem. Marketisation was the solution to bureaucratic inefficiency (Thatcher 1993: 45–9). Sir John Hoskyns (1983) was one of several business leaders seconded to Whitehall. On leaving, he reflected in writing on the experience. In doing so, he criticised the failure of government to agree and define objectives. He complained about the small world of Westminster and Whitehall, and especially about a civil service closed to outsiders, lacking in confidence and energy, and serving political masters with whom it does not agree. He challenged the convention of political neutrality as leading to passionless detachment instead of radically minded officials, and to the low quality of much policy work. His main proposal for change is to break the civil service monopoly of top jobs and to appoint business outsiders on seven-year contracts. In a similar vein, Leslie Chapman (1978), a former regional director in the (then) Ministry of Public Building and Works, castigated the civil service for waste, inefficiency and inadequate management. His solutions included a new investigative audit department and better, accountable management. During the 1979 election campaign he advised Margaret Thatcher on efficiency within the civil service (Metcalfe and Richards 1991: 5–6). Although Chapman was widely tipped to become Thatcher's adviser on efficiency in government, that mantle eventually fell on Sir Derek Rayner, joint managing director of Marks & Spencer.

The recurrent liberal concern with businesslike efficiency, setting clear policy objectives and recruiting better managers pervades various official reports of the last two decades. The Efficiency Unit (1988: 3–5) argues, for example, that 'senior management is dominated by people whose skills are in policy formation and who have relatively little experience of managing or working where services are actually delivered'. It strongly believes that 'developments towards more clearly defined and budgeted management are positive and helpful'. It accepts that senior civil servants must respond to Ministerial priorities but argues the civil service is 'too big and too diverse to manage as a single entity'. So it recommends setting up agencies 'to carry out the executive functions of government within a policy and resources framework set by a department'. Senior management will have the freedom to manage. So there will now be 'a quite different way of conducting the business of government': a central civil service consisting of core departments servicing Ministers and agencies at arm's length with a clearly defined responsibility for service delivery.

Not all liberals focus on reforming public management. Willetts (1992: 71) wants to claim community as a core principle in the liberal tradition. He rejects the idea of community embodied in the nation state for the notion of an 'overlapping network of communities'. He denies that free markets destroy community. On the contrary, liberalism reconciles markets and community with the idea of 'micro-conservatism' or 'the particular network of communities which gives each individual life meaning'. The role of the state is to sustain 'a political order in which this multiplicity of communities can survive' (1992: 105). Micro-communities populate the boundary between state and civil society, an image with a close affinity to nineteenth century notions of governance as private collectivism.

## The Whig tradition

This tradition emphasises the objects that are the historic heart of political science – the study of institutions or the rules, procedures and formal organisations of government, constitutional law and constitutional history. It also has an idealist strand that focuses on the interaction between ideas and institutions. Its most famous expression is the Westminster model of government, which, at times, comes perilously close to telling the story of a single, unilinear, progressive idea, reason or spirit underlying the evolution of British government. It emphasises gradualism and the capacity of British institutions to evolve and cope with crises. It provides 'capacity for independent action, leadership and decision' while ensuring that 'British political institutions would remain flexible and responsive'. This implicit Whig historiography probably added to the appeal of the model to political scientists who 'were largely sympathetic', 'convinced that change needed to be evolutionary' and willing to celebrate 'the practical wisdom embodied in England's constitutional arrangements' (Gamble 1990: 411, 409).

There was a time in the early 1980s when it seemed as if the Conservative maelstrom would sweep aside the traditional civil service. Lord Bancroft (1983: 8), a former head of the home civil service, reflected on these changes in true Whig style:

> I am reminded that Abbot Bower of Inchcolm, commenting on the legislative enthusiasm of James I of Scotland in the Parliament of 1426, applied what he thought an apt quotation: 'to enact new laws with facility, and to change the old with facility, is marvellous damaging to good order'. He was quoting Aristotle. We are heirs to a long inheritance.

Lord Bancroft, again like a true Whig, contrasts his argument 'for organic institutional change, planned at a digestible rate' with a defence of the *status quo*. Indeed, he explicitly criticises 'the overnight fever of a new department here and a new agency there, in order to accommodate a transient personal whim or political tantrum' (see also Bancroft 1983; the concluding remarks in Dale 1941: appendix C; Sisson 1959: 153). He wants gradual evolution through sympathetic reforms that work with, and so perpetuate, all that is salutary in Britain's constitution and political practice.

The White Paper *The Civil Service: Continuity and Change* (Cm 2627, 1994) reflects on a decade of change and, in true Whig fashion, seeks to consolidate the changes in the broader heritage and pattern of historical development. The White Paper's summary of the role and functions of the civil service claims that the civil service has 'a high reputation, nationally and internationally, for its standards of integrity, impartiality and loyal service to the Government of the day'. It suggests 'the particular standards that bind the civil service together are integrity, impartiality, objectivity, selection and promotion on merit and accountability through Ministers to Parliament'. Although recent reforms delegated management responsibility to agencies, the government acknowledges 'the need to ensure that the defining principles and standards of the civil service are not relaxed'. The White Paper instances the new, unified Management Code (1993), which lays down the relevant standards, and promises a statutory code or a New Civil Service Act. The proposed reforms are meagre. The White Paper even phrases its proposals for open competition for top jobs cautiously:

> Departments and agencies will always consider advertising openly at these [senior management] levels when a vacancy occurs, and then will use open competition wherever it is necessary and justifiable in the interests of providing a strong field or introducing new blood.

Such words hardly herald an open season on top posts in the civil service. Equally, the White Paper remains silent on measuring and improving the work of permanent secretaries. The White Paper's title is an accurate reflection of its contents. The Whig tradition's response to public-sector reform, to return to the example provided by Hennessy, is 'wherever possible' to use 'traditional and familiar institutions for new purposes' and so to 'go with the grain of Westminster and Whitehall and their traditions'. Empathy with the British constitution leads to an organic reinvention of that constitution.

## The socialist tradition

The socialist tradition, with its structural explanations focused on economic factors and class, and with its critique of capitalism, mounted a prominent challenge to Whig historiography. The historical story of the socialist tradition is often ambivalent about, or even hostile to, that of the Whigs. For example, David Marquand (1988: 198), former Labour MP and EU official, comments:

> The old Whig historians were not wrong in thinking that Britain's peaceful passage to democracy owed much to the hazy compromises which unprobed ambiguities make possible. By the same token, however, once these compromises cease to be taken for granted . . . arrangements of this sort are bound to run into trouble. . . . Respect for the rules of the game will ebb away. . . . In doing so, they have focused attention . . . on the hidden presuppositions of club government itself . . . And, as a result, these presuppositions have started to come apart at the seams.

The Whig tradition collapses because it confronts a heterogeneous, plural society in which authority has been demystified, cultural values have changed, the political system has lost legitimacy, and territorial politics is in disarray (1988: 199–204).

From the earliest days, a central strand in the socialist tradition is the role accorded to bureaucracy. For example, the leading Fabian, Sidney

Webb, identified socialism with the efficient organisation of society, conceived as co-operative and co-ordinated organisation with state activity
(Bevir 2002). The Fabians, he implied, should act as positivist experts,
providing information and policies to diverse politicians. Although Webb
believed in liberal democracy, he suspected that it would bring a welcome
move away from political conflict towards rule by an administrative and
managerial elite. He had strong faith in experts as a source of neutral compelling advice, although he always restricted their role to providing advice
and implementing policies. Making decisions had to remain the provenance
of elected representatives. Contemporaries such as Graham Wallas (Qualter
1980: 99, 162), and inter-war Fabians such as Greaves (1947), shared
Webb's strong faith in a science of public administration, according bureaucracy a central role in achieving political ends.

Here, because our concern is governance and recent public-sector
reforms, we focus on the New Labour strand in the socialist tradition.
New Labour reinterpreted the concerns highlighted by the New Right
from within the socialist tradition (Bevir and O'Brien 2001). The Old
Labour model built on the Fabians' faith in experts and resembled a top-
down, command-style bureaucracy based on centralised rules. The party
became associated with hierarchic patterns of organisation in which co-
ordination is secured by administrative orders. The New Right rejected
this model, arguing it was inefficient and it eroded individual freedom.
The Thatcher governments tried to make public services more efficient
through privatisation, marketisation and the New Public Management.
Citizens became consumers able to choose between an array of public services. Although command bureaucracy remains a major way of delivering
public services, privatisation, the purchaser–provider split and management techniques from the private sector have become an integral part of
British governance.

New Labour does not defend the command bureaucracy associated with
Old Labour. Rather, we can identify a shift in the socialist tradition inspired
in part by the New Right's concern with market efficiency and choice. For
example, Peter Mandelson, former Secretary of State for Northern Ireland,
and Roger Liddle explicitly reject the 'municipal socialism' and 'centralised
nationalisation' of the past (Mandelson and Liddle 1996: 27). New Labour
'does not seek to provide centralised "statist" solutions to every social and
economic problem'. Instead New Labour promotes the idea of networks of
institutions and individuals acting in partnerships held together by relations
of trust. New Labour's concern with networks based on relations of trust
does not exclude either command bureaucracy or quasi-market competition. Rather, New Labour proposes a mix of hierarchies, markets and networks, with choices depending on the particular nature of the service under
consideration. Government policy is that 'services should be provided
through the sector best placed to provide those services most effectively',
where 'this can be the public, private or voluntary sector, or partnerships

between these sectors' (Cm 4011 1998). Even a simple service is liable to display a mix of structures, strategies and relationships.

Equally, New Labour embodies a critique of the New Right's model of public service delivery. It suggests the New Right has an exaggerated faith in markets. New Labour believes individuals are not just competitive and self-interested but also co-operative and concerned for the welfare of others. So public services should encourage co-operation while continuing to use market mechanisms when they are suitable. For example, David Clark (1997), then the Minister for Public Services, explained that policies such as market testing 'will not be pursued blindly as an article of faith' but they 'will continue where they offer best value for money'. New Labour insists markets are not always the best way to deliver public services. They can go against the public interest, reinforce inequalities and entrench privilege. Besides, much of the public sector simply is not amenable to market competition. Indeed, trust and partnership are essential. Without the conditions for effective markets, one has to rely on either honest co-operation or specify standards in absurd detail. Far from promoting efficiency, therefore, marketisation can undermine standards of service quality.

New Labour's emphasis on individual choice and involvement overlaps with themes found in the New Right. In promoting customer-focused services New Labour adopts features of the New Public Management when it considers them suitable. However, New Labour's model of service delivery does not follow the New Right's vision of the New Public Management. On the contrary, New Labour argues that many features of this New Public Management, such as quasi-markets and contracting out, maintained an unhealthy dichotomy between the public and private sectors: public bodies did not work with private companies but merely contracted services out to them. This argument is used, for example, to justify abolishing the internal market within the National Health Service. The Third Way, in contrast to the vision of the New Right, is supposed to develop networks that enable public and private organisations to collaborate. Examples of such collaboration appear in the partnerships between the public and private sectors that are so important to the delivery of the New Deal for the unemployed.

New Labour's networks for public service delivery are supposed to be based on trust. Prime Minister Tony Blair describes such trust as 'the recognition of a mutual purpose for which we work together and in which we all benefit' (Blair 1996: 292). Trust matters because we are interdependent social beings who achieve more by working together than by competing. Quality public services are best achieved through stable, co-operative relationships. Blair talks of building relations of trust between all actors in society. Trust is promoted between organisations through the Quality Networks programme: organisations should exchange information about their practices to facilitate co-operation. Trust is promoted inside organisations through forms of management that allow individual responsibility and discretion increasingly to replace rigid hierarchies: individuals should be trusted to make decisions and implement policies without the constraint of strict procedures. Trust is promoted between organisations and individuals through the Service First programme: citizens should trust organisations to provide appropriate services, and organisations should trust citizens to use services appropriately.

The Labour government uses networks based on trust to institutionalise its ideals of partnership and an enabling state. Blair (1998) stated the aims succinctly: 'joined-up problems need joined-up solutions'. This theme runs through the *Modernising Government* White Paper with its frequent references to 'joined-up' government and 'holistic governance' (Cm 4310 1999; see also Cabinet Office 1999, 2000; Rhodes 2000b). The term covers both horizontal joining-up between central departments and vertical joining-up between all the agencies involved in delivering services. So services must be effective and co-ordinated and the principles of joined-up government apply across the public sector and to voluntary and private-sector organisations.

Joining up takes various forms. For example, there are area-based programmes or 'action zones' (twenty-six in health, twenty-five in education) linking central and local government, health authorities, the private sector and voluntary organisations; and group-focused programmes such as the 'Better Government for Older People' pilot. The state is an enabling partner that joins and steers flexible networks, and the civil service must adapt. The task is to build bridges between the various organisations involved in designing policies and delivering services. In future civil servants will manage packages of services, packages of organisations and packages of governments.

## Conclusion

In an important sense, there is no such thing as governance, but only the differing constructions of the several traditions. There is no necessary logical or structural process determining the form governance takes, neither a process based on the intrinsic rationality of markets nor one on the path-dependence of institutions. In an equally important sense, however, governance is the diverse actions and practices inspired by the varied beliefs and traditions we have discussed. Patterns of governance arise as the contingent products of diverse actions and political struggles informed by the beliefs of agents as they arise in the context of traditions. These conclusions apply, moreover, whether we are talking about the civil service, public-sector reform, governing structures or state–civil society relations. There may be some agreement that the boundary between state and civil society is being redrawn, and that the form and extent of state intervention are changing, but there is little agreement on how, why or whether it is desirable. At the outset, we noted the emphasis of historians on a broad concept of governance as the relation of the state to civil society. Although the historians we referred to differ in detail, they share the theme of governance as private collectivism being eroded by successive periods of centralisation fuelled by the two world wars. The reinvention of the minimal state by the New Right and the discovery of networks by New Labour are attempts to find a substitute for the voluntaristic bonds diminished by state intervention and the erosion of intermediate institutions such as local government. We are witnessing the search for an extended role for civil society in an era of large organisations.

Appeals to networks can be seen not only as a counterweight to the centralisation of the 1960s and 1970s but also as an example of how rule in late modern society has come to seek involving individuals in their everyday life (as employees, users, citizens) in governance. It has come to do so because of the contingent ways in which politicians from within the various traditions responded to the dilemma of overload by introducing reforms that ask individuals to get involved. So politicians in the liberal tradition sought to involve individuals in markets, while New Labour seeks their involvement in networks. And, again, such citizen involvement is not the result of any necessary structural process but a contingent outcome of political actions and beliefs.

Our decentring of British governance provides a valuable corrective to both the traditional Westminster model of British government and more positivist accounts of governance itself. It offers the hope of finding 'new, better, more interesting, more fruitful ways of speaking about' British government; it is an exercise in 'edification' (Rorty 1980: 360). It does so by decentring networks as well as exploring how their informal authority supplements and supplants the more formal authority of government. We use the notion of governance to develop a more diverse view of state authority in its relation to civil society.

Our decentring of British governance offers a distinctive narrative. It also raises important issues for further research. For example, although there are equivalent trends towards markets and networks in other advanced industrial democracies, we know little or nothing about how national governmental traditions shape responses to these trends. We might perhaps distinguish here between the Anglo-Saxon (no state) tradition, the Germanic Rechtsstaat tradition, the French (Napoleonic) tradition and the Scandinavian tradition, which mixes the Anglo-Saxon and Germanic. In the Germanic tradition state and civil society are part of one organic whole; the state is a transcendent entity. The Anglo-Saxon pluralist tradition draws a more distinct boundary between state and civil society, with contract rather than natural law as the basis of the state. Civil servants have no constitutional position. The Napoleonic tradition sees the French state as the one and indivisible republic, exercising strong central authority to contain the hostile relations between state and civil society. The Scandinavian tradition is also 'organicist', influenced by the ideas of the Rechtsstaat tradition, but differs from the Germanic tradition in being a decentralised unitary state with a strong participation ethic.

National traditions shape patterns of governance. The New Public Management (NPM) is often treated as an example of globalisation but, even allowing that the term refers to a discrete set of reforms, there are marked differences in the way individual countries respond to the 'same' international pressures. For example, the Danish government sought to preserve a popular welfare state by selected reforms aimed at getting better value for money. Public-sector reform was characterised by a negotiated consensus and pragmatism which avoided clear winners and losers. The choice of means was a technical matter, not dictated by party ideology. So privatisation and marketisation were but two choices among many, to be used when there was agreement they were the best way forward. User and citizen roles in public-sector service delivery were strengthened (and for a more detailed comparison of Britain and Denmark see Rhodes 1999).

There are other gaps in our knowledge. Although we can identify different approaches to network management, we know that all these tools of central steering meet problems. Although there is a large democratic shortfall in governance, we know little about the prospects of democratising particular domains. Also we know little about the ethnography of government. Although reducing the size of the civil service and improving efficiency are long-standing policies, we do not know how such change has affected the beliefs and practices of middle-level managers, supervisors and employees. All policies have multiple stakeholders. A decentred approach provides thick descriptions focusing on the beliefs and preferences of these stakeholders. No such accounts exist, whether the subject is management reform or Minister–Permanent Secretary relations.

We had no expectation that we could provide a true account of an objective process unaffected by the mentalities of particular individuals. Rather, we have related governance to the actions of many individuals; described the conflicting but overlapping stories that inform the actions of these individuals; and we have used the concept of tradition to explain why these actors construct their worlds as they do. Individuals are bearers of traditions, and they enact and remake structures in their everyday lives. We argue governing structures can be understood only through the beliefs and actions of individuals located in traditions. Political ethnography enables us to tell the stories of different individuals. Historical analysis is the way to uncover the traditions that shape these stories.

We prefer an interpretative approach with its decentering of governance to the positivism lurking within most accounts of British government, for two reasons. First, the governance narrative is comparatively accurate and comprehensive in its coverage of shared 'facts'. We believe the story of a shift from hierarchies to markets to networks commands a large measure of agreement between academics and practitioners, even if the language varies, encompassing terms such as joining-up, holistic governance and partnerships. Second, we believe our approach will prove to be fruitful, progressive and open. It will open a wide range of new areas and styles of research about the beliefs, preferences and actions of many political actors – from Prime Minister to individual citizens – as they preserve and modify traditions and practices – from Toryism and Parliament to, say, New Age travellers and forms of protest.

To end, we turn to the implications of our governance narrative for practitioners. New patterns of governance bring new problems. Marketisation undermines trust, co-operation and reciprocity in networks. Organisational complexity obscures accountability. The search for co-operation impedes efficient service delivery. Perhaps, as Stoker (2000b) suggests, all we can tell the practitioner is to 'keep on "muddling through" . . . in an appropriately thoughtful and reflexive manner'. Perri 6 (1997: 70) accuses this analysis of fatalism. Yet he is insufficiently cautious about the provisional nature of knowledge in political science, and his optimism for the latest managerial fashion is almost certainly misplaced. But his tool view of governance, with its stress on choosing between and managing resource allocation structures, is widespread. Its prominence is clear from the large and growing literature on how to manage networks. We would argue, in contrast, that the research frontier for the study of governance should not be drawn so tightly. Steering networks is not the only or even the most important question. While a preference for relevance has always been strong in the study of British government, governance is not just about corporate management and marketisation but also about the changing nature of government, how we are governed and how to understand such changes. Our decentred theory, as we have shown, suggests several ways of broadening the research agenda to encompass these topics.

Besides, one important lesson of a decentred approach for those advising government is that there is no toolkit they can use to steer networks. Practitioners might learn from political scientists by listening to and telling stories. Although we can offer only provisional knowledge, this awareness of our limits does not render such knowledge useless. If we cannot offer universal solutions, we can define and redefine problems in novel ways. We can tell policy makers and administrators distinct stories about their world and how it is governed. The language of networks challenges the language of managerialism, markets and contracts. The language of decentring and narratives challenges the language of positivist political science.

In short, therefore, we provide a language for redescribing the world. We open the door to an understanding of how several actors have constructed the meaning, and so the nature, of recent government changes. Simple solutions such as joining-up or holistic governance may have an appealing elegance. Governments will always seek simplicity – but they should distrust it. Our decentring of governance makes no apology for describing a complex world in at least some of its complexity because there are no simple solutions, whether based on hierarchies, markets or networks. We hope that our narrative is edifying. We are convinced it is provisional.

# References

Anderson, J. (1946), 'The machinery of government', *Public Administration* 24: 147–56.

Bancroft, Lord (1983), 'Whitehall: some Personal Reflections', Suntory–Toyota lecture, London School of Economics and Political Science, 1 December.

Barker, R. (1994), *Politics, Peoples and Governments. Themes in British Political Thought since the Nineteenth Century* (London: Macmillan).

Beer, S. (1965), *Modern British Politics* (London: Faber). All page references are to the 1982 edition.

Bevir, M. (2002), 'Sidney Webb: utilitarianism, positivism, and social democracy', *Journal of Modern History* 47 (2): 217–52.

Bevir, M., and O'Brien, D. (2001), 'New Labour and the public sector in Britain', *Public Administration Review* 61: 535–47.

Bevir, M., and Rhodes, R. A. W. (2000), 'Studying British government: reconstructing the research agenda', *British Journal of Politics and International Relations* 1 (2): 215–39.

Blair, T. (1996), *New Britain: My Vision of a Young Country* (London: Fourth Estate).

Blair, T. (1998), in *The Observer*, 31 May.

Blake, R. (1985), *The Conservative Party from Peel to Thatcher* (London: Fontana).

Cabinet Office (1994) *Civil Service Management Code*, London: HMSO.

Cabinet Office (1999), *Modernising Government: Action Plan* (London: Cabinet Office).

Cabinet Office (2000), *Wiring it up* (London: Cabinet Office).

Chapman, L. (1978), *Your Disobedient Servant* (London: Chatto & Windus).

Chapman, R. A., and Greenaway, J. R. (1980), *The Dynamics of Administrative Reform* (London: Croom Helm).

Clark, D. (1997), 'Delivering Better Government from the Bottom Up', speech by the Chancellor of the Duchy of Lancaster, Queen Elizabeth Conference, London, 17 June.

Cm 2627 (1994), *The Civil Service: Continuity and Change* (London: HMSO).

Cm 4011 (1998), *Modern Public Services for Britain: Investing in Reform. Comprehensive Spending Review: New Public Spending Plans, 1999–2002* (London: Stationery Office).

Cm 4310 (1999), *Modernising Government* (London: Stationery Office).

Dale, H. E. (1941), *The Higher Civil Service of Great Britain* (Oxford: Oxford University Press).

Efficiency Unit (1988), *Improving Management in Government: The Next Steps* (London: HMSO).

Efficiency Unit (1993), *Career Management and Succession Planning Study* (Oughton) (London: HMSO).

Finer, S. E. (1970), *Comparative Government* (London: Allen Lane).

Gamble, A. (1988), *The Free Economy and the Strong State* (London: Macmillan).

Gamble, A. (1990), 'Theories of British politics', *Political Studies* 38: 404–20.

Gilmour, I. (1978), *Inside Right* (London: Quartet).

Gilmour, I. (1992), *Dancing with Dogma: Britain under Thatcherism* (London: Simon & Schuster).

Greaves, H. R. G. (1947), *The Civil Service in the Changing State* (London: Harrap).

Harris, J. (1990), 'Society and state in twentieth-century Britain', in F. M. L. Thompson (ed.), *The Cambridge Social History of Britain 1750–1950* III, *Social Agencies and Institutions* (Cambridge: Cambridge University Press).

Honderich, T. (1991), *Conservatism* (Harmondsworth: Penguin Books).

Hoskyns, J. (1983), 'Whitehall and Westminster: an outsider's view', *Parliamentary Affairs* 36: 137–47.

Lee, J. M. (1977), 'Reviewing the Machinery of Government, 1942–1952: an Essay on the Anderson Committee and its Successors' (London: Birkbeck College, mimeo).

Lowe, R., and Rollings, N. (2000), 'Modernising Britain, 1957–64: a classic case of centralisation and fragmentation?' in R. A. W. Rhodes (ed.), *Transforming British Government* I, *Changing Institutions* (London: Macmillan), pp. 99–118.

Mandelson, P., and Liddle, R. (1996), *The Blair Revolution: Can New Labour Deliver?* (London: Faber).

Marquand, D. (1988), *The Unprincipled Society* (London: Cape).

Metcalfe, L., and Richards, S. (1991), *Improving Public Management*. 2nd edn (London: Sage).

Mount, F. (1993), *The British Constitution Now: Recovery or Decline?* (London: Mandarin).

Niskanen, W., *et al.* (1973), *Bureaucracy: Servant or Master?* (London: Institute of Economic Affairs).

Oakeshott, M. (1962), *Rationalism in Politics and other Essays* (London: Oxford University Press).

Oakeshott, M. (1975), *On Human Conduct* (Oxford: Clarendon Press).

One Nation Group (1954) *Change is our Ally* (London: Conservative Political Centre).

Perri 6 (1997), *Holistic Government* (London Demos).

Qualter, T. N. (1980), *Graham Wallas and the Great Society* (London: Macmillan).

Rhodes, R. A. W. (1997), *Understanding Governance: Policy Networks, Governance, Reflexivity and Accountability* (Buckingham: Open University Press).

Rhodes, R. A. W. (1999), 'Traditions and public sector reform; comparing Britain and Denmark', *Scandinavian Political Studies* 22 (4): 341–70.

Rhodes, R. A. W., ed. (2000a), *Transforming British Government*, 2 vols (London: Macmillan).

Rhodes, R. A. W. (2000b), 'New Labour's civil service: summing up *Joining up*', *Political Quarterly* 71 (2): 151–66.

Rorty, R. (1980), *Philosophy and the Mirror of Nature* (Oxford: Blackwell).

Scruton, R. (1984), *The Meaning of Conservatism*, 2nd edn (London: Macmillan).

Sisson, C. H. (1959), *The Spirit of British Administration* (London: Faber).

Stoker, G., ed. (1999), *The New Management of British Local Governance* (London: Macmillan).

Stoker, G., ed. (2000a), *The New Politics of British Local Governance* (London: Macmillan).

Stoker, G. (2000b), 'Urban political science and the challenge of urban governance', in J. Pierre (ed.), *Debating Governance: Authority, Steering and Democracy* (Oxford: Oxford University Press), pp. 91–110.

Thatcher, M. (1993), *The Downing Street Years* (London: Harper Collins).

Tivey, L. (1988), *Interpretations of British Politics* (London: Harvester Wheatsheaf).

Willetts, D. (1992), *Modern Conservatism* (Harmondsworth: Penguin Books).

# 5

# Activation in governance

Jan Kooiman

## Governing as interaction

In the last few decades, alongside traditional patterns of governance, in which governing was basically regarded as 'one-way traffic', we have seen multiple traffic models developing, making 'inter' aspects of governing and governance more apparent. New forms of interactions between governors and governed, between governing bodies, and even between institutions as state, market and civil society attract more and more scholarly curiosity. The bilateral or multilateral aspects of modern governance are emphasised in public public, in public–private as well as in private–private interrelations. Thus we see not only the locus of boundaries between state and society changing, but also those boundaries themselves alter in character and become increasingly permeable. The demarcation line of where the state begins and civil society ends, or where the market begins and the state ends, and even where the market ends and civil society begins, becomes more diffuse. The borderline between public and private responsibilities itself becomes an object of interaction.

The interaction concept has a central place in my social-political or interactive governance perspective (to be indicated as governance in this chapter). Governance issues arise in interactions between 'the political' and 'the social', and are also handled in governing interactions. With those terms I refer to the multilateral relations between social and political actors and entities (individuals, organisations, institutions). In the governance perspective it is assumed that governing interactions also have to be reflected in the governance conceptualisation. Looking from an interaction perspective, the observer will experience the cohesion and disjunction of societal governance issues more clearly and systematically. Day-to-day governing occurrences appear to be complex, layered interaction processes enacted between a variety of actors or entities with discrepant interests and ambitions. In these interaction processes all kinds of tensions and conflicts are articulated, manifest or latent.

An interaction, then, can be considered to be a mutually influencing relation between two or more entities. In an interaction an action and a structural level can be distinguished. Between and within these levels forces are at work, either with a tendency to maintain existing social-political relations or to change them. In these tensions the dynamics of an interaction are implied. In the characteristics of the entities between which the interactions take place the diversity of the social-political reality comes into being. In the mutual cohesion between the many interactions the complexity of the governing world is realised

Actors and interactions mutually determine each other. We are used to considering interacting individuals and organisations as quite independent of the interactions they participate in. Seemingly, they get interactions going and can stop them at will. But basically actors are continuously formed by and in the interactions in which they relate to each other. They form, as it were, intersections in interaction processes.

Governing interactions can be considered to be the crucial analytical concept in analysing governing and governance. Governing I see as the totality of all interactions within the social-political arenas; governance I consider to be the totality of conceptual ideas about these interactions. From my general conceptualisation of governance I discuss for the purposes of this chapter two aspects in particular: from elements of governing I focus on the action component, and from orders of governance I lift out some ideas on meta-governing.[1] In figure 5.1 the place of governing action as one of the three governing elements, and the place of rationality as an aspects of meta-governance as one of the orders of governing, are shown graphically. This conceptual place will be explained in the following two sections.

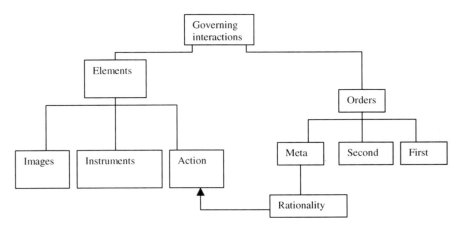

Figure 5.1  *Governing interactions*

cases, different outcomes for individuals' (Coleman 1990: 305). Obligations and expectations, information potential, norms and effective sanctions, but also authority relations and appropriable social organisation and intentional organisation, can be seen as 'direct investment in social capital' (1990: 307).

For Bourdieu, social capital is a theoretical concept to constitute individual identities and strategies, while Coleman employs it as an instrument in the rational calculation of self-interested agents. Both, however, consider social capital as a structural resource with differential access to it, and unevenly distributed as well. This can be expressed in terms of interrelations at different levels of societal aggregation (Edwards and Foley 1998; Foley and Edwards 1999). This makes it possible to conceptualise social capital as sets of interaction, within a broad societal context having historical antecedents and showing broad stratification patterns, such as societal sectors or 'social fields', as Bourdieu calls them. Looked at in this way, social-political capital is a rich concept to be used as a three-level analytical tool to conceptualise the structural component of governing action.

## Types of governing action and their potential

So far I have sketched some conceptual considerations we have to take into account when looking more closely at what action might mean as element of governing. Coming out of this is the notion that governing activities and social capital as societal resource should be seen in close relation to each other. Such a comprehensive action concept can be developed, on the basis of my ideas of governance as a pattern of societal interaction in societies which are characterised by diversity, dynamics and complexity.

### Leadership

There can hardly be any doubt that in social-political governing the role of leadership is important. At all times and in all societies leaders have been and still are essential in staking out a new course or in making changes that take place anyway palatable and thus creating (new) bases of societal governance. Historical studies of leaders have shown these roles, and also nowadays leadership is a subject to which much scholarly attention is paid. The scope has broadened immensely, however, and besides scientific work on 'great leaders', which is still continuing, the emphasis of leadership studies has moved away from these classical or traditional studies of leaders and now focuses on leadership in organisations and groups, informal next to formal leadership, and a systematic analysis of contexts of leadership.

A few words should also be said about the structural features of leadership as an important element of the action component of governing. Social-political capital was conceptualised as the general category comprising the structural level of different forms of governing action; however, it seems possible to introduce a more differentiated structural concept here, which specifies somewhat more precisely in which kind of constraining or enabling context leadership can be seen. For this purpose the concept of stratification or elite structure might do a good job. The question of how leadership as a governing action capacity is embedded in broader societal stratification or elite structures, and what the recent status of stratification and elite theories is, can help in conceptualising the framework within which to approach this question (Grusky 1994). There are different ways to classify stratification/elite theories: some emphasise more classical approaches such as Pareto and Mosca, or Weber and Schumpeter can be distinguished from modern ones such as revised Weberian, revised pluralist or neo-corporatist approaches (Evans 1995). In different ways all these approaches try to explain aspects such as the inevitability of elites, and the nature, structure and circulation of elites.

Elite stratification as distinguished here seems to fit quite well within Bourdieu's view of social capital, and my use of this concept as pointing to the structural context of actual governing action. Continued governance theorising might be able to use this distinction in developing systematic ideas of where and how such differentiated elites will be the social political capital resource from which actual leadership in governing comes about.

For present purposes I deal with leadership in terms of governing interactions, which means that leadership qualities, person-bound and more general, will receive attention (the intentional level of those interactions), and also the structural or processual level. Structural and processual conditions for certain types of leadership will be discussed. A recent example of the kind of leadership I have in mind and the way to analyse this is the way particular types of leaders have been active, and in which social-political leadership expresses itself.

The scientific study of leadership went through different stages, each with its own specific emphases (Chemers 1997). Starting with studying traits, the assumption was that leaders are different from followers, and the most common way to investigate this was to measure all kinds of different personal qualities (Stogdill in Bass, 1990). A new trend was to look at leadership behaviour. And again: some steps were taken, but few 'hard' conclusions could be drawn. And recent insights show that variations in findings often are more to do with the observers' values than with the behaviour of the leaders observed. Another area of research looks at leader–follower relations: exchange approaches, interpersonal relations approaches, legitimation processes, etc. It is the contribution of comparative research that the insight has gained influence such that cultural differences also play an important role.

The area of theory development around leader–follower (influence) processes merits special attention in the present context, as it is the leadership theory that puts most emphasis on the interactional aspect – even on the dynamic character of leadership. A special form of this leadership analysis is that of charismatic leadership. Three major theoretical inputs can be found in the leader–follower processes: social power, exchange and motivation (Conger and Kanungo 1998: 43–5). In the power variant the idea is that the leader–follower interaction is based on resources the leader possesses; the interaction is based upon followers' perception of the need of these resources and way the leader uses them in those interactions. The exchange version of leadership studies puts emphasis on the (often implicit) long-term transactions between leaders and followers and the reciprocal nature of those interactions: the more success the more credit, and vice versa. The motivational school also allots a prominent role to reinforcement (feedback) in those interactions.

In their governing interactions leadership styles in different leader–follower relations enable diversities of perceptions and interests to be brought under one common denominator, and thus order and reorder this diversity on a higher level of abstraction.

*Leadership in partnerships.* A good example of such governing interactions can be found in partnerships between public and private actors collaborating in solving local community problems (Huxham and Vangen 2000). These governing interactions can be described as weakly organised, fluid in membership and quite dynamic in their processes.

In those collaborations that are interactions on a semi-voluntary basis, when hardly anything is fixed, almost all aspects are prone to influence on the part of leaders, even the leadership itself. Two categories of elements of those collaborative interactions to be influenced can be distinguished, what Huxham and Vangen (2000) call media and activities. On the one hand leadership is realised through the triad of media structure, processes and participants, on the other through controlling and managing the agenda, by representing and mobilising member organisations and by enthusing and empowering those who can deliver collaboration aims. Leadership in and of those types of collaborative interaction then can best be seen as being not only enacted in leadership behaviour but also by occurrences or events because of structures, processes and participants which can in some degree be manipulated, but to some extent are outside the control of those interacting and leading the interactions. It seems that for such collaborative interactions to come about their singlemindedness is the key to their success.

Generalising from this example, we might suspect that for leading governing interactions the qualities attributed to 'leaders' (activities) are the more powerful explanatory variable or factor, rather than the qualities attributed to the interactions themselves (media) – with the exception of direct external conditions which are beyond the scope of influence of those involved in them.

*Leadership in mobilisation.* A second example refers to the role of leadership in social mobilisation as through social movements. In those governing efforts it is important that in the mobilisation of these forms of social interaction a relation must be established between goal setting, strategy development and motivational input on the part of leadership and the support, loyalty and voluntary activities of followers/members on the other. Rules of this exchange include incentives such as positional rewards, but also sanctions such as withholding resources. The leadership of such social mobilisation (movements) has to take care that these exchanges are seen as equitable and it must intervene when this balance is distorted. These balancing and intervening processes are not simple one-way traffic but complex networks of exchanges in which influence circulates (Huxham 2000a, b). Structures, processes and participants (media) can be manipulated to some extent, but because of the exchange character of the use of resources leadership activities take place within limits. Generalising from this example to leadership of governing interactions, in those interactions there is a relatively equal balance between leadership qualities and the influence of structural factors.

The third example is *political leadership*. This is an area in which the role of the individual leader in many theories about leadership is quite outspoken. Classic thinkers such as Machiavelli or more recently Weber have set the tone in analysing political leadership qualities as personal traits. There is certainly value in this, although not all studies along these lines allow the contextual aspects the importance they deserve. Even the behaviour of the great political leaders of the past and of our own time needs to be seen in the context of their situation and the interactions between them and their public, however one-sided these interactions might appear at first glance. Leaving aside the exceptions, particularly in the context of modern liberal democracies, with all their complex interrelations of institutional, historical and social forces, political leaders have to work within formal constraints. They operate within the confines of systems where the scope for action is decided largely by their skill in bending them to their advantage, or to the goals they are pursuing. Often it is more fruitful to analyse political leadership in such circumstances as the ability to enlarge and actualise action potential by manipulating those constraints and by turning them into opportunities, more than others could have done in the same circumstances. Political leadership then can be seen as the activation of resources from a 'social field', as conceptualised by Bourdieu, or recombining elements of social capital to be invested for a particular purpose. By doing so political leaders act as broker between more structural conditions of governing interactions and actual governing of this kind. In such brokerage roles the arrow might also point in the other direction, and show how by exercising this power broker role political leaders may also be able to change structural conditions, as one sometimes sees in crises where the brokerage role works both ways: mobilising followers and, through such mobilisation, changing existing institutional frameworks. Again, as with exceptionally 'great' political leaders, those able to change institutional frameworks seem to be the exception, and it would be erroneous to generalise about political leadership on the strength of them alone. It seems to me more fruitful to see political leadership also in role terms, where the essence of the role, as with other categories of leaders, can be found in the relation between the context and the implementation of such role conceptions. Political leadership then can be defined as the ability to make use of existing and sometimes of innovative media with the emphasis on leadership activities in creating opportunities in coping with or reducing the complexity of formal institutional frameworks for a particular purpose.

*Generalising* leadership to governing interactions in the broader analytical sense, it seems that the balance between more personal attributes and features of the context would be tilting towards the personal aspects of those interactions. In interplays (governing diversity of images or interests) the capacity of leaders to influence structural conditions are limited, as are the role of these conditions, because of the 'horizontal' nature of those interactions: the structural conditions (such as of networks or co-management schemes) and the mobilisation capacity of leaders keep each other so to say 'in balance'. Generalising mobilising forms of leadership, it seems that both features, media and activities, can be counted more evenly. Thirdly what is known as leadership in collaborative types of governing the relation between conditional and personal features of such leaders the balance seems to tilt towards the manipulation of contextual aspects for their success. Handling the dynamics of such governing interactions seems to be an important aspect of its leadership. All in all, in the relation between leadership features and contextual aspects of governing interactions, the different forms of governing interactions seem to add to the explanatory power of understanding how these interactions work. At the same time, and related to this, different roles of leadership in coping with the dynamics, diversity and complexity of the situational fields or sectors those governing interactions are embedded in can be a variable of considerable importance.

Leadership in governance has the gift to actualise action potential. It is able to bind societal diversity. Such leaders marshal all sorts and conditions of people, and find terms which cover their diversity and enable those involved to recognise and operationalise their common core.

*Social movements*

Now I move on to the second elaboration of governing action, discussing the action capacity of social movements as a form of social mobilisation for governing purposes. The analysis focuses on these movements as examples of such mobilisation, as there are also other forms of organised action in governance arenas. The other two major forms to be mentioned are interests groups and political parties. Suffice it to say here that all three can be seen as forms of participation in governing processes, as social-political activism on the part of citizens organised in different ways and in somewhat different roles. This has been called a repertory of activism alternatives, and this repertory is seen as growing and becoming more varied (Kaase and Marsh 1979). Recent studies of such activism show that the dividing lines between the three organised forms of such social-political action change and may become diffuse. So the distinction between a social

movement and an interest group is becoming vague and political parties
show a tendency to include elements from this movement (Costain 1992).
It has been argued that parties, interest groups and social movements all
operate on a market of activism, each trying to capture its share of specialised issues, attention and participation (Richardson 1995). I limit myself
in this paragraph to social movements as a means of mobilisation for
governing purposes; however, several of the observations could be generalised *ceteris paribus* to the whole spectrum of this social-political participation and activist market-place. Out of the three social movements, the
latter manifests itself massively on this activist market, and their conceptualisation in the literature provides an opportunity to link up with what has
been said above about social capital as the concept showing some of the
structural characteristics of the action component of governing.

The *actor-oriented perspective* on social movements emphasises questions
of participation in those movements and theories which try to explain why
people become social-politically active in them. In such a perspective social
movements are seen to be populated by individuals who share collective
goals and a collective identity by *engaging in disruptive collective action*
(Klandermans 1997: 3–8). Participation in social movements is far from
commonplace for the society at large. Even large social movements mobilise
only relatively small proportions of the population. Acting according to
one's principles is not always easy, and this is what social movements are
about. If participation in social movements is not very common, how do
people become involved in them, and why do they put so much effort into
them on a voluntary basis? Focusing on the individual, it has been said that
individuals within a movement often disagree about a common course of
action; that each individual is likely to have different motives for participation; that individual participants contribute to the collective enterprise in
different ways, and that this concerted energy may be more than the sum
of its individual parts. Nor is the collective character of this form of social
action self-evident: the way in which social discontent is transformed into
organised action has always been among the key issues discussed in social
movement literature. Participation in a social movement is a good example
of what so-called rationality-based collective action theory has to offer.
This variety of collective action theory states that from a rational actor's
viewpoint there is little reason to engage in collective action (Olsen 1965).
Social movements fight for collective goods (equal or human rights, a clean
environment, democratic government) and/or against collective ills (nuclear
energy, ethnic conflicts, authoritarian regimes). Collective goods and the ter-
mination of collective ills, however, are characterised by jointness of supply.
That is, once a good is made available or an ill eliminated, all the members
of the collective can enjoy the benefits, regardless of whether they participated in the collective action needed to secure it. So why be active in this
form of social-political governing, when history shows time and again that
individuals do participate in collective action, sometimes even at very high

personal cost, and populate social movements? The (collective) rational actor paradigm is unable to solve this dilemma, and thus gives only a partial answer to the question of social movement participation. But how do individuals and social movements solve the social dilemma of movement participation? And why do some people participate in social movements whereas others do not? To answer this question three explanatory elements are used: (1) engagement – how and when individuals become involved in social movements; (2) sustained participation – how and why people continue to participate in social movements, and (3) disengagement – how, when and why people leave.

Now if we turn to the study of social movements from a more *structural perspective* two schools can be distinguished. The first (also seen in time) is the so-called r*esource mobilisation variant*, particularly strong in the United States; the second, under the heading of *new social movement theory* has a predominantly European base.

Resource mobilisation theory develops the idea that a potential for conflict exists in any society and that the actualisation of this potential largely depends upon the proper use of resources and selective incentives to action (Diani and Eyerman 1992). A vocabulary adopted from organisation theory was applied to social movements, and terms such as political entrepreneurs, social movement organisations and even social movement industry were adopted. Resource mobilisation theory focused attention on individuals and the micro-level of analysis, postulating connections between individual properties and protest insurgency, and claimed that it was the most cultivated actors who possessed the necessary resources to act as leaders and organisers of social movements. This had the effect of moving social movement actors from the margins to the centre of society. Resource mobilisation theory also emphasised the rationality of this form of collective action – social actors pursuing their interests, especially those excluded from the established routines of decision making and policy formation (Tilly 1978) – and the decision to join a social movement was treated as just that: a rationally calculated decision distinguishing risks and rewards (Oberschall 1993).

Resource mobilisation theory approaches also face a number of limitations, showing that they cannot be seen as providing the fundamentals for a self-sufficient theory of social movements. Problems deserving special attention in this context include: they say little about the emergence and definition of the stakes involved in the struggle of social movements; they often operate with simplistic models of rational behaviour; they tend to overestimate and over-generalise the importance of formal organisation for collective mobilisation; and viewed from a comparative perspective, resource mobilisation theory approaches primarily reconstruct the dynamics of social movements in particular societies (Kitschfeld 1991: 330).

New social movement theory is rooted in continental European traditions of social theory and political philosophy (Buechler 1995). It has searched for logics of collective action based in politics, ideology and culture, and has looked to other sources of identity such as ethnicity, gender and sexuality. Some theorists of this school seek to update and revise more conventional Marxist assumptions, while others seek to displace and transcend them. There are many variations within the general approach called new social movements, but a number of common themes can be identified. In the first place many scholars of new social movement theory underscore symbolic action in civil society or the cultural sphere as a major arena for collective action, alongside instrumental action in the state or the political sphere. Secondly, the importance of processes that protect autonomy and self-determination instead of strategies for maximising influence and power is stressed. In the third place, some theorists emphasise the role of post-materialist values in this form of collective action, as opposed to conflicts over material resources. Fourthly there is a tendency to problematise the often fragile process of constructing collective identities and identifying group interests, instead of assuming that conflict groups and their interests are structurally determined. Fifth, the socially constructed nature of grievances and ideology is emphasised, rather than assuming that they can be deduced from a group's structural location. And finally, these theories generally recognise a variety of submerged, latent and temporary networks that often undergird collective action, rather than assuming that centralised organisational forms are prerequisites of successful mobilisation. However, it should be noted that various theorists in this approach have put different emphases on the themes.

But new social movement theory has not been without its critics, either (Pichardo 1997). There is significant doubt in terms of whether contemporary social movements are specifically a product of post-industrial society. Do these contemporary movements represent anything unique, except for the issue of identity? It can be argued that they are recent additions to the general repertoire of social movements, and that changes in these repertoires don't need new theories (Tilly 1978). However the main contribution of the new social movement perspective is their emphases on identity, culture and the role of the civic sphere aspects of social movements. This can be seen as an important recent 'European' contribution to social movement literature in general.

For the structural component of social movement as a major form of social mobilisation I recall that I introduced social-political capital for that purpose. Is it plausible that we can see social capital as the action potential from which at a structural resource level such mobilisation can be expected? I think it can be done, and not only for social movements but also for other forms of social-political mobilisation such as interest groups and probably also political parties. As we did with leadership, where stratification was seen as an intermediary concept to take a step operationalising social capital, we may use the same procedure for forms of mobilisation and introduce the concept of *pluralism* for the purpose. Stratification is to be seen as the conceptualisation of the elite structure, indicating how leadership action might be distributed in modern societies; pluralism is the concept with which to indicate how mobilisation, the action potential of modern societies, is distributed. Both these concepts then can be seen as operationalisation of the general action potential structured as social capital. This is certainly in line with Bourdieu's way of applying the concept, and to some extent it is also in agreement with Coleman's opinion here.

But what does pluralism actually mean? Can it be seen as the way in which the mobilisation of action potential is distributed in modern societies? As with many concepts used in social science discourse there are many ways of looking at pluralism: there are pluralist, reformed and neo-pluralist theories (Smith 1990), there are liberal, communal and radical theories of pluralism (Andrain and Apter 1995), and combinations of these (Smith 1995). Although certainly not unproblematic as a concept with at the same time normative, descriptive and analytical qualities to it, it remains an important tool in theorising about the interaction of state and society in general and how power or influence in such interaction is divided. The essence of a plural society is that no single group, organisation or class can dominate its governance (1995: 209). The dispersal of societal sources of power and influence is at the root of pluralist views on the structure of its action potential, and the competition and tensions between these sources give such societies their dynamic quality. There is the continuous upward and downward movement between interest groups and political organisations but also between professions, industries and even classes which show the patterns of plural societal dynamics. The conservation or exchange of social political capital, as the resource base from which social movements and other groups draw, depends heavily on these dynamics, and thus they partly form their structural condition. Although, as Olsen points out, it is not usually made in pluralist literature, there is also a distinction to be drawn between a mobilisation version, which focuses primarily on the role of non-political voluntary associations in mobilising individuals in social-political interactions, and a version that can be called *mediating pluralism*, which is particularly concerned with interest mediating as a form of political influence (Olsen 1993: 148–50). However, as argued above, there also seems to be a tendency for the distinction between movements and interests to become vague – probably depending on the sort of social field or sector we are talking about. This much seems clear, that pluralism from a conceptual point of view sheds light on the diversity of and differences in the structural aspects of sources of influence and thus of action potential in modern societies.

## Meta-norms for governing action

Governors (public or private) with all their ambitions, emotions and intuitions have to be able to underpin their – interactive – governing proposals with reasonable arguments. Governing has in some way to be rational, based upon verifiable facts and data, a logical choice of instruments and defensible action routes. Doubts will always remain, because in governing facts or data are no more than observations having passed through many filters of social-political communication. Instruments are often unreliable and, in combining them, they may even become counterproductive. Action will seldom go undisputed. Rationality in governing thus means the acceptance of a certain degree of uncertainty, the realisation of partial knowledge and provisional insights, and learning by doing (Berting 1996). Still, it is an important normative consideration in modern governance, because rationality implies a condition of 'relevant considerations', as the Dutch philosopher Derksen phrased it (1992). In his view there is nothing particularly 'good' about rationality, but it helps: to act rationally at least relevant considerations are needed; otherwise behaviour can be called irrational – which in social-political governing is not common or advisable.

Despite all this, rationality has strong roots in many (meta-)sciences and is at the same time highly controversial within and between sciences. A symposium on the subject not so long ago, in which almost all philosophy scholars of any note participated, concluded: 'We certainly have not been able to build a general theory of rationality for today's world, not even to lay any firm foundation for such a theory' (Geraets 1979: xi). So claims for an all-embracing rationality concept seem to be overstated, and we had better look for a modest interpretation such as the following:

> [a] rational person is methodical and precise, is tidy and orderly, above all in thought. He does not raise his voice, his tone is steady and equal; that goes for feelings as well as his voice. He separates all separable issues, and deals with them one at a time. By doing so, he avoids muddling up issues and conflating distinct criteria for interaction.[2]

This is the kind of actor I have in mind when I think of a governor acting 'rationally in a governing situation' (see below).

Can something sensible be said about what 'rational' social-political interaction might look like, or, in other words, is there a version of rationality appropriate to meta-norm setting within the governance perspective? There are several ways to approach this question. The first is to start with a view of rationality as applied in public choice theory or game theory and 'stretch' it to serve broader governance purposes. However, even mildly critical reviewers of this theoretical scene seem to agree that we are still a long way from more generally applicable insights into the rationality of governing actors, notwithstanding Scharpf's confident title, *Games Real Actors Play* (1997). Secondly one might start from accepted types of rationality as value and goal–means rationality and work those out. The attraction of such an approach is release from an overall rationality concept, allowing a variety of rationality notions. However, this might open the door to as many rationality concepts as one sees fit – someone even distinguished eight different rationality notions in Weber's writing (Wallace 1994) – thus undermining its normative and synthetic power.

My choice for rationality as a meta-criterion is following a third route, starting from my own ideas on governing and adding some rationality concepts to them. In fact I take the three elements of governing – image formation, choice of instruments and action – and for each of them select a (sub-)rationality concept as yardstick: for 'proper' image formation, communicative rationality (Habermas); for choosing an appropriate instrument, Simon's bounded rationality concept, and, for taking action, Boudon's perception of rationality is a useful one. Boudon's interpretation can also be seen as an integrating one in the sense that in the action component of governing the image and instrumental element are subsumed.

### Rationality of action in a situation

Governing in my perception consists of the formation of governing images, selecting suitable instruments and organising action potential. Images and instruments certainly contribute to governing, but nothing 'happens' if no action is taken. So one might say that action in governing interactions, as it were, comprises the other two, 'binds' them together. In terms of rationality the following line of thought serves this purpose. The least stringent rationality criterion, the communicative one, applies to image building. This governing element is the most 'open' of the three and its rationality yardstick is not so high, for example irrational beliefs are not excluded from consideration. As long as the participants in governing interactions try to reach an understanding by rules and norms as set out by communicative rationality, interaction may lead to shared governing images, in my terms. Interactions in which governing instrument(s) are chosen can be evaluated within the stricter confines of 'bounded' rationality as defined by Simon. After all, choosing a governing instrument usually means going through many stages of deliberation, in which the cognitive limitations of actors are – within limits – overcome by discussions between experts, and the weighing of alternatives. The use of supporting tools and techniques to extend the cognitive limitations of actors by means of thorough interactions is quite common. So, for the choice of instruments the rationality pole can be set a bit higher.

Thirdly, for the action component of governing, rationality demands should be even stricter. Taking action often means making binding decisions, in the public arena, accompanied by strict procedural guarantees. Can a rationality norm be formulated, able to evaluate this last, integrating and decisive step in governing in a meta-perspective? A promising one might be Boudon's concept of *situational rationality*, meaning: if I were in the same situation as the observed actor, pursuing the same goal, with the same information available, wearing the same glasses, 'Would I do the same thing?'

(Boudon, in Berting 1996: 21) In Boudon's view rationality of behaviour can be explained as a function of the structure of the situation of an actor, as an adaptation to the situation. Behaviour directed at reaching a particular goal in a rational manner has to be understandable to an outsider, when this observant has sufficient information at his disposal to judge the way the actor interprets his situation and the goals he or she wants to pursue. Boudon adheres to a rational choice model in which cost–benefit considerations play a central role (Weber's instrumental rationality). At the same time he is aware, that in many – important – situations this model has little explanatory power, e.g. when actions are inspired by beliefs (Weber's value rationality). Boudon interprets value rationality in such a way that such beliefs 'are grounded in the minds of social actors on reasons which they see as valid, and consequently as likely to be considered as valid by others' (1996: 124). Beliefs can be partly scientific, when they are 'trans-subjective', when a generalised other will share the belief – such as 2 + 2 = 4. But we always have to take into consideration that a belief that was once completely valid – as on power and movement in Aristotelian physics – turns to be invalid after all.

This situational rationality – I would do the same thing, *ceteris paribus* – is broad enough and at the same time precise enough to be applicable to the action element of governing. It seems able to integrate the two other rationality criteria, the communicative and the bounded rationality ones. The last word on the use of the rationality concept to evaluate governing activities has yet to be said. At least a first step has been taken towards making meta-governance applicable to this element of governing activities.

## Conclusion

In this chapter I have presented some conceptual ideas on the action element of governing as one aspect of the question how in governance governing actors or entities become activated. These ideas are part of the broader governance perspective I am pursuing. Thinking about activation in relation to governance is not a luxury, because many of the concepts in use to explain governing action are either developed without much regard to the broader context they have to be set in or the distinction between ' fact' and 'norm' has not been clearly spelled out. In this chapter I have tried to overcome these limitations. Only by speaking of action and the action potential of governing in a broader overview can activation for governance get its proper place in the systematic thinking about governance.

## Notes

1 For the whole of my perspective on governance I refer to *On Governance*, to be published in 2002 (London: Sage), and to Kooiman (1999, 20001a, b).
2 Adapted from Gellner (1992: 136–7).

# References

Andrain, C. F., and Apter, D. (1995), *Political Protest and Social Change* (Basingstoke: Macmillan).

Bass, B. M. (1990), *Handbook of Leadership*, 3rd edn (New York: Free Press).

Berting, J. (1996), 'Over rationaliteit en complexiteit', in P. Nijkamp, W. Begeer and J. Berting (eds), *Denken over complexe besluitvorming* (The Hague: SDU), pp. 17–30.

Boudon, R. (1996), 'The "cognivist model"', *Rationality and Society* 8: 123–50.

Bourdieu, P. (1986), 'Three forms of capital', in J. G. Richardson (ed.), *Handbook of Theory and Research in the Sociology of Education* (New York: Greenwood Press), pp. 241–58.

Bourdieu, P., and Wacquant, L. J. D. (1992), *An Invitation to Reflexive Sociology* (Chicago: University of Chicago Press).

Buechler, S. M. (1995), 'New social movement theories', *Sociological Quarterly* 36: 441–64.

Chemers, M. M. (1997), *An Integrative Theory of Leadership* (Mahwah NJ: Erlbaum).

Coleman, J. (1990), *Foundations of Social Theory* (Cambridge MA: Belknap Press), pp. 300–21.

Conger, J. A., and Kanungo, R. N. (1998), *Charismatic Leadership in Organizations* (Thousand Oaks CA: Sage).

Costain, A. N. (1992), 'Social movements as interest groups: the case of the women's movement', in M. P. Petracca (ed.), *The Politics of Interests* (Boulder CO: Westview Press), pp. 285–307.

Crespi, F. (1992), *Social Action and Power* (Oxford: Blackwell).

Derksen, A. A. (1992), 'Wat is rationaliteit en wat is er zo goed aan?' *Algemeen Nederlands Tijdschrift voor Wijsbegeerte* 84: 258–86.

Diani, M., and Eyerman, R., eds (1992), *Studying Collective Action* (London: Sage).

Edwards, B., and Foley, M. W. (1998), 'Civil society and social capital beyond Putnam', *American Behavioral Scientist* 42 (1): 124–39.

Etzioni, A. (1968), *The Active Society* (New York: Free Press).

Evans, M. (1995), 'Elitism', in D. Marsh and G. Stoker (eds), *Theory and Methods in Political Science* (London: Macmillan), pp. 228–48.

Foley, M. W., and Edwards, B. (1999), 'Is it time to disinvest in social capital?' *Journal of Public Policy* 19: 141–73.

Gellner, E (1992), *Reason and culture* (Oxford: Blackwell).

Geraets, T. F., ed. (1979), *Rationality Today* (Ottawa: University of Ottawa Press).

Grusky, D. B. (1994), *Social Stratification* (Boulder CO: Westview Press).

Huxham, C. (2000a), 'Ambiguity, complexity and dynamics in membership of collaboration', *Human Relations* 53 (6): 771–806.

Huxham, C. (2000b), 'The challenge of collaborative governance', *Public Management (Review)* 2: 337–57.

Huxham, C., and Vangen, S. (2000), 'Leadership in the shaping and implementation of collaborate agendas', *Academy of Management Journal* 43: 1159–75.

Kaase, M., and Marsh, A. (1979), 'Political action repertory', in S. Barnes and M. Kaase (eds), *Political Action* (Beverly Hills CA: Sage), pp. 137–66.

Kitschfelt, H. (1991), 'Resource mobilization theory', in D. Rucht (ed.), *Research on Social Movements* (Frankfurt: Campus), pp. 325–54.

Klandermans, B. (1997), *The Social Psychology of Protest* (Oxford: Blackwell).

Kooiman, J. (1988), *Besturen. Wisselwerking tussen Overheid en Maatschappij* (Assen: van Gorcum).

Kooiman, J. (1999), 'Social-political governance: overview, reflections and design', *Public Management (Review)*, 1: 67–92.

Kooiman, J. (2000a), 'Societal governance: levels, modes and orders of social-political interaction', in J. Pierre (ed.), *Debating Governance: Authority, Steering and Democracy* (Oxford: Oxford University Press), pp. 138–66.

Kooiman, J. (2000b), *Working with Governance*, special issue of *Public Management (Review)* 2 (3).

Kooiman, J. (2002), *On Governance* (London: Sage).

Melucci, A. (1996), *Challenging Codes* (Cambridge: Cambridge University Press).

Oberschall, A. (1993), *Social Movements* (New Brunswick NJ: Transaction).

Olsen, M. E. (1993) 'Sociopolitical pluralism', in M. E. Olsen and M. N. Marger (eds), *Power in Modern Societies* (Boulder CO: Westview Press).

Olson, M., Jr (1965), *The Logic of Collective Action* (Cambridge MA: Harvard University Press).

Pichardo, N. A. (1997), 'New social movements', *Annual Review of Sociology* 23: 411–30.

Portes, A. (1998), 'Social capital', *Annual Review of Sociology* 24: 1–24.

Richardson, J. J. (1995), 'The market for political activism: interest groups as a challenge to political parties', *West European Politics* 18: 116–39.

Scharpf, F. W. (1973), *Politische Durchsetzbarkeit innerer Reformen im pluralistisch-demokratischen Gemeinwesen der Bundesrepublik* (Berlin: International Institute of Management).

Scharpf, F. W. (1997), *Games Real Actors Play: Actor-centered Institutionalism in Policy Research* (Boulder CO: Westview Press).

Smith, M. J. (1990), 'Pluralism, reformed pluralism and neopluralism: the role of presssure groups in policy-making', *Political Studies* 38: 302–22.

Smith, M. J. (1995), 'Pluralism', in D. Marsh and G. Stoker (eds), *Theory and Methods in Political Science* (London: Macmillan), pp. 209–27.

Tilly, C. (1978), *From Mobilization to Revolution* (Reading MA: Addison Wesley).

Wallace, W. L. (1994), *A Weberian Theory of Human Society* (New Brunswick NJ: Rutgers University Press).

# Part II
Sociological analyses of meta-governance, governmentality and symbolic violence

# 6

## Governance and meta-governance: on reflexivity, requisite variety and requisite irony

Bob Jessop

There has been growing interest in the past twenty years or so in the potential contribution of new forms of governance to solving co-ordination problems in and across a wide range of specialised social systems (such as the economy, the legal system, the political system, and the health system) and in the life world (or, broadly understood, civil society). This interest is reflected in growing ambiguities about the meaning of governance. For the purposes of this chapter,[1] however, I adopt a relatively narrow definition of governance. Thus governance is defined as the reflexive self-organisation of independent actors involved in complex relations of reciprocal interdependence, with such self-organisation being based on continuing dialogue and resource-sharing to develop mutually beneficial joint projects and to manage the contradictions and dilemmas inevitably involved in such situations. Governance organised on this basis need not entail complete symmetry in power relations or complete equality in the distribution of benefits: indeed, it is highly unlikely to do so, almost regardless of the object of governance or the 'stakeholders' who actually participate in the governance process. All that is involved in this preliminary definition is the commitment on the part of those involved to reflexive self-organisation in the face of complex reciprocal interdependence.

Even on this minimal definition, governance can be distinguished from the 'invisible hand' of unco-ordinated market exchange based on the formally rational pursuit of self-interest by isolated market agents; and from the 'iron fist' (perhaps in a 'velvet glove') of centralised, top-down imperative co-ordination in pursuit of substantive goals established from above. (Some differences between these three modes of co-ordination of complex interdependence and their respective forms of failure are presented in table 6.1.) Governance in this limited sense has become a hot topic for ivory tower academics, this-worldly practitioners, and philosophers seeking to reinterpret the world or even to change it in new ways. It has been hailed as a new social-scientific paradigm, a new approach to problem solving that can overcome the limitations of anarchic market exchange and top-down

**Table 6.1**  *Modalities of governance*

|  | *Exchange* | *Command* | *Dialogue* |
|---|---|---|---|
| *Rationality* | Formal and procedural | Substantive and goal-oriented | Reflexive and procedural |
| *Criterion of success* | Efficient allocation of resources | Effective goal attainment | Negotiated consent |
| *Typical example* | Market | State | Network |
| *Stylised mode of calculation* | Homo economicus | Homo hierarchicus | Homo politicus |
| *Spatio-temporal horizons* | World market, reversible time | National territory, planning horizons | Rescaling and path-shaping |
| *Primary criterion of failure* | Economic inefficiency | Ineffectiveness | 'Noise', 'talking-shop' |
| *Secondary criterion of failure* | Market inadequacies | Bureaucracy, red tape | ? |

planning in an increasingly complex and global world, and as a solution to the perennial ethical, political, and civic problems of securing institutional integration and peaceful social coexistence. As interest in good governance has grown and attempts are made to achieve it; however, there has also been growing recognition of its limitations and the attendant risks of governance failure.

## The appeal of governance

The concept of governance in the sense of reflexive self-organisation is by no means new. During *les trente glorieuses* of the post-war boom in America and Europe, however, the nature and functions of this form of governance were relatively neglected. Instead the emphasis fell on the mixed economy, in which successful state intervention apparently served to compensate for market failure. The concept of governance has since been revitalised and applied to many issues. This has three aspects. First, interest in governance is a response to paradigm crises in the social sciences. Traditional disciplines reflect the organisation of nineteenth-century modern industrial societies: economics focused on markets, political science on sovereign national states, international relations on inter-state *Realpolitik*, and sociology on civil society. Not only has the taken-for-grantedness of national economies, national states, and national societies as units of analysis been challenged by the dialectic of globalisation–regionalisation but conventional conceptual couplets (such as market versus plan, state versus civil society, *bourgeois* versus *citoyen*) also appear less relevant. 'Governance' is being introduced to bridge disciplines and to provide alternative ways of understanding (for a more detailed discussion see Jessop 1998).

For practitioners, governance is attractive for several reasons: (1) it gives a fashionable, new legitimacy to old practices, such as corporatist concertation; (2) it provides a solution, however partial, temporary, and provisional, to the crisis of state planning in the mixed economy and the more recent disillusion with excessively disembedded neo-liberal market forces; and, above all (3) it offers a solution to problems of co-ordination in the face of growing complexity. Thus, as Scharpf notes in relation to hierarchy (but one could apply the same argument to market exchange):

> the advantages of hierarchical co-ordination are lost in a world that is characterised by increasingly dense, extended, and rapidly changing patterns of reciprocal interdependence, and by increasingly frequent, but ephemeral, interactions across all types of pre-established boundaries, intra- and interorganisational, intra- and intersectoral, intra- and international. (Scharpf 1994: 37)

The expansion of governance practices into so many spheres represents a secular response to a dramatic intensification of societal complexity. This has several sources: (1) increased functional differentiation combined with increased interdependence among the resulting functional systems; (2) the increased fuzziness of some institutional boundaries, for example, concerning what counts as 'economic' in an era of increased competitiveness; (3) the multiplication and re-scaling of spatial horizons; (4) the increasing complexity of temporal horizons of action; (5) the multiplication of identities; (6) the increased importance of knowledge and organised learning; and, as a result of the above, (7) the self-potentiating nature of growing complexity, i.e. the fact that complex systems generally function so as to engender further principles of order that possibilise additional complexities (Rescher 1998: 28). Such complexity is reflected in worries about the governability of economic, political, and social life in the face of globalisation and conflicting identities. It implies that important new problems have emerged that cannot be managed or resolved readily, if at all, through top-down state planning or market-mediated anarchy. This has promoted a shift in the institutional centre of gravity (or institutional attractor) around which policy makers choose among possible modes of co-ordination.

Third, philosophically, governance has attracted attention as a solution to co-ordination problems in and across the private and public spheres. Even liberal economists recognise that the market mechanism does not always reflect the true public and/or private costs and benefits of economic activities. This is now reflected in growing interest in modes of institutional design and economic regulation that might obviate the need for state control whilst still guiding the market. Political theorists now suggest that governance is an important means to overcome the division between rulers and ruled in representative regimes and to secure the input and commitment of an increasingly wide range of stakeholders in policy formulation and implementation. In this sense governance also has normative significance. It indicates a revaluation of different modes of co-ordination not just in terms of their economic efficiency or their effectiveness in collective goal attainment but also in terms of their associated values. Thus 'governance' has acquired positive connotations such as 'middle way', 'consultation', 'negotiation', 'subsidiarity', 'reflexivity', 'dialogue', etc., in contrast to the anarchy of the market or the state's 'iron fist'.

## On some conditions for effective governance

Studies suggest that there are four conditions for effective reflexive self-organisation: (1) simplifying models and practices, which reduce the complexity of the world but are still congruent with real-world processes and relevant to actors' objectives; (2) developing the capacity for dynamic, interactive social learning among autonomous but interdependent agencies about causal processes and forms of interdependence, attributions of responsibility and capacity for actions, and possibilities of co-ordination in a complex, turbulent environment; (3) building methods of co-ordinating actions across social forces with different identities, interests, and meaning systems, over different spatio-temporal horizons, and over different domains of action; and (4) establishing a common world view for individual action and a system of 'meta-governance' (see below) to stabilise key players' orientations, expectations, and rules of conduct. Obviously the specific forms of governance will vary with the nature of the objects to be governed: effective governance of local economic development, hypermobile financial capital, international migration, universities, medical practice, the nuclear power industry, and cyberspace, for example, would entail very different sets of partners and practices.

Nonetheless, despite the good press for good governance, it is important to recognise that all modes of co-ordination are prey to dilemmas, contradictions, paradoxes, and failures. These obviously differ. Market failure is said to occur when markets fail to allocate scarce resources efficiently in and through pursuit of monetised private interest; and state failure is seen as a failure to secure substantive collective goals based on political divination of the public interest. There was once a tendency to assume that market failure could be corrected either by extending the logic of the market or by compensatory state action; and that state failure could be corrected either by 'more market, less state' or through improved juridico-political institutional design, knowledge, or political practice. (For a useful review of arguments about market and state failure see Wallis and Dollery 1999.) More recently, however, governance has been seen as an effective response to market and state failure. Unfortunately, growing fascination with governance mechanisms should not lead us to overlook the risks involved in substituting it for markets or hierarchies and the resulting likelihood of governance failure. For it is not just markets and imperative co-ordination that fail; governance is also prone to failure.

## Potential sources of governance failure

Reflexive self-organisation can occur on many different levels of social life from the interpersonal through the interorganisational and interinstitutional to the relations among systems. The following comments on governance failure mainly concern the role of markets, states, and networks in capitalist social formations rather than more amorphous interpersonal relations. There are three sources of governance failure in this regard. The first set is inscribed in the nature of capitalism, which has always depended on a contradictory balance between marketised and non-marketised organisational forms. Although this balance was previously understood mainly in terms of the relative importance of market and state in reproducing the conditions for capital accumulation, governance does not introduce a neutral third term but adds another site upon which the balance can be contested. For new forms of governance provide a new meeting ground for the conflicting logics of accumulation and political mobilisation. This is one of the reasons why the apparent promise of symmetry in social partnership as a form of reflexive self-organisation may not be realised. For there are marked structural asymmetries in the capital–labour relation and in the forms of interdependence between the economic and the extra-economic conditions for accumulation.

The second set of potential sources of governance failure concerns the contingent insertion of partnerships and other reflexive, self-organising arrangements into the more general state system – especially in terms of the relative primacy of different modes of co-ordination and access to institutional support and material resources to pursue reflexively arrived at governance objectives. There are three key aspects of this second set of constraints. First, as both governance and government mechanisms exist on different scales (indeed, one of their functions is to bridge scales), success at one scale may well depend on what occurs on other scales. Second, co-ordination mechanisms may also have different temporal horizons. One function of contemporary forms of governance (as of quangos and corporatist arrangements beforehand) is to enable decisions with long-term implications to be divorced from short-term political (especially electoral) calculations. But disjunctions may still arise between the temporalities of different governance and government mechanisms. Third, although various governance mechanisms may acquire specific techno-economic, political, and/or ideological functions, the state typically monitors their effects on its own capacity to secure social cohesion in divided societies. It reserves to itself the right to open, close, juggle, and re-articulate governance arrangements, not only in terms of particular functions but also from the viewpoint of partisan and overall political advantage.

The third set of constraints is rooted in the specificities of governance as reflexive self-organisation. First, governance attempts may fail because of oversimplification of the conditions of action and/or deficient knowledge about causal connections affecting the object of governance. This is especially problematic when this object is an inherently unstructured but complex system, such as the insertion of the local into the global economy. Indeed, this leads to the more general 'governability' problem, i.e. the question of whether the object of governance could ever be manageable, even with adequate knowledge (Mayntz 1993; Malpas and Wickham 1995). Second, there may be co-ordination problems on one or more of the interpersonal, interorganisational, and intersystemic levels. These three levels are often related in complex ways. Thus interorganisational negotiation often depends on interpersonal trust; and decentred intersystemic steering involves the representation of system logic's through interorganisational and/or interpersonal communication. Third, linked to this is the problematic relationship between those engaged in communication (networking, negotiation, etc.) and those whose interests and identities are being represented. Gaps can open between these groups, leading to representational and legitimacy crises and/or to problems in securing compliance. And, fourth, where there are various partnerships and other governance arrangements concerned with interdependent issues, there is a problem of co-ordination among them. I address this problem below in terms of meta-governance.

## The response to co-ordination failure

In short, markets, states, and governance all fail. This is not surprising. For failure is a central feature of all social relations: 'governance is necessarily incomplete and as a necessary consequence must always fail' (Malpas and Wickham 1995: 40). Indeed, given the growing structural complexity and opacity of the social world, failure is the most likely outcome of most attempts to govern it in terms of multiple objectives over extended spatial and temporal horizons – whatever co-ordination mechanism is adopted. This emphasis on the improbability of success serves to counter the rhetoric of partnership which leads commentators to highlight achievements rather than failures and, where they recognise failure, to see it as exceptional and corrigible in regard to their preferred mode of co-ordination even as they see co-ordination failure elsewhere as inevitable. This polarisation is reflected both in the succession of governments and in policy cycles within governments in which different modes of policy making succeed each other as the difficulties of each become more evident.

There are at least two levels of failure – the failure of particular attempts at governance using a particular governance mechanism and the more general failure of a mode of governance. Failure is a routine feature of every-day life, which is inevitably full of contingency and surprise. Unsurprisingly therefore actors need to reflect on their failures, to adjust their projects, and to consider whether modes of governance should be modified. Even the most cursory review of attempts at governance, whether through the market, imperative co-ordination, or self-organisation, reveals an important role for learning, reflexivity, and meta-governance. Indeed, if markets, states, and governance are each prone to failure, how is economic and political co-ordination for economic and social development ever possible and why is it often judged to have succeeded? In part this can be explained through the existence of a multiplicity of satisficing criteria and through the range and variety of actors with potential vested interests in one or another outcome. This means that at least some aims will be realised to a socially acceptable degree for at least some of those affected. A further explanation can be derived from the observation that 'governing and governance itself should be dynamic, complex and varied' (Kooiman 1993: 36). This highlights the role of the 'meta-structures' of interorganisational co-ordination (Alexander 1995: 52) or, more generally, of 'meta-governance', i.e. the governance of governance. This involves the organisation of the conditions for governance in its broadest sense. Thus, corresponding to the three basic modes of governance (or co-ordination) distinguished above, we can distinguish three basic modes of meta-governance and one umbrella mode.

First, there is 'meta-exchange'. This involves the reflexive redesign of individual markets (e.g. for land, labour, money, commodities, knowledge – or appropriate parts or subdivisions thereof) and/or the reflexive reordering of relations among two or more markets by modifying their operation and articulation. Market agents often resort to market redesign in response to failure and/or hire the services of those who claim some expertise in this field. Among the latter are management gurus, management consultants, human relations experts, corporate lawyers, and accountants. More generally, there has long been interest in issues of the institutional redesign of the market mechanism, the nesting of markets, their embedding in non-market mechanisms, and the conditions for the maximum formal rationality of market forces. There are also 'markets in markets'. This can lead to 'regime shopping', competitive 'races to the bottom', or, in certain conditions, 'races to the top'. Moreover, because markets function in the shadow of hierarchy and/or heterarchy, attempts are also made by non-market agents to modify markets, their institutional supports, and their agents to improve their efficiency and/or compensate for market failures and inadequacies.

Second, there is 'meta-organisation'. This involves the reflexive redesign of organisations, the creation of intermediating organisations, the reordering of interorganisational relations, and the management of organisational ecologies (i.e. the organisation of the conditions of organisational evolution in conditions where many organisations coexist, compete, co-operate, and co-evolve). Reflexive organisational managers can undertake such meta-organisational functions themselves (e.g. through 'macro-management' and organisational innovation) and/or turn to alleged experts such as constitutional lawyers, public choice economists, theorists of public administration, think tanks, advocates of reflexive planning, specialists in policy evaluation, etc. This is reflected in the continuing redesign, re-scaling, and adaptation of the state apparatus, sometimes more ruptural, sometimes more continuous, and the manner in which it is embedded within the wider political system.

Third, there is 'meta-heterarchy'. This involves the organisation of the conditions of self-organisation by redefining the framework for heterarchy or reflexive self-organisation. It therefore involves what my earlier work labelled 'meta-governance'[2] and can range from providing opportunities for 'spontaneous sociability' (Fukuyama 1995; see also Putnam 2000) through various measures to promote networking and negotiation to the introduction of innovations to promote 'institutional thickness' (Amin and Thrift 1995).

Fourth, and finally, there is 'meta-governance'. This involves re-articulating and 'collibrating' the different modes of governance. The key issues for those involved in metagovernance are '(1) how to cope with other actors' self-referentiality; and (2) how to cope with their own self-referentiality' (Dunsire 1996: 320). Meta-governance involves managing the complexity, plurality, and tangled hierarchies found in prevailing modes of co-ordination. It is the organisation of the conditions for governance and involves the judicious mixing of market, hierarchy, and networks to achieve the best possible outcomes from the viewpoint of those engaged in meta-governance. In this sense it also means the organisation of the conditions of governance in terms of their structurally inscribed strategic selectivity, i.e. in terms of their asymmetrical privileging of some outcomes over others. Unfortunately, since every practice is prone to failure, meta-governance and collibration are also likely to fail. This implies that there is no Archimedean point from which governance or collibration can be guaranteed to succeed.

Governments play a major and increasing role in all aspects of meta-governance: they get involved in redesigning markets, in constitutional change and the juridical re-regulation of organisational forms and objectives, in organising the conditions for self-organisation, and, most important, in collibration. They provide the ground rules for governance and the regulatory order in and through which governance partners can pursue their aims; ensure the compatibility or coherence of different governance mechanisms and regimes; act as the primary organiser of the dialogue among policy communities; deploy a relative monopoly of organisational intelligence and information with which to shape cognitive expectations; serve as a 'court of appeal' for disputes arising within and over governance; seek to rebalance power differentials by strengthening weaker forces or systems in the interests of system integration and/or social cohesion; try to modify the self-understanding of identities, strategic capacities, and interests of individual and collective actors in different strategic contexts and hence alter their implications for preferred strategies and tactics; and also assume political responsibility in the event of governance failure. This emerging role means that networking, negotiation, noise reduction, and negative as well as positive co-ordination occur 'in the shadow of hierarchy' (Scharpf 1994: 40). It also suggests the need for almost permanent institutional and organisational innovation to maintain the very possibility (however remote) of sustained economic growth.

Thus meta-governance does not eliminate other modes of co-ordination. Markets, hierarchies, and heterarchies still exist; but they operate in a context of 'negotiated decision making'. On the one hand, market competition will be balanced by co-operation, the invisible hand will be combined with a visible handshake. On the other hand, the state is no longer the sovereign authority. It becomes just one participant among others in the pluralist guidance system and contributes its own distinctive resources to the negotiation process. As the range of networks, partnerships, and other models of economic and political governance expands, official apparatuses remain at best first among equals. For, although public money and law would still be important in underpinning the operation of such networks, partnerships, and analogous governance arrangements, other resources (such as private money, knowledge, or expertise) would also be crucial to their success. The state's involvement would become less hierarchical, less centralised, and less directive in character. The exchange of information and moral suasion become key sources of legitimation and the state's influence depends as much on its role as a prime source and mediator of collective intelligence as on its command over economic resources or legitimate coercion (Willke 1992).

## Meta-governance and meta-governance failure

Recognising the possible contributions of reflexive meta-governance to economic and social co-ordination is no guarantee of success. It is certainly not a purely technical matter that can be resolved by those who are experts in organisational design or public administration. For all the technical activities of the state are conducted under the primacy of the political, i.e. the state's concern with managing the tension between economic and political advantages and its ultimate responsibility for social cohesion. This fact plagues the liberal prescription of an arm's-length relationship between the market and the nightwatchman state – since states (or, at least, state managers) are rarely strong enough to resist pressure to intervene when political advantage is at stake and/or it needs to respond to social unrest. This can be seen in the telling title of Michael Heseltine's report to Cabinet recommending a change in direction on policies for the inner city, *It took a Riot* (1985). More generally, we can safely assume that, *if every mode of governance fails, then so will meta-governance!* This is especially likely where the objects of governance and meta-governance are complicated and interconnected.[3]

Overall, this analysis leads to three conclusions, intellectual, practical and philosophical respectively. For, once the incompleteness of attempts at co-ordination (whether through the market, the state, or heterarchy) is accepted as inevitable, it is necessary to adopt a satisficing approach which has at least three key dimensions:

1 A reflexive orientation about what would be an acceptable outcome in the case of incomplete success, to compare the effects of failure/inadequacies in the market, government, and governance, and regular reassessment of the extent to which current actions are producing desired outcomes.
2 Deliberate cultivation of a flexible repertoire (requisite variety) of responses so that strategies and tactics can be combined in order to reduce the likelihood of failure and to be in a position to modify their balance in the face of failure and turbulence in the policy environment. Moreover, because different periods and conjunctures require different kinds of policy mix, the balance in the repertoire will need to be varied.
3 Self-reflexive 'irony' in the sense that participants must recognise the likelihood of failure but proceed as if success were possible. The supreme irony in this context is that the need for irony holds not only for individual attempts at governance using individual governance mechanisms but also for the practice of meta-governance using appropriate meta-governance mechanisms.

I will comment on each of these in turn, beginning with reflexivity.

By this I mean the ability and commitment to uncover and make explicit to oneself the nature of one's intentions, projects, and actions and their conditions of possibility; and, in this context, to learn about them, critique them, and act upon any lessons that have been learnt. In relation to governance, this involves enquiring in the first instance into the material, social, and discursive construction of possible objects of governance and reflecting on why this rather than another object of governance has become dominant, hegemonic, or naturalised. It also requires thinking critically about the strategically selective implications of adopting one or another definition of a specific object of governance and its properties, a fortiori, of the choice of modes of governance, participants in the governance process, and so forth. (On these particular issues see Larmour 1997.) And it requires learning about how to learn reflexively. There is a general danger of infinite regress here, of course; but this can be limited provided that reflexivity is combined with the second and third principles.

The second principle involves practical recognition of the 'law of requisite variety'. As initially introduced into cybernetics, this law states that, in order to ensure that a given system has a specific value at a given time despite turbulence in its environment, the controller or regulator must be able to produce as many different counteractions as there are significant ways in which variations in the environment can impact on the system (Ashby 1956). This principle has major implications for governance but, as specified, it is essentially static. In a dynamic and changing world the inevitable forces of natural and/or social entropy would soon break down any predefined control mechanism established using this concept. Because of the infinite variety of perturbations that could affect a system in a complex world, one should try to maximise its internal variety (or diversity) so that the system is well prepared for any contingencies. Thus it is appropriate to reformulate the law as follows. To minimise the risks of (meta-)governance failure in the face of a turbulent environment, one needs a repertoire of responses to retain the ability flexibly to alter strategies and select those that are more successful. This may well seem inefficient from an economising viewpoint because it introduces slack or waste. But it also provides major sources of flexibility in the face of failure (Grabher 1994). For, if every mode of economic and political co-ordination is failure-prone, if not failure-laden, relative success in co-ordination over time depends on the capacity to switch modes of co-ordination as the limits of any one mode become evident. This provides the basis for displacing or postponing failures and crises. It also suggests that the ideologically motivated destruction of alternative modes of co-ordination could prove counterproductive: for they may well need to be reinvented in one or another form. The history of Thatcherism in the 1990s and the U-turns under the Bush administration in the wake of 11 September 2001 provide interesting examples of this reinvention. In addition, since different conjunctures and periods require different kinds of policy mix, the balance within the repertoire will need to vary. One should also recognise that, even if specific institutions and organisations are abolished, it may be necessary to safeguard the underlying modes of co-ordination that they embody.[4] Overall this should promote the ability to alter strategies and select those that are relatively successful. Thus a flexible, adaptable political regime should seek to maintain a repertoire of modes of policy making and implementation.

   This need for 'requisite variety' (with its informational, structural, and functional redundancies) is based on the recognition of complexity. For complexity requires a reflexive observer to recognise that she cannot fully understand what she is observing and must therefore make contingency plans for expected as well as unexpected events. This involves monitoring mechanisms to check for problems, resort to collibrating mechanisms to modulate the co-ordination mix, and the reflexive, negotiated re-evaluation of objectives. A further step in strategic self-reflection occurs when actors deliberately build their capacity to switch among different modes of governance. Within this context, however, I want to suggest that self-organisation should be placed at the core of the repertoire with flanking and supportive measures from other modes of co-ordination (see below).

Third, there is a philosophical dimension of meta-governance. This concerns the appropriate stance towards the intellectual and practical requirements of effective governance and meta-governance given 'the centrality of failure and the inevitability of incompleteness' (Malpas and Wickham 1995: 39). This suggests that, in approaching policy making and implementation, one should also respect what can be defined (only half jokingly) as 'the law of requisite irony'. As Booth notes, 'irony is usually seen as something that undermines clarities, opens up vistas of chaos, and either liberates by destroying all dogma or destroys by revealing the inescapable canker of negation at the heart of every affirmation' (1979: ix). For the same reason Kundera suggests that 'Irony is said to irritate "because it denies us our certainties by unmasking the world of ambiguity"' (1988: 134, cited in Hutcheon 1994: 14–15). It might seem odd to call for something that undermines clarities, envisions chaos, and negates affirmation, but, given the problems of complexity posed by governance, these consequences may be no bad thing. Indeed, in a world of increasing complexity, 'irony – with its emphasis on context, perspective, and instability – is simply what defines "the present conditions of knowledge" (Fischer 1986: 224) for *everyone*' (Hutcheon 1994: 33).

To defend this strange idea I distinguish irony from cynicism. The cynic is overly influenced by the 'pessimism of the intellect' and assumes that new policies will work no better than old policies. This leads the cynic into a state of 'being in denial' so that he or she denies failures or else redefines them as successes; it also encourages a manipulative approach, with appearances being stage-managed so that success seems to have occurred. This is the realm of symbolic politics, accelerated policy churning (to give the impression of doing something about intractable problems), and the 'spin doctor' – the realm of 'words that work but policies that fail'. In contrast to the cynic, the ironist is a sceptic. She recognises the wisdom of choosing one's preferred forms of failure: this is irony in the Rortyan sense but it is a public form of irony, not a private form. Rortyan irony primarily concerns a contrast between public confidence about the permanency and validity of one's vocabulary of motives and actions and private doubt about their finality and apodicticity (Rorty 1989: 73–4). Thus, for Rorty:

> An ironist is a person who realizes that all nonpublic convictions and values, and even vocabularies are contingent, contestable, transitory, and exposed to alternatives that arise continually. The ironist's position, therefore, embraces privacy and plurality and denies any one specific view as *a priori* or automatic priority. We must, he says, be *content to treat the demands of self-creation and of human solidarity as equally valid, yet forever incommensurable.* (Rorty 1989: xv, italics in original)

Now, as expressed by Rorty, purely private irony could lead to cynicism or fatalism – a distrust of the motives behind others' expressed motives and actions and self-serving manipulation of their beliefs, on the one hand, or passive resignation, *laissez-penser*, and *laissez-faire vis-à-vis* others' beliefs and actions, on the other. Yet Rorty does go on to spell out one implication of his philosophy, namely 'commitment to political freedom and free discussion' (1989: 84). Thus one could conclude that the ironist is more inclined to an 'optimism of the will' than a 'pessimism of the intelligence'. In this sense the ironist is more romantic than cynical.

Muecke has defined romantic irony as 'the ironical presentation of the ironic position of the fully-conscious artist' (1970: 20). This involves the artist in an ironic position for several reasons:

> in order to write well he must be both creative and critical, subjective and objective, enthusiastic and realistic, emotional and rational, unconsciously inspired and a conscious artist; his work purports to be about the world and yet is fiction; he feels an obligation to give a true or complete account of reality but he knows this is impossible, reality being incomprehensibly vast, full of contradictions, and in a continual state of becoming, so that even a true account would be immediately falsified as soon as it was completed. The only possibility open for a real artist is to stand apart from his work and at the same time incorporate this awareness of his ironic position into the work itself and so create something which will, if a novel, not simply be a story but rather the telling of a story complete with the author and the narrating, the reader and the reading, the style and the choosing of the style, the fiction and its distance from the fact, so that we shall regard it as being ambivalently both art and life. (Muecke 1970: 20)

Transposing these ideas from literature into the art of politics, a romantic ironist would certainly be creative and critical, subjective and objective, enthusiastic and realistic, and, perhaps, emotional and rational. For, given the complexities of all forms of governance and their propensity to fail, the ironist must seek creative solutions whilst acknowledging the limits to any such solution; she must engage in calculation but also make judgements; she must be committed to the governance project but recognise the risk of failure; and she may need to combine passion and reason to mobilise support behind the project. Recognising the inevitable incompleteness of attempts at governance (whether through the market, the state, or partnership), the ironist adopts a satisficing approach. She accepts incompleteness and failure as essential features of social life but continues to act as if completeness and success were possible. Whether the ironic stance in this latter regard is purely private, covert (unstated but implicit), or open (i.e. expressed in a consciously ironic manner) is surely a contingent issue at this level of reflection and analysis. In any case, the political ironist must simplify a complex, contradictory, and changing reality in order to be able to act – knowing full well that any such simplification is also a distortion of reality and, what is worse, that such distortions can sometimes generate failure even as they are also the necessary precondition of relatively successful interventions to manage complex interdependence. The only possibility open for a political ironist, then, is, indeed, to stand apart from her political practice and at the same time incorporate this awareness of her ironic position into the practice itself.

Moreover, if the political ironist is also to involve the 'reader and the reading' in her ironic attempts at governance, then she must also choose the style in and through which to do so. The law of requisite irony entails that those involved in governance choose among forms of failure and make a reasoned decision in favour of one or another form of failure. In this respect it is important to note that, in contrast to the cynic, the ironist acts in 'good faith' and seeks to involve others in the process of policy making, not for manipulative purposes but in order to bring about conditions for negotiated consent and self-reflexive learning. In line with the law of requisite variety, moreover, they must be prepared to change the modes of governance as appropriate. But for good philosophical reasons to do with empowerment and accountability, they should ideally place self-organisation at the heart of governance in preference to the anarchy of the market or the top-down command of more or less unaccountable rulers. In this sense self-reflexive forms of governance are performative – they are both an art form and a life form. Like all forms of governance they are constitutive of their objects of governance but they also become a self-reflexive means of coping with the failures, contradictions, dilemmas, and paradoxes that are an inevitable feature of life.

## Conclusion

I have suggested that there are different modes of governance (or co-ordination of complex reciprocal interdependence) and have focused on the self-reflexive self-organisation of substantively interdependent but formally independent actors. Interest in self-organisation has grown in recent years in response to the experience of market and state failure and in response to the increasing complexity of the social world. But, as I have also argued, self-reflexive self-organisation itself is prone to failure. There are different ways of coping with the inevitability of failure, ranging from small-scale incremental adjustments based on trial-and-error learning to comprehensive attempts at constitutional and institutional redesign. Indeed, without learning *and forgetting*, social order, such as it is, would be impossible. Finally, in addressing the four main forms of meta-governance (concerned respectively with the reflexive reorganisation of markets, hierarchies, and networks and with the collibration of these different modes of governance), I have emphasised three general principles of governance in the face of complexity: these are the principles of requisite reflexivity, requisite variety, and requisite irony. Since reflexivity and variety are relatively familiar principles, if not always fully integrated into the analysis of governance, I have paid most attention to the role of a 'romantic' public irony in dealing with the problems posed by the likelihood of governance failure. This is the most effective way, I believe, of combining the 'pessimism of the intelligence' and 'optimism of the will' that was recommended by Romain Rolland and popularised by Antonio Gramsci as the masthead slogan of his journal, *L'ordine nuovo*. It further implies the desirability of involving a wide range of 'stakeholders' in attempts at governance. This will affect in turn the definition of the objects of governance and, in so far as governance practices help to constitute these objects, it will also transform the social world that is being so governed.

## Notes

1  The arguments presented in this chapter have been developed intermittently over the last five years following my involvement in an ESRC-funded research project on local governance and subsequent reflection on the conditions for effective governance in social formations marked by structural contradictions, strategic dilemmas and discursive paradoxes. I have benefited from opportunities to present earlier trial versions of some of the arguments at the Centre for Organisation and Management (COS, Copenhagen), Roskilde University Centre, the University of Lausanne, Mannheim University, the University of Illinois at Chicago and the University of Strathclyde. Useful criticisms have also been received from Henrik Bang, Mick Dillon, Rod Rhodes and Gerry Stoker. The final version was written while I was in receipt of a Canterbury Fellowship at the University of Canterbury at Christchurch, New Zealand.
2  I would now reserve the concept of 'meta-governance' for what Dunsire (1996) calls 'collibration'. Meta-governance is best employed as an umbrella concept for the redesign of the relationship among different modes of governance.
3  '[S]ince every project is always a part of some more extensive assemblage, so every project is always enmeshed with other projective activities, and there can be no guarantee that such projects, though connected, will even be wholly consistent with one another' (Malpas and Wickham 1995: 46).
4  There are further dilemmas here from an evolutionary viewpoint: (1) learning versus forgetting; and (2) removing particulars versus retaining the general. If one affirms the maxim that 'it is necessary to change society to preserve it', there should be mechanisms for social forgetting as well as for social learning.

## References

Alexander, E. R. (1995), *How Organizations Act Together: Interorganizational Co-ordination in Theory and Practice* (Amsterdam: Overseas Publishers).
Amin, A., and Thrift, N. (1995), 'Globalisation, institutional "thickness" and the local economy', in P. Healey, S. Cameron, S. Davoudi, S. Graham and A. Madani-Pour (eds), *Managing Cities: The New Urban Context* (Chichester: Wiley).
Ashby, W. R. (1956), *Introduction to Cybernetics* (London: Chapman & Hall).
Booth, W. C. (1979), *A Rhetoric of Irony* (Chicago: University of Chicago Press).
Dunsire, A. (1996), 'Tipping the balance: autopoiesis and governance', *Administration and Society* 28 (3): 299–334.
Fischer, M. J. M. (1986), 'Ethnicity and the postmodern arts of memory', in J. Clifford and G. E. Marcus (eds), *Writing Culture: The Poetics and Politics of Ethnography* (Berkeley CA: University of California Press), pp. 194–233.

Fukuyama, F. (1995), *Trust: The Social Virtues and the Creation of Prosperity* (New York: Free Press).

Grabher, G. (1994), *Lob der Verschwendung* (Berlin: Sigma).

Gramsci, A. (1971), *Selections from the Prison Notebooks* (London: Lawrence & Wishart).

Heseltine, M. (1985), *It took a Riot* (London: HMSO).

Hutcheon, L. (1994), *Irony's Edge: The Theory and Politics of Irony* (London: Routledge).

Jessop, B. (1998), 'The rise of governance and the risks of failure: the case of economic development', *International Social Science Journal* 50 (1): 29–46.

Kooiman, W. (1993), 'Governance and governability: using complexity, dynamics and diversity', in W. Kooiman (ed.), *Modern Governance: New Government–Society Interactions* (London: Sage), pp. 35–48.

Kundera, M. (1988), *The Art of the Novel* (London: Faber).

Larmour, P. (1997), 'Models of governance and public administration', *International Review of Administrative Sciences* 63 (4): 383–94.

Malpas, J., and Wickham, G. (1995), 'Governance and failure: on the limits of sociology', *Australian and New Zealand Journal of Sociology* 31 (3): 37–50.

Mayntz, R. (1993), 'Governing failures and the problem of governability: some comments on a theoretical paradigm', in J. Kooiman (ed.), *Modern Governance: New Government–Society Interactions* (London: Sage), pp. 9–20.

Mayntz, R. (1993), 'Modernization and the logic of interorganizational networks', in J. Child, M. Crozier, R. Mayntz *et al.*, *Societal Change: Between Market and Organization* (Aldershot: Avebury), pp. 3–18.

Muecke, D. C. (1970), *Irony* (London: Methuen).

Putnam, R. D. (2000), *Bowling Alone: The Collapse and Revival of American Community* (New York: Simon & Schuster).

Rescher, N. (1998), *Complexity: A Philosophical Overview* (New Brunswick NJ: Transaction).

Rorty, R. (1989) 'Private irony and liberal hope', in *Contingency, Irony, and Solidarity* (Cambridge: Cambridge University Press), pp. 73–95.

Scharpf, F. W. (1994), 'Games real actors could play: positive and negative co-ordination in embedded negotiations', *Journal of Theoretical Politics* 6 (1): 27–53.

Wallis, J., and Dollery, B. (1999), *Market Failure, Government Failure, Leadership and Public Policy* (Basingstoke: Macmillan).

Willke, H. (1992), *Ironie des Staates. Grundlinien einer Staatstheorie polyzentrischer Gesellschaft* (Frankfurt: Suhrkamp).

# 7
# Culture governance and individualisation

Mitchell Dean

There are a whole host of themes in recent social and political thought that link the individual with issues of its governance and self-governance: the 'politics of identity/difference', the 'postmodern fragmentation of self', 'individualisation', a 'life politics', 'cosmopolitanism' and so on. At some distance from, but related, to these themes stand a number of theoretico-political views of the role, capacities and obligations, of the citizen as a governable and self-governing individual in contemporary liberal democracy. The latter include such formations as 'neo-liberalism' (e.g. Hayek 1978), the 'new paternalism' (e.g. Mead 1997), the 'third way' (e.g. Giddens 1998) and communitarianism (e.g. Etzioni 1995).

Doubtless there are large divergences between these theories and diagnoses. Common to many of them, however, I believe there stands a barely articulated thesis I would like to call *culture governance*. This is the view that rule in contemporary liberal democracies increasingly operates through capacities for self-government and thus needs to act upon, reform and utilise individual and collective conduct so that it might be amenable to such rule. The reform of institutions and practices must then be articulated in a particular discursive modality. This is neither the fundamentally suspect and anyway outmoded modality of the political, tied as it to a fading nation and state and to adversarial relations, nor the discredited domain of the social, connected with the rigidities of the welfare state and the homogeneous ideals of solidarity. The modality will be cultural, in which the reform of institutions will be tied to the attributes and capacities individuals and the transformation and self-transformation of their conduct (Dean 1998). At its best, such a reform will act in the name of a cultural pluralism constituted through generous recognition of the agonism of culturally constituted differences within the public sphere (Connolly 1999). If the memory of the welfare state belongs to the left, and the nostalgia for the nation to the Old Right, the thesis of culture governance is said to be 'beyond left and right'.

These themes call to mind Michel Foucault's later lectures, interviews and books. There, as you will know, he opened up two distinct but related domains of reflection. The first is on 'government' understood as a term for the heterogeneous forms of the direction of conduct for various ends (the 'conduct of conduct') rather than as delineating the limited institutional domain of the state in the liberal fashion. In this regard, Foucault perhaps anticipated our current concern with governance. The second concerns 'ethics', considered not simply as the arena of moral codes and commands but also as a set of practices, exercises, or arts of existence, which entail an action of 'self on self'. Here, Foucault speaks to our concern about individuality, lifestyle and self-actualisation. These analytical domains, taken separately or together, are valuable resources for the analysis of the themes that underlie both our theoretical and our programmatic approaches to governing individuals and groups. They also shed some light, I think, on this thesis of culture governance, on the practices it codifies and invests with particular aims and orientations.

There is no necessary relationship between governmental and ethical practices so conceived. The connections between them are contingent and thus open to empirical and historical study. In this chapter I shall thus often take recourse to widely different examples from very different historical and spatial contexts. Because, however, both governmental and ethical practices can be understood as attempts to direct and regulate human conduct, they are open to a style of analysis that facilitates the study of their interconnections. Here, then, I present this way of thinking about government and 'individualising power' (Foucault 2001) in the context of the thesis of culture governance. I first sketch a composite account of how contemporary social theory with its twin themes of globalisation and individualisation is linked with this idea of culture governance. I then use the themes of governmentality and the care of the self, and the resources of what I call a 'critical history of ourselves', to raise some questions about the contemporary analysis of individualisation in the social and political sciences. I want finally to reflect upon the nature and effects of the diagnosis of cultural governance upon the political constitution of the present.

## Individualisation and modernity[1]

Studies of governmentality and of techniques of the self are hardly alone in raising the question of the practices through which selves and individuals, and persons and citizens, are formed. There are many exemplary sociological, historical and anthropological accounts that can assist us with our task here. I shall refer to them later. However, beside these accounts is a style of theory that attempts to produce a detailed and authoritative account of the nature and dilemmas of the individual subject or self in contemporary social life. This theoretical literature is vast and complicated. For the sake of brevity, I simply draw a hopefully not too fanciful composite sketch of how these questions of individuality are played out in recent discussions. My excuse for doing this is that my major aim is not so much to offer a detailed critique of contemporary social theory as to provide a sense of how its diagnosis of the fate of the individual is linked with the thesis of culture governance. I also hope to be able to give a sense of the ethos that has animated the studies of practices of government and techniques of the self.

Our types of society, according to these accounts, have undergone a fundamental transformation, even if somewhat behind our backs. All variants of this narrative tell the story of a continuation, completion, or transcendence of the story of modernity. Hence there is a proliferation of diagnoses of the present all relating to 'modernity' as the dominant term: postmodernity, an 'incomplete modernity' (Habermas 1985), 'late modernity' (Giddens 1991) or most recently the 'Second Age of Modernity' (Beck 2000b). What is common to these accounts can be approached by what they view as in decline. First, there is the relativisation of the authority of the legitimating truths of an earlier phase of modernity. The meta-narratives of reason and progress that accompanied the early stages of modernisation begin to fail, instanced by the loss of an unquestioned faith in the benefits of science, of economic growth and industrial production. Truth is contested within the public spaces provided by social movements (Greens, those against genetically modified food, etc.) and the news and information media. This occasions a new awareness of risk, so much so that contemporary modernisation is organised around the production and distribution of risk as much as of wealth (Beck 1989: 86–7). Secondly, the role of the national economy and actors tied to it such as organised labour has been bypassed by the effects of economic 'globalisation'; a term that principally refers to the flows of financial capital through electronic information networks (Castells 1996). Together with the emergence of trans- and international political associations, and international non-government organisations, there is, thirdly, a parallel decline of structures of national state sovereignty (Rosenau 2000). Fourthly, the institutions of these states such as welfare, income support, state expenditure and industrial relations legislation 'melt under the withering sun of globalisation' (Beck 2000b: 1). We thus have a fundamental delegitimation of bureaucratic and welfarist forms of rule so that within and outside the borders of the territorial national state we witness the emergence of an authoritative order which is best described as 'governance without government', one in which states 'steer' but do not 'row'. There is a sense in which the 'authority of authority' has come into question. Science has lost its monopoly of truth. The state has lost its monopoly of legitimate power over a given territory. The nation has lost the legitimacy of its claim on the identity of its citizens. Bureaucratic organisation has lost its monopoly of the welfare of the population.

These economic and political developments undermine the old solidarities based on class. So too the postmodern fragmenting, mixing and invention of cultures and identities, the new information and communication networks, the global cultural industries and the patterns of consumption they foster, break down solidarities and dependences of neighbourhood, community, locality and even family (Beck 2000a). There is thus an undoing of the stable identities of class, gender, sexuality, ethnicity and nation. From a more critical perspective, what emerges has been called the 'naked individual' (Hardt and Negri 2001: 203–4), which can be diagnosed as a new merging of political life with 'bare life' (Agamben 1998). This naked individual is nevertheless institutionally mediated and needs to invent itself to give itself some kind of identity in the face of the uncertainty of these changes. Put in a more sophisticated way, the subject is always in a process of ethico-political becoming through arts of existence (Connolly 1999: 143–53). As Ulrich Beck puts it, 'Choosing, deciding, shaping individuals who aspire to be the authors of their lives, the creators of their identities, are the central characters of our time' (1998: 28). He goes on:

> Let's be clear what individualism means. It is not Thatcherism, not market-individualism, not atomisation. On the contrary, it means 'institutionalised individualism'. Most of the rights and entitlements of the welfare state, for example, are designed for individuals rather than for families. In many cases they presuppose employment. Employment in turn implies education, and both of these presuppose mobility. By all these requirements people are invited to constitute themselves as individual: to plan, understand, design themselves as individuals and, should they fail, to blame themselves. Individualisation thus implies, paradoxically, a collective lifestyle.[2]

The story of the Second Age of Modernity is the story of the coming into being of this naked individual or, to give it a more favourable title, 'cosmopolitan' individual. Cosmopolitan individuals make their own lifestyle and with a little goodwill might come to realise themselves as a part of a world democracy in which they have rights as individuals and are obligated to the defence of the rights of other such individuals wherever they might be violated. Thus 'living alone means living socially'.

But there is also a darker side to this individualisation. The second modernity is organised as much around the production and distribution of risk as of wealth (Beck 1989: 86–7). It thus brings a proliferation of frequently incalculable industrial and technological hazards. While distributed differentially among populations and subject to constant attempts at risk assessment and monitoring, these are nonetheless global in that they no longer respect the borders between nations. Contemporary modernity is thus a 'risk society' marked by an increasing publicity of, and indeed contestation around, the threats posed by the application of techno-science, and its application in the energy, biotechnology and chemical sectors (Beck 1992a: 101–6). Individuals are left in the fateful situation of attempting to control their own proneness to risk by the use of expert knowledge that has been deprived of intrinsic authority.

The impact of risk culture on individual and collective conduct raises questions of trust in abstract systems and expertise and calls into question individual and collective security in ways that resonate with other general features of the Second Age of Modernity. The relentless tide of globalisation and the undoing of traditional, familial, communal and even societal bonds leave the naked individual in a state of ontological insecurity no longer able to take confidence in gender, class or national identities. He or she is forced to choose among the multiplicity of forms of life and consciously adopted lifestyles. The net result can be a present in which identities are decentred, dislocated, fragmented and placed in crisis (Hall 1992). More subtly, there is a kind of dialectic between existential anxiety and ontological insecurity. On the one hand, the search for authentic forms of life becomes subverted by the debased and commodified lifestyle provided by the mass media and advertising that leaves genuine needs in a permanent state of dissatisfaction (Giddens 1991: 196–201). On the other, ontological security can be achieved by constructing the self, turning it into coherent narrative and autobiography, with the help of the multiplying numbers of therapists, counsellors, writers of self-help manuals and other experts. The self becomes a 'reflexive project'. Traditional politics is displaced by a life politics geared to self-actualisation rather than emancipation. This politics is practised first of all by ethnic and sexual minorities, feminists, Greens and others.

All this has an impact upon how we must conceive of the role of government and gives rise to what I have called the thesis of culture governance. Wherever one looks, authority, the hierarchy and the chain of command it entails, has lost its justification with the decline of the moral, legal, religious and even epistemological foundations of its legitimacy. Even more broadly, under the onslaught of the relentless forces of globalisation and the emergence of the polycentric 'steering mechanisms' inside and outside nation states, power has lost its centre and notions of the state and its sovereignty have lost their purchase on contemporary political realities. One rather extreme version of this has been put forward by James Rosenau (2000: 184):

> it might well be observed that a new form of anarchy has evolved in the current period – one that involves not only the absence of a highest authority, but that also encompasses such an extensive disaggregation of authority as to allow for a much greater flexibility, innovation and experimentation in the development and application of new control mechanisms.

These interdependent and proliferating mechanisms at sub-national and supranational levels constitute a form of 'governance without government' (Rosenau, 2000: 182). If power is to be exercised, this story continues, it must and will be exercised in such a way that it is consistent with the freedom, values and choices of individuals and the communities and collectivities in which they live. Sometimes this freedom is something that is immediately found in the capacities of certain types of motivated and enterprising individuals and communities. At other times, subjects need to be 'empowered' to exercise such freedom by therapeutic or other means.

Arrangements need to be made through which those choices and that freedom can be shaped or constructed in some way, e.g. by the construction of quasi-markets or market-like arrangements for the delivery of services to customers. We are leaving behind a sovereign government that is hierarchical, totalising, territorialised, centred on nations and states, exclusionary, and operating through commands and law. We are witnessing the emergence of a culture governance, which works through networks and flows rather than structures and hierarchies. It is inclusive, individualising, pluralist, borderless and polycentric, operating to include through choice and agency and the transformations and becoming of identity and difference.

## From social theory to critical history

Contemporary grand sociological theory views the self-fashioning individual as the outcome of large-scale process such as globalisation and individualisation and as the presupposition of new forms of rule and authority. We call this post-sovereigntist 'governance without government' culture governance. What are we to make of this, from the perspective of issues of governmentality and techniques of the self and form the broader resources that might constitute a 'critical history of ourselves' of which they are a part? Such a critical history concerns the practices through which we have come to understand and know ourselves in certain ways, and to act upon ourselves and others accordingly.

*First*, we might note the concern for self-identity is neither as new nor as prolific as is thought in contemporary social and political thought. Rather than an anxiety about self, identity or conduct being a general feature of our modernity, it should be treated as something relatively rare, as arising in particular circumstances, at certain times, in specific locations, and having definite purposes. It is bound up with conflicts of not only how to govern but who should and has the right to govern. This concern for the self or identity is to be approached not as a symptom of forces that have broken down traditional bonds, but through the singular practices of the self in which it appears. These practices can be analysed through many dimensions (Foucault 1985: 25–32; Dean 1995, 1996). There are the questions that are put to aspects of conduct or 'problematisations'. There are the specifically conceived topographies of the 'individual', 'the person' or 'the self' through which this conduct is viewed. There are the distinctive techniques that work on variously thought-out aspects of the self. There are the reasons given for doing this and the ends and goals sought. There are the singular hierarchies and capacities these practices establish, which can become resources for political struggles, for the functioning of organisations, and for systems of production and consumption. In other words, the focus of a critical history is not on the general nature of the self in an epoch or civilisation but on the practices through which we come to know and act upon ourselves and others in a certain way. At heart, a critical history of ourselves analyses and seeks the intelligibility of practices (Foucault 1981). Applied to one contemporary theme, rather than assuming a risk culture of society, one can analyse the range of quite different practices through which we come to perceive and know risk and to act upon our individual or collective risk (Castel 1991; Ewald 1991; O'Malley 1996; Weir 1996; Dean 1999:176–97). Most important, to constitute oneself or be constituted as a subject of risk in the management of one's own life, reproduction, health, safety and economic security is not simply a feature of subterranean sociological processes of late modernity. It is to adopt or be given an ethical mode of being with political consequences. It can lead to an opposition between the normal form of life and population to a risky and dangerous one; it can mark the defeat of one political programme (the collectivisation of risk under the welfare state) by another (its devolution and privatisation). There are stakes and resources, which are fought over, won and lost, in the process of the adoption of such identities.

*The Use of Pleasure* (Foucault 1985) analyses the ethical problematisations of sexual conduct posed by the ancient Greeks as they arise in particular domains of practice. These domains include the 'dietetic' management of the health and life of the body, the 'economic' matters of marriage and the management of the household, the 'erotic' field of love relations, and 'philosophical' practices concerned with attaining wisdom or truth. There are many and different ethical problematisations we could describe today, e.g. of the lack of self-esteem of those at risk of teenage pregnancy, of the lack of mutuality in intimate relationships or of welfare dependence among the poor. We could then show how these problematisations are made in relation to particular practices: the production and consumption of self-help literature and confessional television programmes; the attempt to reform welfare systems so that they are more efficient and render recipients more active. These practices borrow, generate and deploy particular techniques and mechanisms such as 'bibliotherapy' to prevent teenage pregnancy and Workfare programmes to combat welfare dependence (Cruikshank 1999; Theodore and Peck 1999). But just as the governing males of antiquity gave themselves a mode of being suited to ruling, so today the teenage mum and the long-term unemployed are fitted out with identities which make them suitable to be ruled in a certain ways with specific techniques.

*Second*, we should be wary of a millenarian approach to the present which sees it as moment of fundamental rupture, an 'epochal break' (Beck 2000a: 88). A critical history might show that many of our techniques for caring for the self have a long trajectory. Hence many of the features held to be specific to the quest for self-identity in late modernity are part of the longer and more complex trajectory of techniques of the self. Thus we find the use of 'autobiographical' techniques among Roman philosophical schools, including the keeping of notebooks, writing letters to friends and mnemonic devices such as the nightly self-examination recommended by Seneca (Foucault 1988, 1993). Continual or regular acts of self-interrogation, the scrutiny of innermost thoughts in the search for truth and authenticity, and the verbalisation of that which provokes resistance, are all present in John Cassian's fourth-century exposition of the practice of confession. The point is not that we should erase all historical narratives of the way we have sought to act on selves but that attention to particular practices of the self and the techniques that sustain them reveals awkward continuities for those seeking to claim the ruptural nature of the present.

*Third*, we must be careful not to erase power, conflict and struggle from accounts of identity and self. But by making the new individualism a feature of general social processes, current grand sociological theory does precisely that. To counter it, a critical history would show how different ways of governing ourselves are related to power relations, to social and political struggles and to the right to exercise authority over others. Ethical relations and arts of existence are conditions of possibility of certain political relations. Thus, rather than positing processes of individualisation, we should be concerned to chart the genealogy of 'individualising power' (Foucault 2001: 300) and to analyse the politics of individualisation. Contemporary forms of this individualising power are present in those approaches to public service provision in which the recipients are to be regarded or formed as certain types of individuals: customers or consumers, enterprising individuals who are members of an enterprise community, active citizens, 'job seekers', and so on. These contemporary developments can be placed in the series that constitutes the *longue durée* of pastoral power and its technologies (Foucault 1982: 213–15).

Moreover, different forms of individuality and different ways of working on and forming ourselves are related to political struggles. The 'No Logo' thematic of the anti-globalisation movement is one example of how an alternative way of forming oneself is counterposed to the consumerist images of the self promoted by multinational corporations and advertising agencies. The attempt to work on oneself by the technique of 'consciousness raising' was a staple of early second-wave feminism and provided a resource to conduct struggle. But such localised 'arts of existence' have no univocal political meaning. The anti-corporate identity stance, for example, can be used in different marketing strategies (and indeed it has with so-called 'generic' brands). 'Consciousness raising' has become the staple of daytime Oprah-style talk shows.

Nevertheless, different political and social orders entail different forms of ethical comportment, different ways of directing oneself and hence of seeking to govern others. And sometimes, indeed, these differences are central to even cataclysmic social and political transformations, such as the emergence and spread of early Christianity. In late antiquity Peter Brown (1987: 253–85, 1992) has found a striking contrast between the leaders of the Christian Church and the Roman ruling class. There the studied and cultivated comportment of the Roman notable grounded in specific educational practices of *paideia* met the Christian ideal of the desert monks which sought singlemindedness, simplicity, transparency to God and openness to others. This difference was linked to different relations with the governed. The Roman ruler saw himself as kind of patrician benefactor to the city who gave to citizens as equals to enforce the hardened solidarity of equals (Veyne 1987b: 105–15, 1990). The new bishops by contrast grounded their authority in universal charity as 'lovers of the poor'. This would include all those outside the confines of the Roman world and would give a new role to women in public life in charity and in nursing (Brown 1987: 292; Nelson 1996). Without doubt, social and political conflicts can be driven by ideology or belief. However, the way that contending groups know, govern and present themselves, and the consequent forms of ethical comportment, can become resources in their claims to authority over others. While we need to maintain the irreducibility of the political to the ethical, ethical practices and arts of existence help form the agencies which can be put into play in agonistic or solidaristic relations, relations of dominance and of combat.

*Fourth*, the sociological model assumes a general form of the relation between society, its institutions and structures and the self and its personality. A critical history, however, would start from the assumption that there is no natural, necessary or given, mode of determination of selves and identities. The latter is not concerned with a general figure of the self bound by a necessary social determination. Rather it is concerned with the more or less explicit attempts to problematise our lives, our forms of conduct and our selves found in a variety of pronouncements and texts, employed in a variety of locales, using particular techniques, and addressed to different social sectors and groups. Its raw material, then, includes books of manners and etiquette, catechisms and poems (Elias 1978) or systems of military discipline, schooling or tracts on sexology or erotic arts. It could also include lifestyle television programmes and magazine and newspaper columns, much popular psychological and sociological writing, and all types of 'how to' texts, manuals and pamphlets concerned with success in work, business, school, money matters, childbearing and child rearing, marriage, love and sex.

Rather than analyse 'socialisation' as a general way in which 'society' affects 'individuals', we need to analyse socialising, disciplining and civilising practices, the historical forms they take, the rationalities they deploy, the techniques, mechanisms, practices and institutions through which they operate. Thus the real innovation of Jacques Donzelot's *The Policing of Families* (1979) was that it provided a hitherto lacking analysis of the mechanisms by which the modern family was socialised without reference to the effect of general social processes on biological norms. To do so, it demonstrated how families, differentiated by class and capacity for self-governance, became variegated spaces in which their various members came to be entrusted with differential obligations and statuses (mother, housewife, breadwinner, child). The latter were specified by a range of medical, educational and philanthropic practices of intervention and grids of perception and evaluation that, in turn, constituted particular bodies of expertise and a range of institutional authorities (cf. Hodges and Hussain 1979; Hirst 1981; Minson 1985: 180–224). From this point of view, the problem with contemporary sociological accounts is that they are pitched at too general a level and propose a mysterious, even occult, relation between general social processes and events (e.g. globalisation, detraditionalisation) and features of self and identity (fragmentation, fluidity, reflexivity, the desire for self-actualisation, etc.).

Associated with this presupposition of a necessary and general relation between society and individual identity is the assumption of a continuity and sedimentation of the subject form that is supported, built upon or even undermined by successive social processes. Here is a model of a continuous form of the subject, made up of layer upon layer of the historical sedimentation of affects, sensibilities, capacities, habits, manners and morals. It is certainly present in the work of the Frankfurt school and in phenomenological accounts of the personhood and culture (Merleau-Ponty 1974). It is present – for all their other merits – in Elias's conception of the civilising process and the social moulding of the economy of drives and affects of individuals (1978, 1982) and in perhaps even in Mauss's seminal essay on the notion of the person (1985). These layers, then, form a series of strata that become the raw material of new social processes. If, however, we are dealing with the rarity and materiality of problematisations that have singular times and spaces, and the practices that give rise to them, the question of continuity and discontinuity becomes, above all, an empirical one. Thus whether specific practices of the government of conduct and techniques of living continue to be of consequence, whether they continue to have the same effects, whether they continue to operate in tandem with the same rationality, or whether they have been placed within different strategies and oriented toward different ends, and whether certain capacities, affects or habits are generalised among specific populations, all become questions for empirical enquiry and argument. A critical history of ourselves is necessary, precisely because those spaces and relations we designate by the terms 'self', 'individual', 'person' or 'citizen' cannot be assumed to be either continuous or discontinuous. They are subject to particular domains of governmental and ethical practice and to local problematisations that might foster the maintenance or undermining of various human attributes and capacities in the same or different forms for new purposes or for the same old reasons.

*Fifth*, and following from this, we can say there is no single figure that can capture the form of the subject for a particular society or culture or even for the historical trajectory of forms of self in a civilisation. The characterisation of a fragmented subject endlessly becoming and reconstructing itself is heir to a long historical and sociological heritage that has indeed tried to do just that. Notions of social and cultural types of individuals, from the bourgeois individual and *homo oeconomicus* to one-dimensional man and the administered subject, to the fragmented self or self as reflexive project, are so many versions of this motif. In fact, this approach has one of its ancestors in the writings of the Frankfurt school of the 1940s. Horkheimer, in his *Eclipse of Reason* (1974: 128–61), provides something of a general history of the self in the West. Here a narrative is charted of the ebb and flow of individualism, from tribal societies to late capitalism. It moves from a primitive pre-individuality living in the gratification and frustrations of the moment, through the model of the Greek hero, the flowering of individuality in the Hellenic city states with Socratic conscience and Platonic objective reason, and its retreat into Stoic resignation with the subjugation of the cities by the Roman empire. This is followed by the investment of the individual with a unique and immortal soul in Christianity, and its secularisation and humanisation in the Renaissance, Reformation and Enlightenment. The 'era of free enterprise' leads to an open proclamation of bourgeois individuality that proves to be evanescent under administered capitalism and mass culture with the arrival of what would later be called 'one-dimensional man'. In such an account there is a curious simultaneous historicising and naturalising of the individual or self. The self is a historical product, transformed through different phases of the historical development of features of society such as the division of labour and the forms of social domination. Yet it retains a general form throughout this trajectory as an entity that represses and instrumentalises its own inner being and external nature in the interests of self-preservation. There is, then, both a general form of subject underlying both the spurious unity of 'the West' and the distinctive versions corresponding to each socio-cultural period.

This positing of a general form of the subject, whether for a particular epoch or for an entire civilisation, is undermined, however, not only by its own implausibility but by the crucial work of recent cultural historians of private life (Ariès and Duby, 1987–91) and the work of other social thinkers such as Norbert Elias. The collective work of the historians of private life is exemplary in that, as Georges Duby notes (1987: viii), it remains conscious of the retrospective nature of reading over two millennia of European history in terms of a concept of personal existence barely a century old and that it seeks to avoid using these histories as evidence for a general history of individualism. Here studies of education, marriage, slavery, religion, domestic architecture, notions of the sacred and the secret, and private belief – to cite some of the contents of the first volume of four (Veyne 1987a) – become so many occasions for an exploration of the myriad ways in different societies and at different times in which humans have carved out domains of private and public life, employing a vast array of techniques and means to construct an existence for themselves and others made up of a bewildering variety of reasons and purposes. At their best, the work of the historians of private life shows how specific aspects of conduct and person were problematised, by various agents and authorities, among distinct populations, employing certain techniques and with particular aspirations, goals and consequences. The danger with such cultural history, however, is that it is always at risk of viewing this multiplicity of concepts and practices as evidence of the quest of a universal subject seeking to give meaning to its activities or turning private life into the *telos* of civilisation.

The work of Elias (e.g. 1978, 1982, 1983; Dean 1994: 202–8) illustrates the very same point. His history of manners demonstrates the specificity of the aspects of conduct that are problematised in poems, songs and written treatises of manners (from table manners, nose blowing, spitting, excretion, aggression, to relations between the sexes), the heterogeneous locale in which conduct is problematised (at the table, in the bedroom, in the street and market place, the castle on the feudal estate, the absolutist court), the diverse ends invoked (courtesy, civility), and the diverse groups addressed (the knights, the *noblesse de robe*, the *noblesse d'épee*, the clergy, the urban bourgeoisie and financiers) by very different authorities (secular, municipal, ecclesiastical, military). This is genealogy as 'grey, meticulous and patiently documentary' (Foucault 1977: 139). However, Elias seeks to encapsulate this within a global thesis of the 'civilising process' in which there is an assumed fit between the rationalisation of conduct and the development of the state, a concern ultimately with the 'sociogenesis' of modern personality types. Moreover, he proposes a psychoanalytic mode of the moulding of persons through the regulation of drives by the social implantation of habits that later become unconscious mechanisms of constraint. Despite his genuine breakthrough in making the analysis of the mechanisms of self-moulding central to his historical-sociological enterprise, Elias – in both these moves – suffers the same problem as afflicts the social and cultural theorists of the Frankfurt school (cf. Bogner 1987). He assumes a general topography of the self that is shaped and moulded by civilising processes to produce a definite form of the modern individual.

The aim of a critical history of ourselves is not to provide an account of the genesis of the 'modern' subject, of its fragmentation self-reconstruction in late modernity, or even to align processes of 'sociogenesis' with ones of 'psychogenesis', as Elias might have put it (1978). Its aim is to understand how human beings came to be *thought of* and *characterised* as having a certain psychological interiority in which the determinations of culture could be inscribed, organised and shaped into a distinct personality or character (Rose 1995). Its point is to make it intelligible how we came to understand ourselves as an essential innerness or wholeness from which flow our thoughts, our expressions, our conduct and our emotions, or how we understand ourselves as fragmented and ambiguous identities in a process of becoming. Its object is to show how these experiences of personhood are given to us within the myriad ways we are made transparent to ourselves and others so that we may be rendered calculable and ultimately governable, or so that we may calculate and govern. The object, moreover, is not the subject that is produced by specific practices, whether these are governmental or ethical ones. It is the relation between the forms of truth by which we have come to know ourselves and the kinds of practices by which we seek to shape our conduct and that of others. Ultimately the constitution of selves and identities occurs within the horizon of material practices and the authoritative discourses linked to them; and the capacities released by such practices equip individuals and collectives to enter relations of dominance, enable forms of appropriation and production, and are set to work in antagonisms and struggles. While the political is irreducible to these ethical practices, such practices can have definite political consequences, and the political can become a struggle over and between different ethical discourses, practices and dispositions.

*Finally*, social theory tends to pose the question of the historical relationship between politics and the individual self at the level of the development of citizenship and its rights (Marshall 1963) or the relationship between state formation and the 'moral regulation' or civilising of the modern individual (Elias 1978; Corrigan and Sayer, 1985). A critical history, by contrast, might turn its attention to the very situations in which the regulation of personal conduct becomes linked with the regulation of political or civic conduct, even allowing that this might be undertaken by the agencies of national states or programmes of the national and international government of the state. Two extraordinarily different examples of the interleaving of a problematisation of personal existence and identity with political and governmental considerations will suffice here. As a first example, we can refer to the instructive history of 'welfare reform' over the last two decades in many liberal democracies. In an initial phase, there was the advocacy and implementation of a so-called 'active system' of the treatment of the unemployed and other beneficiaries in many OECD member countries (Dean 1995). Here the individual is regarded as a 'job seeker' who is required to agree to perform certain tasks (job search, retraining, undergoing counselling, joining job clubs, voluntary work) in return for state allowances. The point of these 'obligations' is to require the individual to adopt a particular form of comportment in which he or she is to present himself or herself in a certain fashion and to plan his or her life in rational manner. The rationale for this is to ensure that the individual can become an active citizen, a condition in which one is held to maintain self-esteem, networks of social obligation, life skills and enthusiasm. There is certainly a form of administratively guided asceticism at work here such that the practices of active systems of income support are neither strictly a governmental regime nor an ethical regime but a hybrid assemblage of multiform dimensions. Such a regime typically involves the 'partnership' of different kinds of agencies in the delivery of services such as departments of state, 'voluntary', 'community' or 'third sector' bodies and businesses.

One of the rationales for such a system was that the long-term unemployed, the single parent or the person with a disability would avoid the
characteristics of welfare dependence. In these earlier formulations, the
ethical and ascetic characteristics of the individual were to be managed with
the guided consent and agreement of the welfare beneficiary. More recently,
however, the use of sanctions such as the restriction or cutting off of benefits for breaches of agreements and requirements, and the enforcement of
work in Workfare or 'welfare-to-work' programmes, have brought a new
dimension to this task of transforming the marginal or excluded self. In US-
style Workfare programmes (Peck 1998; Theodore and Peck 1999; Schram
2000) and the writings of 'new paternalists' such as Lawrence Mead and
his colleagues (1997: 23) we find the principle that 'those who would be
free must first be bound'. This means that state-sponsored coercion, underwritten by the use of sovereign powers, acts as a condition for attaining
the ethical state of self-government. More generally, many contemporary
theoretico-political programmes we have cited, from Third Way social
democracy and the new paternalism to communitarianism, agree that the
individual is under a 'mutual obligation' to the state and/or 'community'
that maintains him or her. The example of welfare reform reveals that, while
the transformation of the self can take a liberal and pluralist form of
working through the self-governing capacities of individuals, this does not
preclude the use of sovereign kinds of rule in local contexts that link governing through self-governing and self-becoming with the enforcement of
obligations. This example demonstrates a limit of the thesis of 'culture governance'. Far from emerging at the point of the decline of sovereignty and
sovereign powers, the attempt to govern through the freedom of the individual in a process of becoming links arms with the enforcement and closure
of a particular kind of positive freedom by sovereign means, albeit delegated on to a range of authorities, much as Isaiah Berlin (1997) would have
expected.

As a second example we can cite Foucault's own analysis (1985) of how
a minority of men who were free and equal citizens in Antiquity came to
problematise their capacities of self-government as a consequence of their
government of others in both the *polis* and the *oikos* as citizens and heads
of households. In contrast to the government of the unemployed, here the
problematisation of one's own conduct is a feature not of being governed
but of the exercise of authority over others. There is a long trajectory of
problematisations of the conduct of statesmen, from early modern 'mirror
of princes' literature (Foucault 1991) to media coverage of contemporary
US politicians. They ask: what characteristics are required to exercise
authority – probity, wisdom, restraint, virtue, fortitude, honour? What kind
of behaviour is appropriate – in relations with others, with subjects, with
agents and so on? We can also examine the way a certain ethos of the rule
is called into question and displaced by another. Thus there is a long history,
tied to notions of 'responsible government', of the delineation and forma-

tion of the comportment of the bureaucrat who is held to exhibit an 'ethos of office' (Minson 1998). Such an ethos includes party-political neutrality, a willingness to give impartial and dispassionate advice, and to subjugate private beliefs to public duty. We can examine the role of certain recent attempts to reform public sectors – the New Public Management, moves to devolution and contractualisation, and their successors – in calling that ethos into question (Minson 1998; du Gay 2000). A similar trajectory can be traced concerning the role of the officer in the military and the challenge of moves to implement, for instance, sexual harassment policies (Smith 1998).

In short, to pose the question of political identities at either or both the level of nation and state (or their supposed demise) and the individual (*however* conceived) is both too general and empty. Rather than a general form of citizenship based on national identity, or a unitary state morally regulating its subjects, or even self-reflexive subjects transforming themselves in the public sphere, the political shaping and self-shaping of individuals occur through singular practices of the regulation of conduct from discipline and civility to arts of existence found in and across different and definite locales, the problematisations that are linked with them, the goals they seek, the kinds of subjects they attempt to make or to become, and the diverse instrumentation they deploy. Most important, such forms of ethical being and subjectivity entered the political as capacities and attributes which divide and unify in the course of struggles and which can become the stakes within such struggles. These struggles, however much framed as cultural identities and ethical dispositions, concern the appropriation, development and distribution of material and symbolic resources, of space and of territory.

## Truth, norms and power

Doubtless I have strayed far from my initial concerns here. I have sought, however, to raise a series of questions and introduce a set of resources that might contribute to our concerns about how issues of self and the individual intersect with how we govern and are governed and the effects in the political domain. But this excursus does permit us to return to the more contemporary theme. It allows us to identify some crucial moves of a discourse that is composed of the story of globalisation and individualisation, on the one hand, and what I have called the thesis of culture governance, on the other. This discourse is premised upon a certain – *hubris* that of the newness of the present and its ruptural characteristics. It claims to discover this newness in the thematic of a prolific individualisation that gives us the general form of a deterritorialised cosmopolitan subject or naked individual. This subject is held to be the outcome of a reflexive project and its processes of self-narration and self-construction, possibly conducted with the help of experts. The individual is a DIY (do-it-yourself) artefact. It is also a subject of risk, of the attempt to manage and navigate the reefs found in its voyage of security. Strangely, however, while the individual might confront power structures in a life politics in order to achieve 'self-actualisation', its formation is divorced from power relations, from programmes of rule, practices of government and self-government and their effects, and indeed from the political itself. In part this is because the story of the naked individual is the story of the emancipation of the subject from older systems of domination of class, of gender, ethnicity, community and nationality. It is thus a subject that is freed from power relations and from political structures rather than fabricated through them and within them. In part, this emancipation of the individual is the story of the decline of the state and its sovereign powers, and the rise of the sovereignty of the individual over its own life. It is hence a story of depoliticisation.

The self-reflexive, cosmopolitan individual is thus a single figure of the Second Age modern self. It corresponds to a deterritorialised political sphere and a detraditionalised social sphere. Thus the contemporary self is the effect of a fairly simple dialectical overcoming of the dominated individual and dominating state and society. The first stage of modernity liberates individuals from traditional and feudal statuses and dependences. However, it blocks their full development as self-governing individuals in a process of becoming by reinscribing them within the territorial domination of the state and the 'traditional' structures and cultural identities of modernity and nation. It is only with emergent globality, undermining the very concept of a national society, and the displacement of state sovereignty with networks of governance, that full individualisation can occur. Because the exercise of authority will now be forced to route itself through the agency of the free individual, the political logic of state and sovereignty structures, with all its 'demonic' potential (Foucault 2001: 311), will re-emerge full exorcised in a multi-layered governance that has to draw upon the cultural resources of individuals and use that culture as its means and agency.

What are we to make of this story? How are we to analyse it? It would be easy to dismiss it as mere mythology, as an ideology of the intellectual mandarins of the new global elite. There are those who would be better placed to make such judgements than myself. I simply want to suggest three effects of the story of culture governance: a truth effect, a norm effect and a power effect.

The truth effect of such a discourse is to erase the sphere of contestation, appropriation and domination. It is to make what might be contested appear as inevitable or necessary, whether we like it or not. Whether it is given a triumphalist or critical modulation, its truth effect is to 'black-box' certain practices and to render them immune to inspection. An apparently neutral description or analysis of this kind acts a kind of 'condition of acceptability' for certain practices, which it only dimly acknowledges (Foucault 1981). Thus despite his view that globalisation is to be subject to political moulding, Beck (2000b: 1) can tell us that its consequences are that:

> The premises of the welfare state and the pension system, of income support, local government and infrastructural policies, the power of organised labour, industry-wide free collective bargaining, state expenditure, the fiscal system and 'fair taxation' – all this melts under the withering sun of globalisation and becomes susceptible to demands for political moulding. Every social actor must respond in one way or another and the typical responses do *not* fit in the old left–right schema political action. (Original emphasis)

Thus the discourse of globalisation provides the conditions of acceptability for those practices that seek and demand the reform of public-sector organisation, taxation and industrial relations systems and so on. While there is no necessary form in which these practices of reform should operate, the necessity of reform is not doubted. *How* reform will proceed links the truth effect with the norm effect.

The thesis of individualisation presents us with a sociological *fait accompli* that institutions, policy makers and indeed national and international organisations need to respond to. On the one hand, as we have seen, the thesis presents a description of how people in the Second Age of Modernity will behave. They will turn their lives into a 'planning project' (Beck-Gernsheim 1995). 'In the individualised society, the individual must learn, on pain of permanent disadvantage, to conceive of himself or herself as the centre of activity, as the planning office with respect to his or her own biography, abilities, orientations, relationships and so on' (Beck 1992b: 135, cited in Beck-Gernsheim 1995: 140). Whether we like it or not, there is a 'tendency towards *planning and rationalisation in conduct of life*, which is increasingly becoming the task of individuals' (Beck-Gernsheim 1995: 139, original emphasis). On the other, this description is capable of generating a set of norms that might govern the reform of institutions. For Giddens (1998: 36–7):

> If institutional individualism is not the same as egoism, it poses less of a threat to social solidarity, but it does imply that we have to look for new means of producing that solidarity. We have to make our lives in a more active way than was true of previous generations, and we need more actively to accept responsibility for the consequences of what we do and the lifestyle habits we adopt. The theme of responsibility, or mutual obligation, was there in old-style social democracy but was dormant, since it was submerged within the concept of collective provision, We have to find a new balance between individual and collective responsibilities today.

Thus this discourse is capable not only of codifying the operation of practices and providing authoritative descriptions and justifications for them. It is also capable of converting its authoritative descriptions into normative judgements. It is thus able to generate a kind of programme for the reform of the operation of institutions and institutional practices and orienting them to a new set of ends such as making individuals the head office of their own lives. A perfunctory familiarity with welfare reform over the last two decades, as noted previously, would show that these norms, and the kinds of programmes of reform they might justify, are hardly novel or inventive.

These norms are norms of inclusion and difference, rather than exclusion and stratification. The prudential subject, the active citizen, the enterprising individual, the life-planning person and the cosmopolitan self – and, on a more abstract level, the perpetual becoming individual – are all so many manifestations of a kind of norm that works to include by combating those attributes and orientations that leave individuals and populations in a condition of social exclusion and dependence and those which would form the basis of political struggle. If there are capacities, expectations and attitudes derived from 'traditional' class, gender, ethnic or national identities, these are reconfigured as 'indices of disadvantage' and 'risk factors', as obstacles and forces of resistance to be overcome. Once stripped of these, the individual is left with depoliticised cultural differences that are put into play as the agencies and energies that are to be transformed by the work of government. These differences provide opportunities for enterprise, activity and consumerism, sources of communal identification, celebration and cultural plurality that displace the social and fragment early modern solidarities, and become energies and desires for transformation (e.g. the empowerment and self-determination of indigenous populations). They also provide a norm of government and the management of populations which links us with the question of power and its effects.

The story of culture governance is a dialectical one. The opposition between state and individual is overcome by the new, multi-layered, polycentric networks of 'governance' that need to become 'cultural' because it must work through, shape and be shaped by the agency and energies of self-governing individuals and the communities they might form. The power effects of this truth are to make it impossible to ask certain kinds of questions and to render specific kinds of forces invisible. We might want to ask when, in what contexts, how, and for which individuals and groups, 'governance' conducted with the aim of 'activating' individuals comes to place obligations above freedom, and use sanctions and coercive measures in the establishment of a particular form of life. Is it a case of governing through freedom for some (the consumer of services, those participating in community development programmes), obligation for others (the welfare-dependent) and sovereign force for still others (the illegal immigrant)? How is the diagram of a polycentric, individualising, enabling and networking, form of governance laid upon a centric, totalising, commanding and hierarchical form of territorial power (and the international order made up of relations between such powers)? In other words, how is cultural governance connected with new figurations of disciplinary and sovereign forms of power? These are the types of questions the dialectical narrative precludes or downplays in relation to emergence of governance through self-governing individuals. It may be that, for example, rather than a movement from state-centric sovereignty to polycentric governance we have transformations and interlacing of the sovereign and the governmental and a new kind of language of politics. If the sovereign decides upon the state of exception, in the famous definition of Schmitt (1985: 5), the governmental works to generate the norm (Dean 2002). This norm, itself, generates further sovereign exceptions. The cosmopolitan individual is today a key version of this norm. It provides a norm of political inclusion that constrains and enables in a singular fashion. It simultaneously strips individuals of the capacities derived from their historically given identities and puts into play depoliticised cultural differences and identifications. There is a simultaneous negative/positive, constraining/enabling, operation of power. Its power effect, then, is to generate norms of government that transform cultural energies and identifications into the material and the objectives of rule. They also allow the sovereign to decide the exceptions in which sanction and force are to be used.

Finally, the image of the anarchic – or even 'heterarchic' (Jessop 1998) – and multi-layered governance at supranational and sub-national level deprives us of seeking the intelligibility of the world balance of forces. 'A globally *disorganized* capitalism is spreading out. For there is no hegemonic power and no international regime, either political or economic' (Beck 2000b: 13). This precludes what some, not least the anti-globalisation movements from Seattle to Genoa, most urgently want to ask, and which the events of 11 September and the War on Terror pose. What is the political constitution of the international order in the present? How are we to describe it? What capacities do we have to form ourselves as subjects of its contestation and resistance? What do current identities offer in the way of such capacities?

The problem with the thesis of culture governance is not its falsity. It is its truth that requires our contestation. That contestation might require use to think about how we are asked to constitute ourselves today and how we might think differently about that request. It might require us to think of the consequences of the entry of cultural governance and its valorisation of the arts of existence as a specifically political problem.

## Notes

1 This and the following section draw upon but significantly rewrite, clarify, amend and develop the arguments of passages found in Dean (1996).
2 This passage is quoted by Giddens (1998: 36). Interestingly, in view of his use of it (see below) to discuss the creation of social solidarity, he stops before the conjunction 'and' in the second last sentence. This omits both the key insights of the collective character of individualism and the individualisation of responsibility for failure.

## References

Agamben, G. (1998), *Homo sacer: Sovereign Power and Bare Life*, trans. D. Heller-Roazen (Stanford CA: Stanford University Press).

Ariès, P., and Duby, G., eds (1987–91), *A History of Private Life*, 5 vols (Cambridge MA: Belknap Press).

Barry, A., Osborne, T., and Rose, N., eds (1996), *Foucault and Political Reason: Liberalism, Neo-liberalism and Rationalities of Government* (London: UCL Press).

Beck, U. (1989), 'On the way to the industrial risk society? Outline of an argument', *Thesis Eleven* 23: 86–103.

Beck, U. (1992a), 'From industrial society to risk society', *Theory, Culture and Society* 9: 97–123.

Beck, U. (1992b), *Risk Society: Towards a new Modernity*, trans. M. Ritter (London: Sage).

Beck, U. (1998), 'The cosmopolitan manifesto', *New Statesman*, 20 March.

Beck, U. (2000a), 'The cosmopolitan perspective: sociology of the Second Age of Modernity', *British Journal of Sociology* 51 (1): 79–105.

Beck, U. (2000b), *What is Globalization?* trans. P. Camiller (Cambridge: Polity Press).

Beck-Gernsheim, E. (1996) 'Life as a planning project', in S. Lash, B. Szerszynski and B. Wynne (eds), *Risk, Environment and Modernity: Towards a New Ecology*, London: Sage.

Berlin, I. (1997), 'Two concepts of liberty', in *The Proper Study of Mankind* (London: Chatto & Windus).

Bogner, A. (1987), 'Elias and the Frankfurt school', *Theory, Culture and Society* 4: 249–85.

Brown, P. (1987), 'Late antiquity', in P. Veyne (ed.), *From Pagan Rome to Byzantium*, trans. A. Goldhammer (*A History of Private Life* I, Cambridge MA: Belknap Press), pp. 235–311.

Brown, P. (1992), *Power and Persuasion in late Antiquity: Towards a Christian Empire* (Madison WI: University of Wisconsin Press).

Burchell, G., Gordon, C., and Miller, P., eds (1991), *The Foucault Effect: Studies in Governmentality* (Brighton: Harvester Wheatsheaf).

Castel, R. (1991), 'From dangerousness to risk', in G. Burchell, C. Gordon and P. Miller (eds), *The Foucault Effect: Studies in Governmentality* (Brighton: Harvester Wheatsheaf), pp. 281–98.

Castells, M. (1996), *The Information Age* I, *The Rise of the Network Society* (Oxford: Blackwell).

Connolly, W. E. (1999), *Why I am not a Secularist* (Minneapolis MN: University of Minnesota Press).

Corrigan, P., and Sayer, D. (1985), *The Great Arch: English State Formation as Cultural Revolution* (Oxford: Blackwell).

Cruikshank, B. (1999), *The Will to Empower: Democratic Citizens and other Subjects* (Ithaca NY: Cornell University Press).

Dean, M. (1994), *Critical and Effective Histories: Foucault's Methods and Historical Sociology* (London: Routledge).

Dean, M. (1995), 'Governing the unemployed self in an active society', *Economy and Society* 24 (4): 559–83.

Dean, M. (1996), 'Foucault, government and the enfolding of authority', in A. Barry, T. Osborne and N. Rose (eds), *Foucault and Political Reason: Liberalism, Neo-liberalism and Rationalities of Government* (London: UCL Press), pp. 209–29.

Dean, M. (1998), 'Neoliberalism as counter-Enlightenment cultural critique', in S. Hänninen (ed.), *The Displacement of Social Policies* (Jyväskylä: SoPhi), pp. 198–226.

Dean, M. (1999), *Governmentality: Power and Rule in Modern Society* (London: Sage).

Dean, M. (2002), 'Liberal government and authoritarianism', *Economy and Society* 31 (1): 37–61.

Dean, M., and Hindess, B., eds (1998), *Governing Australia: Studies in Contemporary Rationalities of Government* (Cambridge: Cambridge University Press).

Donzelot, J. (1979), *The Policing of Families*, trans. R. Hurley (London: Hutchinson).

Du Gay, P. (2000), *In praise of Bureaucracy* (London: Sage).

Duby, G. (1987), Foreword, in P. Veyne (ed.), *A History of Private Life* I, *From Pagan Rome to Byzantium*, trans. A. Goldhammer (Cambridge MA: Belknap Press), pp. vii–ix.

Elias, N. (1978), *The Civilizing Process* I, *The History of Manners*, trans. E. Jephcott (New York: Urizen).

Elias, N. (1982), *The Civilizing Process* II, *State Formation and Civilization*, trans. E. Jephcott (Oxford: Blackwell).

Elias, N. (1983), *The Court Society*, trans. E. Jephcott (Oxford: Blackwell).

Etzioni, A. (1995), *The Spirit of Community: Rights, Responsibilities and the Communitarian Agenda* (London: Fontana).

Ewald, F. (1991), 'Insurance and risk', in G. Burchell, C. Gordon and P. Miller (eds), *The Foucault Effect: Studies in Governmentality* (Brighton: Harvester Wheatsheaf), pp. 197–210.

Foucault, M. (1977), 'Nietzsche, genealogy, history', in D. Bouchard (ed.), *Language, Counter-memory, Practice* (Oxford: Blackwell), pp. 139–64.

Foucault, M. (1981), 'Questions of method', *I and C* 8: 3–14; reprinted in G. Burchell, C. Gordon and P. Miller (eds), *The Foucault Effect: Studies in Governmentality* (Brighton: Harvester Wheatsheaf), pp. 73–86.

Foucault, M. (1982), 'The subject and power', in H. Dreyfus and P. Rabinow (eds), *Michel Foucault: Beyond Structuralism and Hermeneutics* (Brighton: Harvester), pp. 210–26.

Foucault, M. (1985), *The Use of Pleasure*, trans. R. Hurley (New York: Pantheon).

Foucault, M. (1988), 'Technologies of the self', in L. H. Martin, H. Gutman and P. H. Hutton (eds), *Technologies of the Self: A Seminar with Michel Foucault* (London: Tavistock), pp. 16–49.

Foucault, M. (1991), 'Governmentality', in G. Burchell, C. Gordon and P. Miller (eds), *The Foucault Effect: Studies in Governmentality* (Brighton: Harvester Wheatsheaf), pp. 87–104.

Foucault, M. (1993), 'About the beginnings of the hermeneutics of the self', *Political Theory* 21 (2): 198–227.

Foucault, M. (2001), ' "Omnes et singulatum": toward a critique of political reason', in J. Faubian (ed.), *The Essential Works, 1954–1984*, III *Power* (London: Allen Lane), pp. 298–325.

Giddens, A. (1991), *Modernity and Self-identity* (Cambridge: Polity Press).

Giddens, A. (1998), *The Third Way: The Renewal of Social Democracy* (Cambridge: Polity Press).

Habermas, J. (1985). 'Modernity: an incomplete project', in H. Foster (ed.), *Postmodern Culture* (London: Pluto Press).

Hall, S. (1992), 'The question of cultural identity', in S. Hall, D. Held and T. McGrew (eds), *Modernity and its Futures* (Cambridge: Polity Press), pp. 274–316.

Hardt, M., and Negri, A. (2001), *Empire* (Cambridge MA: Harvard University Press).

Hayek, F. A. (1979), *Law, Legislation and Liberty* III, *The Political Order of a Free People* (London: Routledge).

Hirst, P. Q. (1981), 'The genesis of the social', *Politics and Power* 3: 67–82.

Hodges, J., and Hussain, A. (1979), review article '*La Police des familles*', *Ideology and Consciousness* 5: 87–123.

Horkheimer, M. (1974), *Eclipse of Reason* (New York: Continuum).

Jessop, B. (1998) 'The rise of governance and the risks of failure: the case of economic development', *International Social Science Journal* 50 (1): 29–45.

Marshall, T. H. (1963), 'Citizenship and social class', in *Sociology at the Crossroads and other Essays* (London: Heinemann), pp. 67–127.

Mauss, M. (1985), 'A category of the human mind: the notion of the person; the notion of the self', in M. Carrithers, S. Collins and S. Lukes (eds), *The Category of the Person* (Cambridge: Cambridge University Press), pp. 1–35.

Mead, L., ed. (1997), *The New Paternalism: Supervisory Approaches to Poverty* (Washington DC: Brookings Institution).

Merleau-Ponty, M. (1974), *Phenomenology, Language and Sociology*, ed. J. O'Neill (London: Heinemann).

Minson, J. (1985), *Genealogies of Morals: Nietzsche, Foucault and Donzelot and the Eccentricity of Ethics* (London: Macmillan).

Minson, J. (1993), *Questions of Conduct: Sexual Harassment, Citizenship and Government* (London: Macmillan).

Minson, J. (1998), 'Ethics in the service of the state', in M. Dean and B. Hindess (eds), *Governing Australia: Studies in Contemporary Rationalities of Government* (Cambridge: Cambridge University Press), pp. 47–69.

Nelson, S. (1996), 'Care of the Sick: Nursing, Holism and Pious Practice', PhD thesis, Nathan Qld: Griffith University.

O'Malley, P. (1996), 'Risk and responsibility', in A. Barry, T. Osborne and N. Rose (eds), *Foucault and Political Reason: Liberalism, Neo-liberalism and Rationalities of Government* (London: UCL Press), pp. 189–207.

Oestreich, G. (1982), *Neostoicism and the Early Modern State*, trans. D. McLintock (Cambridge: Cambridge University Press).

Osborne, T. (1994), 'Sociology, liberalism and the historicity of conduct', *Economy and Society* 23 (4): 484–501.

Peck, J. (1998), 'Workfare; a geopolitical etymology', *Environment and Planning D, Society and Space* 16: 133–61.

Rose, N. (1995), 'Authority and the genealogy of subjectivity', in P. Heelas, P. Morris and S. Lash (eds), *De-traditionalization: Authority and Self in an Age of Cultural Uncertainty* (Oxford: Blackwell).

Rosenau, J. (2000), 'Governance in a globalising world', in D. Held and A. McGrew (eds), *The Global Transformations Reader* (Cambridge: Polity Press), pp. 181–90.

Schmitt, C. (1985), *Political Theology: Four Chapters on the Concept of Sovereignty*, trans. G. Schwab (Cambridge MA: MIT Press).

Schram, S. F. (2000) *After Welfare: The Culture of Postindustrial Social Policy* (New York: New York University Press).

Smith, A. (1998), 'Bad habits or bad conscience? Sexual harassment in the Australian Defence Force', in M. Dean and B. Hindess (eds), *Governing Australia: Studies in Contemporary Rationalities of Government* (Cambridge: Cambridge University Press), pp. 70–86.

Theodore, N., and Peck, J. (1999), 'Welfare-to-work: national problems, local solutions', *Critical Social Policy* 19 (4): 485–510.

Veyne, P., ed. (1987a), *From Pagan Rome to Byzantium*, trans. A. Goldhammer (*A History of Private Life* I, Cambridge MA: Belknap Press).

Veyne, P. (1987b), 'The Roman empire', in P. Veyne (ed.), *From Pagan Rome to Byzantium*, trans. A. Goldhammer (*A History of Private Life* I, Cambridge MA: Belknap Press), pp. 5–234.

Veyne, P. (1990), *Bread and Circuses: Political Pluralism and Historical Sociology*, trans. B. Pearce (London: Allen Lane).

Weir, Lorna (1996) 'Recent developments in the government of pregnancy', *Economy and Society* 25 (3): 372–92.

# 8

# Pierre Bourdieu's political sociology and governance perspectives

David L. Swartz

The multi-faceted work of Pierre Bourdieu has been widely discussed, if not always understood, outside France. All his major books have received extensive attention and discussion. Many sociologists are by now familiar with most of his principal concepts and arguments. Yet neglected by most observers is the underlying political analysis in Bourdieu's work, both his political sociology and his underlying political project.[1] The purpose of this chapter is to address this gap in the Anglo-American literature on Bourdieu's political sociology. I will argue that there is a strong theory of politics within Bourdieu's work.

Some observers charge that a shortcoming of Bourdieu's sociology is his lack of systematic attention to institutions, including political ones (e.g. Lamont 1989: 782). Bon and Schemeil (1980: 1203), for example, observe that his emphasis on 'symbolic violence' is paralleled by neglect of the specific character of political institutions, such as the control of 'physical violence'. Indeed, Bourdieu does not devote much attention to public demonstrations, strikes, police, army, prisons or war.[2] Nor does he devote much attention to those political units, such as legislatures or constitutions, commonly treated as institutions by political scientists and historians. Except for the act of delegating political power, Bourdieu has not devoted much attention to political *processes*, such as decision making, coalition building or leadership selection.[3]

Many of these criticisms reflect traditional concerns that animate the academic disciplines of political sociology and political science. But Bourdieu's sociology attempts a broader sweep of political issues than those delineated by the boundaries of these academic disciplines. Indeed, I would argue that Bourdieu's sociology makes no distinction between the sociological approach to the study of the social world and the study of the political power. Bourdieu sees *all* of sociology as fundamentally dealing with power. He therefore rejects the validity of a substantive area of investigation that might be considered as specialised in the study of only the power dimension of social life. He rejects the traditional academic division of labour between sociology, political sociology and political science.[4]

Politics in fact stand at the very core of Bourdieu's sociology even though he has not devoted much attention to traditional political science concerns, such as the state, elections and voting, parties, pressure groups, polling, and forms of physical coercion and violence.[5] He has, however, been a sharp critic of public opinion polling by arguing that political participation, as in voting, is highly skewed by social class. While the rise of the modern state has not been an ongoing topic of interest, in recent years he has defined a possible extension of Max Weber's (1978: 56, 65) view of the state as that instance that monopolises the means of symbolic violence. Yet Bourdieu's study of politics, like his study of the social world more generally, is framed by his concern for 'modes of domination'. The key guiding question is how non-egalitarian social orders reproduce intergenerationally through the misrecognition of the arbitrary powers that order them (Swartz 1997: 6). Bourdieu's sociology of symbolic power is in this sense an original, cross-disciplinary political sociology.[6]

## Bourdieu and governance

For the purposes of this particular volume on governance, this chapter relates Bourdieu's work to the governance orientation to politics. It should be stated at the outside that Bourdieu is *not* a governance theorist. Bourdieu himself does not use the language of governance. He does not cast his work within disciplinary boundaries of political sociology, political science or administrative science where the idea of governance is most widely discussed. Indeed, Bourdieu rejects much of what is advocated under a governance perspective, particularly where normative claims are made about how public policy should be implemented. For example, he is sharply critical of privatising public enterprises and services and decreasing the role of the state, policy preferences favoured by many governance theorists (Merrien 1998: 59). In recent years Bourdieu (1998c) has become a sharp public critic of neo-liberalism, decrying the increasing reliance on market mechanisms for social welfare provision. The focus of Bourdieu's work is on power, particularly the more subtle forms of cultural power, and not on the concerns of efficiency in political decision making that seem to drive the governance imagination.

Nonetheless, there are points of overlap. Bourdieu has devoted considerable attention to the crisis of education and social service provision in France (e.g. 1998a). He therefore shares with many governance theorists the concern that modern welfare societies face a severe crisis. He has been sharply critical of French state leadership for pursuing its own particular interests to the neglect of broader social interests, particularly where the lower social classes are concerned. He wants, as do many governance theorists, to render public services more democratic. Bourdieu's approach to the study of power in terms of fields of conflict rather than focusing exclusive attention on particular institutions, such as the centralised state, gives a relational and multi-centred analytical view of power that overlaps to some extent with the concerns of governance thinkers. In the course of the chapter I call attention to such points of potential convergence between Bourdieu's sociology and certain concerns that find expression today in the governance orientation to the study of politics. This chapter, however, does not attempt to transform Bourdieu into an unwitting governance theorist. Moreover I would note, along with numerous other observers (Stoker 1998), that governance today remains an eclectic orientation, designating a great variety of descriptive, analytical and theoretical concerns. I necessarily have been selective in choice of themes by selecting only those that seem central to Bourdieu's thinking about politics while drawing comparisons with the general governance framework where appropriate.

### The politics of symbolic power

What are politics for Bourdieu? What would be his sociology of politics? It is useful to distinguish two different ways Bourdieu approaches these questions. First, he sees power as a central organising dimension of all social life. Power is not an independent domain that can be separated from culture or economics but a force that pervades all human relations. Politics concern the structures and exercise of power; the sociology of politics must reveal that fundamental dimension of social relations regardless of level of analysis or substantive area. Bourdieu's sociology of symbolic power and violence calls attention to that political dimension of all social life.[7]

Secondly, Bourdieu also thinks of politics as a specific sphere of activity where the conquest of power is the specific objective. Here his thinking follows much the lines of Max Weber when Bourdieu proposes his idea of the political field as an arena of struggle for political capital. I begin the presentation of Bourdieu's thinking with the first dimension before taking up his concept of the political field.

A very important feature of Bourdieu's sociology of politics is his social constructionist emphasis on the symbolic struggle of social life where individuals and groups compete to impose their respective views of the social world as universal (Bourdieu and Wacquant 1998: 117). For Bourdieu the political dimension of social life goes to the very foundation of any collectivity, since he sees all instituted groups as emerging out of a symbolic struggle (struggle over representations) to impose selected representations as legitimate social identity. Any distribution of properties, such as age, gender, education or wealth, can serve as the basis of group divisions and therefore become the basis of political struggle (Bourdieu 1981: 71). Such properties, or 'capitals', as Bourdieu calls them, require legitimation to function as power resources. His concepts of symbolic power and violence call attention to that power dimension where there are particular interests that go misrecognised as representing universal interests. Symbolic power is a *world-making*[8] power, for it involves the capacity to impose the 'legitimate vision of the social world and of its divisions' (Bourdieu 1987b: 13, 1989b). Bourdieu sees the very foundation of the social order as a struggle among various collectivities to impose as legitimate their particular identities and definitions of the social world. Symbolic power is a group-making power, for it is able to constitute social realities as legitimate entities. This occurs through struggle over the right to exercise that symbolic function. The task of sociology is to reveal the underlying character of those legitimation struggles. Viewed this way, all sociology for Bourdieu is in fact a sociology of politics.

Bourdieu (1981: 69) argues that political action is possible only because actors have a knowledge or understanding of the social world and are able to act on the basis of that understanding. He rejects the idea that political action is 'determined mechanically' by the social world in which actors are located. Rather, the external economic and social worlds operate on actors through their knowledge and perceptions. In other words, political action is mediated by symbolic representations (e.g., mental, verbal, graphical, theatrical).

Bourdieu analyses political action as practices that attempt to produce and impose representations on the social world, representations that either lend support to the existing social order or attempt to subvert it. Political protest, for example, begins by a break with, or 'denunciation' of, the taken-for-granted understanding of the social world (the *doxa*). Bourdieu writes:

> Politics begins, strictly speaking, with the denunciation of this tacit contract of adherence to the established order which defines the original doxa; in other words, political subversion presupposes cognitive subversion, a conversion of the vision of the world. (1991b: 127–8)

Here he makes the foundational claim that politics begin when the social order is questioned, that is, when the doxa is challenged. He goes on to say (1991b: 128) that a critical break with the presuppositions of the established social order 'presupposes a conjuncture of critical discourse and an objective crisis, capable of disrupting the close correspondence between the incorporated structures and the objective structures which produce them'. Political action presupposes, therefore, both a 'critical discourse' and an 'objective crisis' (1981: 69).

This political orientation can be seen in the social constructionist perspective he brings to naming and classification. The formation of individual and group identities points to the power to name, to give symbolic identity that both reflects and forms collective social reality. Naming brings into existence. It creates symbolic power. Politics are the cultural construction of collective identities and practices. They are fundamentally linked with the formation of group identities. Bourdieu writes that politics are the site *par excellence* of symbolic effectiveness, an activity which works through signs capable of producing social entities and, above all, groups.[9]

In *Distinction* Bourdieu (1984a) makes a compelling case for why classification struggles are class struggles. Classification struggles are also political struggles, since they concern processes and effects of drawing boundaries and establishing hierarchies. Bourdieu (1991c) forcefully argues for a social constructionist view that public identity, whether individual or collective, is forged through classification struggles. Bourdieu's stratification analysis of modern societies is also his political sociology.

*Sociological method and politics*
Bourdieu's sociology of politics is connected with his constructionist sociological method. Already in 1977 he (Bourdieu 1977) posed a fundamental epistemological problem for the sociological study of politics: how can one study politics sociologically without simply imposing a partisan political agenda. In a paper on the state he (1993b) opens the discussion by stressing how difficult it is to construct sociological knowledge that is independent of the official categories and classifications imposed by the state. He stresses the difficulty of doing a good sociological analysis of politics because we are 'immersed' in politics through the mass media. Politics are such a familiar, taken-for-granted world that it is difficult to gain the requisite distance from received views in order to gain a reasonably objective view of politics as a field of struggle (1988c: 2). This calls for a critical and reflexive practice of sociology. Since for Bourdieu, following Durkheim (1966), the sociological method requires breaking with received views of the social world, how is it possible to gain some vantage point on contemporary political life when politics shape much of our everyday lives?[10] Bourdieu's answer lies in his field analytical approach to the study of the social world. Constructing the field of political conflict and tracing out its historical development are to key to Bourdieu's method. It is by introducing the notion of a 'political field' that Bourdieu believes he has found an answer to this dilemma.

In a discussion of the 'political field' he (2000a) also identifies this question as an ongoing concern and suggests that the concept of a 'political field' has three methodological 'advantages' for addressing the problem. First, the field approach makes the very definition of what is political an object of study. Politics is sociologically a constructed object rather than a taken-for-granted reality. Second, his method is comparative historical. Tracing out the historical context that leads to the instituted and commonly accepted political ideas (such as the opposition between the left and the right) is a key technique for breaking with the received views of the political world. Political ideas and institutions are not universal but historically specific. And third, his method is critical rather than prescriptive.

But Bourdieu's answer is not that sociology can achieve value neutrality in political analysis. He rejects that form of objectivism. Following the field analytical method, sociology can, he believes, transcend the partisanship of choosing sides among available political options. But at a deeper level 'science – and particularly science of the political game – is never totally freed of political force, at least the negative force of critique' (Bourdieu 2000b: 69). Bourdieu holds that scientific analysis of the social world unveils the taken-for-granted power relations of social life; by debunking the received wisdom of social life science exercises a political effect (Swartz 1997: 259–62). Bourdieu's sociology of politics is therefore intimately connected with his politics of sociology.

### The field analysis of politics

Political practices, as all practices, occur in structured arenas of conflict called *fields*.[11] Fields denote arenas of production, circulation and appropriation of goods, services, knowledge or status, and the competitive positions held by actors in their struggle to accumulate and monopolise these different kinds of valued resources, or capitals. Fields may be thought of as structured spaces that are organised around specific types of capital or combinations of capital.[12]

### General characteristics of fields

Bourdieu (1993c: 72) speaks of the 'invariant laws' or 'universal mechanisms' that are structural properties characteristic of all fields. First, fields are arenas of struggle for control over valued resources, which Bourdieu calls *capitals*. Field struggle centres around particular forms of capital, such as economic, cultural, scientific or religious. Second, fields are structured spaces of dominant and subordinate positions based on types and amounts of capital. Fields are stratified by the unequal distribution of relevant capitals and field struggle pits those in dominant positions with more capital against those in subordinate positions with less. Third, fields impose on actors specific forms of struggle. Both dominants and subordinates share a fundamental doxa, or set of rules of the game that specify, often tacitly, the specific forms of struggle that are legitimate. Fourth, fields are structured to a significant extent by their own internal mechanisms of development and thus hold some degree of autonomy from the external environment. Cultural fields, for example, develop their own specific laws of exercise that relate to but do not reduce to economic or political interests. Bourdieu uses the language of 'relative autonomy' and 'structural and functional homologies' to talk about inter-field relations in terms of isomorphic patterns, or similarity of function, but devoid of instrumental design.

Each field is internally differentiated by a 'homologous structure' of an economically dominant and culturally dominated pole and a culturally dominant and economically dominated pole (Bourdieu 1989a: 383). Two major competing principles of social hierarchy – what Bourdieu calls a 'chiasmatic structure' – shape the struggle for power in modern industrial societies: the distribution of *economic capital* (wealth, income and property), which Bourdieu calls the 'dominant principle of hierarchy', and the distribution of *cultural capital* (knowledge, culture and educational credentials), which Bourdieu calls the 'second principle of hierarchy'. This fundamental opposition between cultural capital and economic capital delineates what Bourdieu (1989a: 373–85) calls the 'field of power'.[13]

Bourdieu's field-analytic approach to the study of the social world consists of identifying the various forms that this oppositional structure takes in specific arenas of struggle. The chiasmatic structure of economic capital and cultural capital functions as the bedrock of Bourdieu's field analysis and his understanding of social stratification and politics.

Field of power also designates for Bourdieu the dominant class, that group of individuals and families richest in total volume of the most valued forms of capital in modern societies. This dominant class is in turn internally differentiated by an unequal distribution of economic capital and cultural capital.[14] The chiasmatic structure of economic capital and cultural capital differentiates intra-class groups in the lower regions of the social class structure as well. The fundamental cultural capital/economic capital opposition in Bourdieu's field-analytic framework, therefore, distributes and ranks *all* fields of struggle (e.g. economic, administrative, university, artistic, scientific, religious, intellectual), including the social class structure. His field analysis consists of an internal analysis of this cultural capital/economic capital opposition in particular fields of struggle and an externally oriented dimension that situates each particular field relative to the dominant class, or field of power.

Fields vary in terms of their own internal differentiation around their own specific forms of the fundamental cultural capital/economic capital opposition and in terms of their respective proximity to the competing poles in the field of power. For example, even in the economic field one can identify a fundamental opposition between technocratic big business leaders who are rich inheritors of cultural capital and accumulators of scholastic capital and owners of large private-sector family firms who are inheritors primarily of economic capital. Relative to the field of power, the economic field stands at one end where the artistic field centred around cultural capital stands at the other end. The administrative and university fields occupy intermediate positions, with the administrative being situated closer to the economic and the university closer to the artistic. The juridical field, Bourdieu (1987a: 851) observes, obtains less autonomy than the artistic and scientific fields, since it is more closely tied to the political field. This means that art and science are less dependent upon the economy and polity than is law for rewarding careers and developing symbolic systems. The journalistic field, by contrast, is the most dependent upon the administrative and political circles. Thus fields vary in their degree of autonomy from economic interest, political power and cultural authority, and a central objective of Bourdieu's sociology consists of situating different fields of cultural activity relative to the field of power.[15]

## The political field

Bourdieu does not offer as detailed or elaborated an analysis of the political field as he does of cultural fields, such as the scientific field or the artistic field (Bon and Schemeil 1980; Caro 1980: 1172). Yet the political field appears to share many of the same properties of other fields: it is a relatively autonomous arena of struggle with its own specific type of capital that has developed historically. But there is some overlap in Bourdieu's conceptual terminology that confuses and reflects usage in different contexts. For example, at one point (1988a: 545) he specifies that ' "political field" refers to specifically political institutions and actors (*champ politique*) *and also* to the whole field of power relations in politics and society (*champ du pouvoir*)' (emphasis added). Nonetheless, the economic capital/cultural capital opposition applied to the field of French politics reveals a pattern of oppositions homologous to that of the class structure.[16] Predictably, one finds occupations, newspapers and magazines and political parties with a considerable volume of total capital distributed toward the political right whereas those with less total volume of capital are distributed toward the political left. Among those on the political left one finds the French socialists and radical left to hold relatively more cultural capital than members of the French Communist Party.

The political field, however, also has some distinctive properties. The political field is a specific sphere of activity where the conquest of power is the central objective.[17] It is an arena of conflict over the definition and implementation of public policies that are struggled over by political professionals who are increasingly linked with the state. The political field can be described as 'a game in which the stakes are the legitimate imposition of the principles of vision and division of the social world' (Bourdieu 2000b: 67). In this respect the political field is similar to other cultural fields of struggle over symbolic power. Both involve symbolic struggle to impose legitimate standards. Indeed, Bourdieu (2000b: 60) draws an analogy in this respect between the religious field and the political field. Both are arenas of struggle over belief in what is the legitimate way to characterise how the social world is organised or should be organised. What is distinctively political in Bourdieu's eyes is that the political field involves struggles not just over ideas but for a particular type of ideas, that is, ' "force ideas", which are ideas capable of bringing about collective mobilisation' (Bourdieu 2000b: 63). Politics is about the mobilisation of public support for particular views of the social world.[18]

### Political capital

The political field has its own specific currency. Bourdieu (1988c: 1) speaks of 'political capital' and refers to it as a 'particular kind of symbolic capital'. It is 'a reputational capital linked to notoriety', a 'symbolic capital linked to the manner of being perceived' (Bourdieu 2000b: 64, 65). Political capital can mean the capacity to get the vote out, the capacity to organise support for particular public decisions. The capacity to hold a political opinion, to which Bourdieu devotes considerable attention, also represents a form of political capital. The political capital of an individual is largely dependent on the importance of his or her political party and his or her position within that party (Bourdieu 2000b: 65). It is also related to other forms of capital, particularly cultural capital and social capital.

*Relative autonomy*
The political field in modern France is a self-regulated sphere of public decision relatively independent of moneyed and cultural interests. Here Bourdieu's analysis is similar to that of Weber, who in critical dialogue with orthodox Marxism stressed the autonomy of the political realm from economic interests.

Bourdieu (1993a: 164) says that 'politics can be described by analogy with a phenomenon of the market: supply and demand'. That relationship, however, is not direct but mediated by the relatively autonomous structure and history of the field in which politics as a form of culture (i.e. political opinion) is produced and consumed. Here Bourdieu's field perspective on politics differs significantly from a straightforward supply/demand market perspective. He argues (1993a: 165) that supply of political options does not develop in direct response to popular demand 'but to the constraints peculiar to a political space that has a history of its own'. By this he means that the supply of political views is shaped by the positions of the producers of political views in the field of political cultural production less by conscious reference to competitors than by virtue of the competitive positions occupied. Demand likewise is determined by competitive position within the class structure. In both cases one needs to understand the relatively autonomous history of each field. Bourdieu's field analysis of politics entails a broader, more complex analysis than a simple supply/demand equation.

A key implication of the relative autonomy of the political field is that political professionals (party leaders, pollsters, political commentators, etc.) do and say things not in direct reference to voters but in reference to other political professionals holding different positions in the field (Bourdieu 2000b: 57). Their behaviour reflects more directly 'the structure of the political field' than the interests of their constituencies (Bourdieu 1985: 738). Bourdieu writes:

> It is the structure of the political field, in other words the objective relationship to the occupants of the other positions, and the relationship to the competing stances that they offer, which, as much as the direct relationship to their mandators, determines the stances they take, i.e., the supply of political products. (1985: 738)

In other words, there is an internal dynamic of self-referencing among political professionals that shapes decisively the array of political options

available to the public. Much behaviour of political professionals, according to Bourdieu's field perspective, entails more posturing to differentiate
positions or enhance their scope of representation than responsiveness to
the direct interests of their constituencies.

Political field analysis implies that political professionals pursue their own
specific interests of position that do not necessarily reflect the interests of
their constituencies (Bourdieu 2000b: 58). There must be of course some
degree of overlap between the political leadership interests and constituency
interests for leadership to maintain a minimum of legitimacy. Bourdieu
acknowledges this but stresses the disjuncture. Most important among those
interests are the 'reproduction of the political apparatus' and maintaining
one's position within it. Here he draws an analogy with the Church. The
strength of political institutions, just like that of the Church, lies in their
capacity to control positions (Bourdieu 2000b: 66–7). Much political
behaviour is motivated by the desire to reproduce the political institution
by maintaining positions for its members. Thus the idea of field autonomy
and its focus on particular interests present a formidable challenge to the
ideals of democratic representation.[19] His field analysis is also more relational than traditional structural and state-centred approaches to welfare
state politics and thus overlaps with the new thinking of certain governance
theorists.[20]

The idea that political positions are likely to reflect the immediate
professional interests of field position more than broader class or cultural
affiliations provides a useful meso-level of analysis that improves upon
one-sided micro or macro-perspectives. It improves upon the traditional
class reductionism of Marxism and the various forms of cultural determinism, such as a functionalist adaptation to societal norms or to the interests of rationally calculating actors. Yet the problems of reductionism and
determinism do not go away but re-emerge in a kind of field reductionism
and determinism. Bourdieu's politics tend to reduce to field positions.[21]
Moreover the political field perspective leaves unexamined the *social
processes* through which political alliance might be formed or broken.
Bourdieu's field analysis of politics needs a social movement component that
would examine the actual processes of political action and mobilisation.

*Professionalisation and delegation*
One of Bourdieu's principal concerns in analysing the French political field
is the political effects of the *professionalisation* and *specialisation* of the
division of labour of symbolic production in modern political life. One
effect he stresses concerns the dynamics and consequences of delegated
political authority. He examines the mechanism of political delegation by
which individual representation and group identity come to be expressed
through spokespersons. He explores the complex and circular relationship
between the group that selects and creates its spokesperson and the
spokesperson who in turn creates the group. He sees in the delegation of

authority a kind of generic antimony between the individual and the group. On the one hand, the individual cannot exist politically without being part of a group. Any delegation is an act of group creation (Bourdieu 1991a: 205). Delegation is an 'act of magic' that enables a collection of individuals to form a corporate body that transcends individuals in significance and purpose (Bourdieu 1991a: 208). On the other hand, by becoming part of a group, individuals 'dispossess themselves in favour of a spokesperson' (Bourdieu 1991a: 204). Bourdieu speaks of this process of delegation in the language of 'bad faith', 'usurpatory ventriloquism' and 'usurpation'. He analyses the situation of the delegate as a 'sort of structural bad faith' in which the delegate conflates personal interests with those of the group, where both individual and group interests coincide. The individual delegate perceives his actions solely in terms of group interests and thereby fails to recognise his own individual interests at work as well. Not bad intentions but formative group processes drive delegation and consequence dispossession (Bourdieu 1991a: 209).[22]

The effects of delegation are 'dispossession', where subordinate groups give up their political voice to delegated representatives who usurp that delegated power in pursuit of their own individual and organisational interests. Dispossession is enhanced by professionalisation and bureaucratisation. The 'specific logic of *delegation*' tends to dispossess, in favour of professional officials (Bourdieu 1993a: 166). Dispossession is more likely to occur to those in the dominated classes without much cultural capital. Lacking cultural capital, individuals are more constrained to rely on delegates for their political voice (Bourdieu 1991a: 206). Bourdieu (1991a) clearly has in mind the French Communist Party and its affiliated labour unions in his analysis of political dispossession through delegation. Individuals without alternative sources of symbolic identity – the French working class – are more dependent upon their political party than are those with cultural capital. This enhances centralised party power but at the price of individual freedom and local control.

Thus the delegation of political authority for Bourdieu (1991a: 205) is an important form of political alienation. Ironically, like Michels (1962) in the 'iron law of oligarchy', Bourdieu too finds political alienation precisely in those political organisations whose political ideology seems most committed to combating it. In his words (1991e: 174), 'the concentration of political capital is at its greatest . . . in parties whose aim is to struggle against the concentration of economic capital'.

Bourdieu's analysis of delegation suggests that governance perspectives need to be attentive to the potentially stratifying effects of culture in the newly emerging patterns of political arrangements. A shift from the administrative centralism of the traditional Western European welfare state need not necessarily signal a radical step toward more democratic life. Traditional welfare state roles may be displaced by new cultural elites who become significant players in the more decentralised and diversified realm of political life. Yet the broad masses of people may not find a new voice or increased representation – a point not sufficiently appreciated in much governance thinking.

### The political doxa

Like other fields, the political field develops its own doxa, or political culture, a 'specific competence' which is learned through experience of how to behave politically (Bourdieu 2000b: 58). To be a serious contender in the political field requires a shared belief, regardless of political affiliation, that politics are important, that it takes experience to be a successful political leader, and that political leadership should be reserved for those with the requisite experience (2000b: 56). This political doxa is shared by all political professionals who otherwise compete for political capital.

Bourdieu (2000b: 60) stresses how the political doxa acts as a closure mechanism that erects a barrier to effective political expression for all but the well initiated. While acquired through professional experience, that political culture in France is increasingly becoming part of formal training in a few elite higher education institutions, such as the Paris Institut de science politique and the Ecole nationale d'administration (Bourdieu 2000b: 58–9). French political leadership has progressively passed from the hands of political activists to political professionals.

Bourdieu has been highly critical of the contemporary French political field arguing that it has largely become an enclosed, self-contained universe with less and less contact and understanding of everyday problems faced by French citizens. He sees French political leaders, technocrats, journalists, and intellectuals, all in their particular ways, caught within this closed world and unable to be genuine representatives of the larger public.

Bourdieu's criticism of the French political elite resonates with those governance voices who want to broaden the reach of democratic processes in modern societies. But in the case of France, Bourdieu sees the French state as occupying a central role in the distribution of power and yet abdicating moral responsibility in ways not found in most governance perspectives.

Bourdieu's field analytical framework has several features that overlap with concerns expressed by governance theorists. Politics need not be centred around a centralised state. There can be multiple and crosscutting levels and arenas of political conflict and policy formation that involve a great variety of actors and organisations. Field analysis brings Bourdieu close to the analytical level and strategy recommended by Rod Rhodes (1997: 29) for a governance perspective; namely, a 'meso-level' approach that links micro expressions of particular interests with macro power concerns. Thus Bourdieu's field analytical approach to politics, like the new governance perspective, brings into play a broader range of power centres contributing to political life than do approaches focused on the central organism of government.

Despite the social construction emphasis in much of Bourdieu's work, an emphasis suggesting that politics is a struggle over classifications, meanings, and boundaries one finds a growing emphasis in his later work on the dominating role in politics played by the centralised French state.[23] The state is the ultimate source of symbolic power. It is the ultimate referee of all classification struggles. Thus the state contributes to the unification of a cultural market (Bourdieu 1993b: 54). It is the basis of a national culture. From a governance perspective, this portion of Bourdieu's thinking remains very much in the traditional political theorist mode.

### Conclusion

I have outlined key features of Bourdieu's political sociology and suggested comparisons with some of the emerging governance perspectives regarding changing relations between modern welfare states, civil society and markets. Bourdieu anticipates some of the concerns found in governance perspectives, though he himself is not a governance theorist; indeed, he strongly opposes the normative neo-liberal ideas advocated by many governance thinkers. While a sharp critic of the centralised French state and the elitist character of its political class, Bourdieu nonetheless opposes privatisation of health, education and welfare services. He defends (1998c: 110) the need for state power to counterbalance the effects of markets, which, if left unchecked, will ultimately prove 'destructive' of 'collective structures' at the level of the nation, work groups, unions and the family. He urges (1998b) the mobilisation of citizens, particularly critical intellectuals, labour organisations and civil servants in the health, education and welfare sectors of the state, in defence of the social welfare functions historically assumed by Western European states. In response to the challenge of financial globalisation Bourdieu (1998b) would advocate the development of supranational state structures able to regulate international capital flows and markets and protect established collectivities. These views put him quite at odds with much governance thinking.

Nevertheless, other elements of his thought overlap with key concerns of many governance theorists. His theory of symbolic power opens the way to being attentive to new emerging forms of political practices that appear to transcend the boundaries of traditional political institutions (Bang and Sørensen 1999). His field-analytical perspective anticipates new forms of public/private interface that governance theorists stress. Yet the general tone of his political sociology is quite different from that of much governance writing. Jan Kooiman (1993: 1, 6), for example, employs the language of 'co-managing, co-steering and co-guidance' to describe and stress the new forms of co-operation between public and private sectors, and between different levels of decision making. This is strikingly different from Bourdieu's language of 'distinction', 'struggle' and 'domination'. Bourdieu has little to say about modes of co-operation; his fundamental concern is modes of domination. So while one finds in Bourdieu elements that echo concerns of the growing governance literature, the general tone of Bourdieu's conflict sociology is quite different from much governance thinking. Still, the impulse to expand democratic processes and to find new ways of doing so is shared by all.

## Notes

1  Alford and Friedland (1985), for example, situate Raymond Boudon in the pluralist camp but say nothing of Bourdieu. Bon and Schemeil (1980), Caro (1980), Robbins (1991), Wacquant (1992), Swartz (1997), Pinto (1998) and Fritsch (2000) are notable exceptions, devoting attention to both his political sociology and his underlying political project.

2  I have argued (Swartz 1997) that Bourdieu's stress on the symbolic aspects of power may lead one to lose sight of the physical and economic aspects. Bon and Schemeil (1980: 1202) also make the observation that Bourdieu does not pay enough attention to physical violence, a shortcoming, I might add, shared by many social scientists. Bourdieu sees the material and symbolic aspects as intimately interconnected, but his emphasis on the symbolic dimension may overshadow the physical and material aspects.

3  In contrast to Alain Touraine (1968), Bourdieu has devoted little attention to social movements, including the May 1968 student movement, which was analysed by virtually every French sociologist at the time. Bourdieu's (1988b; Bourdieu et al. 1971) observations on May 1968 come later and stress the effects of academic professionalisation and social stratification rather than the dynamics of a social movement.

4  Indeed, as Bon and Schemeil (1980: 1203) point out, Bourdieu refuses to grant political science the status of a genuine social science. He considers it a form of practical knowledge designed to assist professional politicians in advancing their interests within the political field. He calls it a 'false science' in that it legitimates this political practice as ostensibly scientific.

5  Bon and Schemeil (1980) and Pinto (1998) make similar assessments of the fundamentally political character of Bourdieu's sociology.

6  It is noteworthy that changes in American political sociology over the last several years seem more attentive today to the concerns animating Bourdieu's sociology. American political sociology has experienced a significant shift over the last thirty years from a behavioural to an institutional orientation (Robertson 1993; Orum 1996). There has been a shift away from behavioural studies of parties, voting, political participation, political attitudes, etc., and toward an increased interest in social institutions, particularly the welfare state, and social movements. Moreover, studies are increasingly informed by a historical perspective. With the important exception of his interest in French elites, Bourdieu has never shown much interest in the behavioural orientation of the old political sociology – focus voting, political parties, political participation, etc. Nor did Bourdieu participate in the neo-Marxist-inspired emphasis on the state that grew out of the turmoil of the 1960s. The work of Louis Althusser (1970) and Nicos Poulantzas (1975) contributed significantly to the rise in the 1970s in importance of the sub-fields of world systems, historical sociology and Marxist

sociology (Orum 1996: 140–1). Bourdieu was in fact quite critical of this Altusserian–Poulantzas emphasis that influenced American political sociology during that period. Bourdieu is much closer to the more recent emphasis on social institutions and the history of the modern welfare state that can be found, for example, in the work of Theda Skocpol (1992; Skocpol and Campbell 1995) and Charles Tilly (1978) than in the older behaviour orientation in political sociology. And Bourdieu has been a sharp critic of rational actor theory (Coleman *et al.* 1966; Hecter 1987), a rival trend to the New Institutionalism. Indeed, it is the explosion of interest in culture in American sociology, not the declining fortunes of political sociology, that has made Bourdieu's writings so attractive in the United States.

7 The all-pervading influence of power in human relations is stressed by certain governance theorists (see chapter 7 of this volume) who are careful not to divorce new forms of individualism in contemporary political life from power conflicts.

8 The term comes from Nelson Goodman (1978).

9 Bourdieu's emphasis on symbolic power overlaps with the anti-essentialist concerns of the governance perspective. Both stress the socially constructed character of political life.

10 Bourdieu (1988c) is sharply critical of most media-oriented political commentators, who, he believes, do not impose such a break on their observations and analyses. Rather, they have one foot in science and one foot in politics, performing a pseudo-science that in fact is oriented to specific political ends.

11 Bourdieu (Bourdieu and Wacquant 1992: 97) defines field as a network, or configuration, of objective relations between positions. These positions are objectively defined, in their existence and in the determinations they impose upon their occupants, agents or institutions, by their present and potential situation (*situs*) in the structure of the distribution of species of power (or capital) whose possession commands access to the specific profits that are at stake in the field, as well as by their objective relation to other positions (domination, subordination, homology, etc.).

12 See Swartz (1997: 118–22) for discussion of the origins and meta-theory of Bourdieu's concept of field.

13 He in fact sees this field of power as a 'transhistorical' structure whose existence pre-dates the rise of modern industrial societies. At its most general level, this chiasmatic structure represents the 'fundamental opposition of the division of labour of domination' across all societies that occurs 'between temporal and spiritual powers' (Wacquant 1993: 24).

14 Bourdieu's most comprehensive statement of this conceptualisation of the dominant class is to be found in *Distinction* (1984a: 114–15).

15 Clearly Bourdieu's political sociology, while seemingly informed by the class-conflict thinking of Marxism, breaks decisively with Marxist class analysis and economic determination of politics. Bourdieu (1985: 736) proposes a multi-dimensional stratification analysis (multiple fields of struggle develop degrees of autonomy from each other) and attributes to the political field in modern societies a degree of autonomy from the economy that is much closer to Weber than to Marx.

16 This is diagrammed explicitly in *Distinction* (Bourdieu 1984a: 452).

17 This is similar to Weber's (Gerth and Mills 1970; Weber 1978) idea of the political order.

18 The idea of 'force ideas' to distinguish the political from the religious, the cultural or intellectual is not fully satisfying, however. Religious ideas could also be thought of as mobilising forces; otherwise they secure no following. This points to ambiguity in defining what exactly is in the political field and what is not. Bourdieu acknowledges this ambiguity but contends that the problem lies not in his conceptualisation but in political reality itself. There is ambiguity precisely because the boundaries of what is political and what is not are themselves objects of struggle (2000: 74). Bourdieu has a point here, for the act of politicising an issue points up precisely a struggle over field boundaries – a good theoretical point but methodologically difficult to operationalise.

19 Bourdieu's view of political leadership as pursuing its own institutional interests resonates with the neo-Marxist view (Block 1977) of the role of state managers within a relatively autonomous state and with democratic elite pluralism (Bachrach 1966; Dahl 1967, 1972; Dye and Zeigler 1978). Bourdieu, however, sees the French state as a good deal more unified than pluralists suggest and more culturally determined than Marxists would allow.

20 I am indebted to Henrik Bang for suggesting this point. Bourdieu, however, would not go so far as Jessop (chapter 6 of this volume) to suggest that the state has lost so much of its sovereign authority that it competes virtually on a par with other centres of power. For Bourdieu the state remains central and should do so.

21 This field reductionist tendency is most striking in *Homo Academicus* (Bourdieu 1988b: xvii–xviii), where he boldly asserts that political stances among the Parisian professorate originate from their academic field positions rather than from broader class and political influences. Yet his analysis of the literary field seems to guard against this kind of field position reductionism. In this work he says that political stances are mediated more by strategies than by positions alone, that the field of political stances can take on a degree of autonomy of its own, since it is generated by strategies of differentiation in a field where to exist means to differ (1984b: 7, 1991d: 7). Thus the exact relationship of strategies to field positions seems unclear; perhaps Bourdieu sees that relationship varying from one field to another.

22 Bourdieu (1991a: 214) rejects the 'cynical view of the delegate as a conscious and organised usurper' as 'a very naive view, for all its apparent lucidity'. He stresses that the delegation process is generally perceived as a legitimate process and the 'legitimate imposture succeeds only because the usurper is not a cynical calculator who consciously deceives the people, but someone who in all good faith *takes himself to be* something that he is not'.

23 The dominant role of the French state in Bourdieu's analysis of politics undoubtedly reflects the particular type of state formation in France, reflecting a long national tradition of a highly centralised state with its origins extending back to the old regime. Yet it also stands in tension with the social constructionist orientation of his other work that stresses the micro-level of human agency. Bourdieu aims to incorporate and transcend micro and macro-levels of analysis in his sociology. Yet this part of his political sociology is decidedly more macro in orientation.

## References

Alford, R. A., and Friedland, R. (1985), *Powers of Theory: Capitalism, the State and Democracy* (New York: Cambridge University Press).

Althusser, L. (1970), *For Marx* (New York: Vintage Books).

Bachrach, P. (1966), *The Theory of Democratic Elitism* (Boston MA: Little Brown).

Bang, H. P., and Sørensen, E. (1999), 'The everyday maker: a new challenge to democratic governance', *Administrative Theory and Praxis* 21: 325–41.

Block, F. (1977), 'The ruling class does not rule: notes on the Marxist theory of the state', *Socialist Revolution* 33: 6–28.

Bon, F., and Schemeil, Y. (1980), 'La rationalisation de l'inconduite: comprendre le statut du politique chez Pierre Bourdieu', *Revue française de sociologie* 30: 1198–230.

Bourdieu, P. (1977), 'Questions de politique', *Actes de la recherche en sciences sociales* 16: 55–89.

Bourdieu, P. (1981), 'Décrire et préscrire: note sur les conditions de possibilité et les limites de l'efficacité', *Actes de la recherche en sciences sociales* 38: 69–73.

Bourdieu, P. (1984a), *Distinction: A Social Critique of the Judgement of Taste* (Cambridge MA: Harvard University Press).

Bourdieu, P. (1984b), 'Le champ littéraire: préalables critiques et principes de méthode', *Lendemains* 36: 5–20.

Bourdieu, P. (1985), 'Social space and the genesis of groups', *Theory and Society* 14: 723–44.

Bourdieu, P. (1987a), 'The force of law: toward a sociology of the juridical field', *Hastings Journal of Law* 38: 209–48.

Bourdieu, P. (1987b), 'What makes a social class? On the theoretical and practical existence of groups', *Berkeley Journal of Sociology* 32: 1–18.

Bourdieu, P. (1988a), 'Flaubert's point of view', *Critical Inquiry* 14: 539–62.

Bourdieu, P. (1988b), *Homo Academicus* (Stanford CA: Stanford University Press).

Bourdieu, P. (1988c), 'Penser la politique', *Actes de la recherche en sciences sociales* 71–2: 2–3.

Bourdieu, P. (1989a), *La Noblesse d'Etat: grandes corps et grandes écoles* (Paris: Minuit).

Bourdieu, P. (1989b), 'Social space and symbolic power', *Sociological Theory* 7: 14–25.

Bourdieu, P. (1991a), 'Delegation and political fetishism', in J. B. Thompson (ed.), *Language and Symbolic Power* (Cambridge MA: Harvard University Press), pp. 203–19.

Bourdieu, P. (1991b), 'Description and prescription: the conditions of possibility and the limits of political effectiveness', in J. B. Thompson (ed.), *Language and Symbolic Power* (Cambridge MA: Harvard University Press), pp. 127–36.

Bourdieu, P. (1991c), 'Identity and representation: elements for a critical reflection on the idea of region', in J. B. Thompson (ed.), *Language and Symbolic Power* (Cambridge MA: Harvard University Press), pp. 220–8.

Bourdieu, P. (1991d), 'Le champ littéraire', *Actes de la recherche en sciences sociales* 89: 4–46.

Bourdieu, P. (1991e), 'Political representation: elements for a theory of the political field', in J. B. Thompson (ed.), *Language and Symbolic Power* (Cambridge MA: Harvard University Press), pp. 171–201.

Bourdieu, P. (1993a), 'Culture and politics', in *Sociology in Question* (Thousand Oaks CA and London: Sage), pp. 158–67.

Bourdieu, P. (1993b), 'Esprits d'Etat: genèse et structure du champ bureaucratique', *Actes de la recherche en sciences sociales* 96–7: 49–62.

Bourdieu, P. (1993c), *Sociology in Question* (Thousand Oaks CA and London: Sage).

Bourdieu, P. (1998a), 'La pécarité est aujourd'hui partout', in P. Bourdieu (ed.), *Contre-feux* (Paris: Libre-Raisons d'Agir), pp. 95–101.

Bourdieu, P. (1998b), 'Le mythe de la "mondialisation" de l'Etat social européen', in P. Bourdieu (ed.), *Contre-feux* (Paris: Libre-Raisons d'Agir), pp. 34–50.

Bourdieu, P. (1998c), 'Le neo-liberalism, utopie (en voie de realisation) d'une exploitation sans limites', in P. Bourdieu (ed.), *Contre-feux* (Paris: Libre-Raisons d'Agir), pp. 108–19.

Bourdieu, P. (2000a), *Propos sur le champ politique* (Lyons: Presses Universitaires de Lyon).

Bourdieu, P. (2000b), 'Conférence: le champ politique', in *Propos sur le champ politique* (Lyons: Presses Universitaires de Lyon), pp. 49–80.

Bourdieu, P., and Wacquant, L. J. D. (1992), *An Invitation to Reflexive Sociology* (Chicago: University of Chicago Press).

Bourdieu, P., and Wacquant, L. J. D. (1998), 'Sur les ruses de la raison imperialiste', *Actes de la recherche en sciences sociales* 121–2: 109–18.

Bourdieu, P., Boltanski, L., and Maldidier, P. (1971), 'La défense du corps', *Social Science Information* 10: 45–86.

Caro, J-Y. (1980), 'La sociologie de Pierre Bourdieu: éléments pour une théorie du champ politique', *Revue française de science politique* 6: 1171–97.

Coleman, J. S., Campbell, E. Q., Hobson, C. J., McPartland, J., Mood, A. M., Weinfeld, F. D., and York, R. L. (1966), *Equality of Educational Opportunity* (Washington DC: US Government Printing Office).

Dahl, R. A. (1967), *Pluralist Democracy in the United States: Conflict and Consensus* (Chicago: Rand McNally).

Dahl, R. A. (1972), *Democracy in the United States: Promise and Performance* (Chicago: Rand McNally).

Durkheim, E. (1966), *The Rules of Sociological Method* (New York: Free Press).

Dye, T. R., and Zeigler, L. H. (1978), *The Irony of Democracy* (North Scituate MA: Duxbury).

Fritsch, P. (2000), 'Introduction', in P. Bourdieu (ed.), *Propos sur le champ politique* (Lyons: Presses Universitaires de Lyon), pp. 7–31.

Gerth, H. H., and Wright Mills, C. (1970), *From Max Weber: Essays in Sociology* (London: Routledge).

Goodman, N. (1978), *Ways of Worldmaking* (Indianapolis IN: Hackett).

Hecter, M. (1987), *Principles of Group Solidarity* (Berkeley CA: University of California Press).

Kooiman, J. (1993), 'Social-political governance: introduction', in J. Kooiman (ed.), *Modern Governance: New Government–Society Interactions* (London: Sage), pp. 1–6.

Lamont, M. (1989), 'Slipping the world back in: Bourdieu on Heidegger', *Contemporary Sociology* 18: 781–83.

Merrien, F-X. (1998), 'Governance and modern welfare states', *International Social Science Journal* 50: 57–67.

Michels, R. (1962), *Political Parties*, trans. E. a. C. Paul (New York: Free Press).

Orum, A. M. (1996), 'Almost a half century of political sociology: trends in the United States', *Current Sociology* 44: 108–31.

Pinto, L. (1998), *Pierre Bourdieu et la théorie du monde social* (Paris: Albin Michel).

Poulantzas, N. (1975), *Classes in Contemporary Capitalism* (London: Schocken).

Rhodes, R. A. W. (1997), *Understanding Governance: Policy Networks, Governance, Reflexivity and Accountability* (Buckingham: Open University Press).

Robbins, D. (1991), *The Work of Pierre Bourdieu: Recognizing Society* (Boulder CO: Westview Press).

Robertson, D. B. (1993), 'The return to history and the New Institutionalism in American political science', *Social Science History* 17: 1–36.

Skocpol, T. (1992), *Protecting Soldiers and Mothers: The Political Origins of Social Policy in the United States* (Cambridge MA: Belknap Press).

Skocpol, T., and Campbell, J. L. (1995), *American Society and Politics* (New York: McGraw-Hill).

Stoker, G. (1998). 'Governance as theory: five propositions', *International Social Science Journal* 50: 17–28.

Swartz, D. (1997), *Culture and Power: The Sociology of Pierre Bourdieu* (Chicago: University of Chicago Press).

Thompson, J. B. (ed.), *Language and Symbolic Power* (Cambridge MA: Harvard University Press).

Tilly, C. (1978), *From Mobalization to Revolution* (Reading MA: Addison Wesley).

Touraine, A. (1968), *Le Mouvement de Mai, ou le communisme utopique* (Paris: Seuil).

Wacquant, L. J. D. (1992), 'Toward a social praxeology: the structure and logic of Bourdieu's sociology', in P. Bourdieu and L. J. D. Wacquant (eds), *An Invitation to Reflexive Sociology* (Chicago: University of Chicago Press), pp. 2–59.

Wacquant, L. J. D. (1993), 'From ruling class to field of power: an interview with Pierre Bourdieu on *La Noblesse d'Etat*', *Theory, Culture, and Society* 10: 19–44.

Weber, M. (1978), *Economy and Society*, ed. G. W. Roth and C. Wittich (Berkeley CA: University of California Press).

# Part III
## Political theory and democratic governance

# 9

# The language of democracy and the democracy of language

John G. Gunnell

Custom is our nature. (Pascal)
>  . . . here we strike rock bottom, that is, we have come down
>  to conventions. (Wittgenstein)

The question that I am posing is one that underlies, either explicitly or implicitly, a great deal of contemporary political theory and, particularly, those dimensions of democratic theory that focus on discourse and deliberation. The question is whether it is possible to extrapolate, logically or by convincing warrants, democratic values and a demand for democratic governance from the fact, or facts, of language or speech. Is there something about the nature of language that requires or points toward democratic practice and are standards of democratic judgement inherent in language? A broader, but still further submerged, question is whether, in principle, any moral or political norms are entailed by linguistic theory.[1] What might be construed as an affirmative answer to this question has been most fully and familiarly elaborated in the work of Jürgen Habermas, but a variety of arguments about deliberative democracy as well as claims associated with the 'new institutionalism' also suggest something of this sort. Theorists as diverse, in some respects, as Charles Taylor and Chantal Mouffe have urged the idea of an essential connection between language and democratic practice, and, in a somewhat looser sense, both Michael Oakeshott and Richard Rorty have suggested that the polyphony and openness of the 'conversation of mankind' embody and sustain democratic values and practice (Oakeshott 1962; Rorty 1979). Although my basic purpose is neither to analyse nor to recount these arguments in any great detail, I will deal with some more fully at a later point. In the end, however, the question must be raised to a yet more general level.

Although an analysis of language and speech is often a convenient way of engaging more general issues regarding the explanation and judgement of human conduct,[2] language, narrowly conceived, is only one mode of conventionality, that is, of the practices and mediums that constitute social phenomena. Yet, in both philosophy and social theory, a general theoretical account of conventions has been lacking, and while many exponents of some form of connection between language and democracy stress the identity of conventionality and social reality, they are often ultimately nervous about what they fear to be the lack of limits, and substantive demands, that conventionalism seems to imply. I will, in the end, argue that there is a connection between conventionality and democratic values, but the claim will be parsed in a significantly different manner from that represented in the work of most contemporary theorists.

The general idea of a connection between conventionality and some form of self-rule, and attending values such as freedom and equality, is hardly novel. Much of traditional contract theory suggested a logical link between convention and what might be called popular sovereignty. Although contemporary interpretations of this literature have usually focused on the matter of natural rights, the work of thinkers such as Thomas Hobbes, John Locke, and J-J. Rousseau suggest that the basic concern, whether they advocated solidifying or limiting political order, was less with postulating individual rights than with demonstrating that a certain kind of rights claim was not valid, that is, a natural or extraconventional right to domination. The implication was that, since political rule was artificial, only consent and agreement could make it legitimate – either in its constitution or in its execution. This was, paradoxically, the essential message of the symbolism regarding a prior natural condition, just as it continues to be in John Rawls's more recent hypothetical postulate of an 'original position' (Rawls 1971). Although an image of such a situation was in various ways advanced as a standard, either positive or negative, the focus on nature served principally to demonstrate the conventional origins and character of civil society and sovereignty. Although we may sometimes attribute to these theorists, or their rhetoric may suggest, the view that the political realm could be somehow compared with or judged by the characteristics of a logically or temporally prior condition, any sharp distinction, either historical or analytical, was, in the end, illusory.

For Locke, the state of nature was, in fact, already social and conventional, even though he stressed the constructed character of civil society and government. Not only were language and the conditions of social intercourse in operation, but institutions such as property were in effect. Even in the case of Hobbes, the state of nature, despite the highly conflictual character he attributed to it, was not prior to language and agreement but only prior to certainty regarding linguistic meaning and the viability of such performances as promising. In the case of Rousseau, human beings in the primordial state of nature did not possess language and other attributes that would distinguish them on any other basis than physical form. In each case, then, any fundamental distinction between nature and convention dissolved. The real issue was what conventionality entailed with respect to the form of political society. For all these individuals, the conventionality of political society, despite the enigmas of representation, pointed in the direction of what amounted, at least, to popular sovereignty. Even in the case of Hobbes, essentially free and equal individuals both authored and embodied the sovereign, just as the existence of a sovereign constituted the people. Hobbes stressed the futility of both subjective and transcendental bases of judgement, that is, the claims of both Protestants and Catholics, and he noted that beliefs were, after all, usually belief in what someone had said. And Locke was no less a critic of the 'enthusiasm' of religious and political claims that were not the subject of communal agreement. In the seventeenth century, the idea of 'the people' was, from the beginning, as much a fiction as divine right, but in the political philosophy of the period the concept did underscore the conventionality of civil society in that 'the people' was a radically constructed entity. But the political implications of conventionality run deeper, both philosophically and historically.

A persistent theme in what is usually taken to be the canon of Western political thought, from Plato to Marx, is the claim that the human condition is naturally unnatural, that is, irreducibly conventional. What nature bestowed upon human beings was, ironically, the capacity, and the need, to transcend nature. While this idea carried with it a sense of freedom and openness, it also manifested an aura of fear from which political theory has been unable to extricate itself, fear not only regarding the integrity and stability of political life but with respect to the theorist's claim to the authority of knowledge as a basis of critical claims about particular configurations of politics. The idea of conventionality generates anxiety, since it might imply, in the manner which some may read Hobbes, that any political arrangement is equally justified, and it raises questions about the grounds and stability of standards of judgement. Thus there would seem to be two basic choices in thinking about democracy: to revert to seeking a non-conventional standard or to pursue a justification within conventionality itself. Both these choices have been manifest in the history of political thought, and they remain involved in the 'linguistic turn' in contemporary democratic theory.

The idea of an intrinsic and necessary connection between conventionality and democracy might be construed as beginning with Aristotle. For Aristotle, the *polis* was natural and necessary not in that it was a product of nature and biologically inevitable but rather in that human institutions tended, because of natural human needs and capacities, to evolve in that direction. Politics was an arena within which the capacities with which humans were naturally endowed, such as speech, reason, and collective action, could be developed and exercised. While nature might place certain limits, both contingent and necessary, on convention, and while there was a natural tendency for human associations to develop into a *polis*, nature did not dictate what specific conventions could and should exist. If human beings were denied the exercise of their basic or potential capacity, however, they would be less than human, and thus without the *polis* they were alienated from what Marx would later refer to as their 'species being', that is, their capacity to choose and construct. Furthermore, if, within society, some individuals were, unnaturally, denied their potential for equality and freedom with respect to the exercise of human capacities, especially with regard to participating in public discussion and decisions, they were diminished as humans and lost autonomy and identity. Consequently, it could be said that self-governance was natural and morally demanded – precisely, however, because human beings stand outside nature. This was also the basic trust of Rousseau's formulation.

Like Aristotle, Rousseau eschewed the term 'democracy' as a synonym for the proper conformation of political society – both because of certain historical connotations of the word and because he wished to reserve it for specifying a particular type of governmental institution. As in the case of all instances of government, he wished to construe it as serving an executive or administrative function distinct from sovereignty which was lodged in the people *qua* legislature. For Rousseau, the conventional constitution of the political realm released the individual, in part, from the necessitous forms of domination characteristic of private and social life and opened up a space, and dimension of freedom, characterised by equality and collective self-rule. Since there was no natural right to domination, political authority could be legitimised only by consent, but consent should yield true self-domination rather than some surrogate such as representation if it were to also give full play to the human potential for conventional action.

Thus there is reason to suggest that the 'traditional' justification for democracy or self-rule has rested on two basic principles: there is no natural right to domination and there must be equal freedom for the exercise of human conventional capacity. It is not difficult to see these basic claims reflected in the work of Marx, and, in the twentieth century, it was Hannah Arendt who most distinctly resurrected this line of argument. She rejected the idea of a human nature in favour of what she referred to as the 'human condition', and the core of that condition was conventionality. Human beings were distinguished by their possession of the capacity for making and, above all, doing. The political or public realm was a conventional realm, a product of artifice, and it was the space within which individuals realised themselves, literally created themselves, through speech and action. Through conventional behaviour in a public space, they transcended the private and social worlds which, while in the case of humans was also conventional, represented the dimensions of life which were generically or functionally shared by all animals. The human condition was natural to human beings but distinctly non-natural in that only by extending themselves into the realm of relatively unconstrained conventionality, despite the uncertainties that this entailed, did they become fully human. Thus one might say that, for Arendt, the very idea of democracy is once again rooted in language and convention.

To understand the more recent expression of this type of argument in democratic theory, it is necessary to recognise that it represents more than an emphasis on recapitulating the traditional idea of a public realm or public space and attending ideas of democracy. Most contemporary versions of 'linguistic democracy' are closely tied to images of what might be called critical theorising, that is, the pursuit of how, at least in principle, to bring philosophy to bear on political practice and distinguish between appearance and reality. While what is often termed the theory/practice problem was deeply embedded in the classic literature, the distribution of emphasis was more in the direction of coming to grips with the particularities of politics than in vouchsafing the claims of the theorist. This difference in emphasis is in part a consequence of the increasingly institutionalised distinctions between public and academic discourse, but it has served to accentuate the inherent ambivalence about conventionality. While the arguments are rooted in the premise of conventionality, they seek, at the same time, to transcend conventionality and assert grounds of epistemic, and practical, authority.

The most prominent example is Habermas's claim that there are 'conditions of rationality inherent in communicative action' and that rationality and democracy are mutually entailed (Habermas 1984: ix). Habermas has been one of several individuals who have found in the 'linguistic turn' in philosophy a way to retain an image of social science as an interpretive or hermeneutical form of cognition and yet escape the charges of intuitionism and subjectivity that have often plagued such a conception. The emphasis on the public character of language, as elaborated by Ludwig Wittgenstein, J. L. Austin, Peter Winch and others, seemed to offer an answer to the perennial problem of gaining access to 'other minds' and reducing the suspicion that haunted images of social enquiry based on 'consciousness philosophy'. But Habermas was uneasy with what he took to be the 'relativistic' implications of this position and sought a further 'public' significance in 'linguistic philosophy'. The very character of language, he suggested, might not only underwrite an image of the public sphere as a sharing of subjectivity but provide standards of rational democratic judgement and action.

From a conception of language in use, that is, speech, Habermas attempts to extrapolate quasi-transcendental criteria of rationality – the somewhat oxymoronic image of 'universal pragmatics'. Although he claims that all language, whatever the time and place, has inherent truth conditions, he argues that the grammar and propositional form characteristic of the speech and writing in modern Western natural languages has escaped the parochialism, that is, the context and particular referents, of oral culture in ancient and primitive societies and achieved a certain autonomy. It also provides a vehicle for the identity of the individual subject with respect to its relationship to the objective world as well as a basis for bridging subjectivities. Language is more than an instrument for representing the external world and communicating individual experience – and it carries with it general criteria for assessing truth in the sphere of human relations. Speech is a medium for reaching rational mutual understanding and contains standards for raising and redeeming validity claims. Consequently, modern society possesses the potential for general enlightenment and agreement, and the idea of democracy, which involves such things as uncoerced open discourse and consensus, is inherent in this condition. The spectre of relativism, the dark side of conventionality, can, he believes, be exorcised, since formal universal standards of judgement are derivable from the structure of communicative or illocutionary action and offer something comparable to 'scientific rationality' which, he argues, can 'claim validity beyond the context of particular cultures' (1984: 65).

Despite all the attention that Habermas's work has elicited, there has been little discussion of specific elements of his theory of action and the linguistic premises on which it is predicated. This is in part because his claims involve very complex philosophical issues which commentators are usually neither willing nor equipped to engage in detail. It is also because Habermas's account of language and human action is less argued than asserted and because the fundamental concern is not, in the final analysis, with a theory of language and human action but with advancing an image of critical theory. Habermas has taken aspects of very diverse philosophies and theories of language, ranging from the structuralism of Naom Chomsky to the transcendental pragmatics of K. O. Apel, linked them with certain elements of speech-act theory, placed them within the context of a philosophy of history, and woven them together into a corpus designed to support a theory that would 'validate its own critical standards' (1984: xxxix).

A less explicit attempt to establish a connection between language and democracy, with respect to both democratic values and democratic processes, characterises some of the claims associated with the New Institutionalism. As in the case of Habermas, this work has been influenced by the post-positivist linguistic focus in the philosophy of social science. The major assumption of individuals such as James March and Johan Olsen is that 'the perspectives of political discourse come to constitute political realities' and that 'institution-based' theories create 'political perspectives' that are more consistent with 'democratic hopes' than some of the prevailing forms of empirical political analysis such as rational choice theory and other approaches which focus on individual self-interest and aggregate political behaviour (March and Olsen 1989, 1995: 241). For the most part, the argument is the relatively straightforward one that action is a function of 'identities', both of individuals and of groups, and that these identities are formed – and transformed – through the medium of language. They present this approach as rescuing the significance of institutions as a whole, and stress that, in effect, conventionally constituted institutions are themselves political actors. And, as in the case of Habermas, they wish to reclaim the very idea of the public realm or the idea of the 'political' and the 'polity' as something with 'autonomy' and 'coherence' which cannot be reduced to a functional category or viewed merely as an arena for private and social behaviour. Political action, they claim, is guided by rules and institutions which 'constrain and shape politics through the construction and elaboration of meaning' and thereby 'enact social reality' (March and Olsen 1989: 3, 17, 38–9). Also, as with Habermas, there is an assumption that this approach has purchase as a way of solving the theory/practice problem and contributing to the creation of democratic institutions and identities. Exactly how language, democracy, and institutions come together in this approach as well as the precise terms of the theory that underlies it and its relevance to political practice remains somewhat vague.[3]

Although based on quite different assumptions about the nature of language and speech, Chantal Mouffe has also attempted to find in language a basis for defending the autonomy of 'the political' and, as in the case of Habermas's later work (1996), a pluralist theory of democracy that would also move in the direction of a neo-Marxist solution to the theory/practice problem (Mouffe 1993). The model of language to which she turns, however, is derived from the work of Jacques Derrida and concepts such as difference and undecidability. While Habermas looks to language for universal norms, Mouffe seeks support for democracy in the porousness and diversity of language. She argues that what is required is a political theory that reflects the contemporary philosophical critique of rational essentialism and universalism. It is now possible, she claims, 'thanks to post-structuralism', to formulate a radical democratic theory which accepts pluralism and other liberal democratic values while protecting pluralism from the pathology of closure that has haunted it in the past. Such a theory would, she argues, also provide the basis of a critical theory with political purchase.

Rather than attempting to transcend pluralism by relegating it to the private and social spheres and focusing on universal individual rights, Mouffe claims that it is 'constitutive *at the conceptual level* of the very nature of modern democracy' and 'something we should celebrate and enhance' (1996: 246). Traditional images of unanimity and homogeneity are fictions and, in the end, really based on subtle acts of exclusion. Yet, she claims, there must be 'essential limits' to difference, and it is necessary to reconstitute, but in a weaker (postmodern) sense, the republican idea of 'commonality' and common good, a 'we', or collective identity and citizen community as well as the idea of 'the *political*' as such. Her conception of 'the political', however, is basically a functional one grounded in the idea of the 'ineradicable character' of 'power and antagonism' and the manner in which they are constitutive of social phenomena. 'The political' is 'a discursively constituted ensemble of social relations' which mirrors the fact that the human subject is an ensemble of subject positions (1992: 11). Politics is the realm in which inevitable social antagonisms are expressed and is 'a practice of creation, reproduction, and transformation of social relations' which underlies all social relations (Laclau and Mouffe 1986: 111). Thus any social entity or position is 'ultimately political' and manifests what Derrida has called its 'constitutive outside' or the 'traces of acts of exclusion that govern its constitution' (Mouffe 1996: 247).

The moral that Mouffe draws from these claims is that every attempt to achieve hegemony is contingent, society never really 'is', so to speak, since there is fundamental antagonism at the base of every association which defeats its ability to be a stable whole. Since identity is ultimately based on difference, the normative conclusion is that everyone must accept the particularity and partiality of their position and abjure any claim to a special place. Democracy is belied by claims to a universal rational consensus, since such claims are always based on covert prejudice and a position of power. Like meaning in language, human affairs are distinguished by ultimate 'undecidability' which cannot be eliminated and which is the essence of 'the political' and can be repressed only at our own risk. Although we should not relinquish totally the idea of universality, it should, like truth and meaning, be 'conceived as a horizon that can never be reached' rather than a basis of closure (1996: 254).

Charles Taylor's image of the connection between language and democracy, as well as his concern about the authority of the theorist, is somewhat less schematic than that of either Habermas or Mouffe, but similar assumptions and concerns hover behind much of his work. First of all, Taylor subscribes to the general proposition that language is a peculiarly human way of being together and 'serves to place some matters out in the open between interlocutors. One might say that language enables us to put things in public space' and even 'serves to found public space' and that 'a flourishing public space is essential to democracy' (1985: 258–9, 1995: 278). Very early on, Taylor challenged positivist and behaviourist accounts of social scientific explanation in favour of an image of the 'sciences of man' as interpretive or hermeneutic endeavours and of social reality as linguistically constituted and intersubjectively shared (1964, 1970, 1971). While the scientific method, as described by positivist philosophies, could be applied to the 'brute data' of natural science, the autonomy of the social sciences and their methodology are predicated on the distinctness of the phenomena which they study.

Taylor's ultimate concern, however, was not simply to establish the hermeneutic character of social science but to argue for the possibility of a critical meta-science that through gains in 'insight' would expose 'inauthenticity, bad faith, and self-delusion' and 'replace this confused, incomplete, partly erroneous self-interpretation by a correct one' or one with 'greater clarity'. Such an image, however, required overcoming what he feared were the relativistic implications of conventionality. Taylor sought something comparable to the certainty of natural scientific judgement and its epistemology 'whose validity cannot be questioned by offering another interpretation or reading' and to which the 'progress of science has lent great credibility' (Taylor 1971: 112–113). First, as opposed to postmodern and post-structural construals, he postulated, although vaguely, a tran-scendental subject that was the bearer and determiner of meaning. Second, much like Habermas, and explicitly in contradiction to what he understands to be the arguments of individuals such as Michel Foucault, he adopts a philosophy of history which assumes increasing rationality and a 'signifi-cant gain of truth' (Taylor 1984: 179) represented, for example, in the progress of natural science. Taylor believes that progress and the attainment of truth that transcends configurations of power is also evident in the evo-lution of liberal democracy, which has been, and can be further, enhanced by the enlightening impact of 'valid theory' on practice (Taylor 1983: 74, 85). The criteria of such 'validation' are not easily specified, but, for Taylor, it has to do with the 'sensibility' and 'superiority' of certain interpreters and interpretative positions that allows distinctions between 'error' and 'illu-sion' (Taylor 1971: 127).

For Taylor, the pressing issue in democratic theory and practice today is that of multiculturalism and other issues involving equal status of various groups (Taylor 1992). He believes that the demand for authenticity can go too far and obscure the 'horizonal' and 'dialogical' character and diversity of human life. What is required, he argues, is a liberalism rooted in a 'politics of difference' and 'recognition' that acknowledges and respects the identity and integrity of groups while retaining a traditional concern with basic individual rights and immunities. Too often, however, the abstract 'universalisms' of liberal democracy reflect substantive hidden values of society and fail to affirm adequately the worth of particular groups. Yet Taylor remains concerned not only about the epistemic issue of relativism but with the concomitant extreme social pluralism implied in the work of individuals such as Derrida and Foucault. While he claims that we should begin by presuming the 'equal worth' of all groups and cultures and accord-ing them equal respect, we cannot, in the end, escape comparative judge-ment. Taylor is not very specific about the criteria of such judgement apart from suggesting, in accordance with his general philosophy of history, that we should assume that 'all human cultures that have animated whole soci-eties over some considerable stretch of time have something important to say to all human beings' (1992: 66).

One basic problem with all these claims about language and democracy is that they do not get to grips with the details of a theory of language, let alone conventionality as such. And while much of this literature involves assumptions and claims about the relationship between types or levels of practice and forms of discourse, such as social science and politics, these relationships are not very thoroughly explored, either analytically or his-torically. What follows is some specific but summary claims about such matters[4] which I will offer as a preface to reconsidering the issue of the rela-tionship between language and democracy.

Conventions are manifest in three basic modes: thought, language or sym-bolisation, and action. Once we give an account of these modalities, we have, in effect, given an account of conventionality. As modes of conventionality, none has a particular privileged theoretical status, and they each bear no general explanatory relationship to one another even though an instance of one can, in particular circumstances, be construed as the cause of, or giving rise to, an instance of another. The reason that we often find it so compelling to conceive, for example, of social reality in terms of the model of a text, or to think of speech as a manner of 'doing', or to describe thought linguistically, is because we are talking about forms of theoretically identical things, that is, conventions. The structures and properties that are common to thought, speech, and action and that make them theoretically the same constitute too large an issue to explore fully in this context, but the basic point is the theoretical autonomy of conventions.

Conventionality can also be analysed in terms of the generic forms of practice and discourse in which thought, speech, and action are manifest. The most fundamental distinction is between *first-order* practices and *meta-practices*. Meta-practices are, simply, those supervenient practices that have other practices or activities as their object of knowledge and gain much of their identity in terms of their real and perceived *cognitive* and *practical* relationship to that object. Examples of meta-practices of the *second order*, that is, those that study *first-order* practices, include political science and political theory, sociology, history, philosophy, literary criticism, and a number of enterprises less associated with the academy – such as sportscasting, theatre criticism, and journalism.

First-order practices are, by definition, what second-order practices talk about – that is, they include natural science, religion, politics, and common sense and other forms of ordinary language. Political societies have their own embedded meta-discourses, so, already, identifying first-order practices is not a matter of finding realms in which first-order discourses govern exclusively. What most fundamentally distinguishes first-order symbolic configurations, however, is that they not only define and conceptually and practically constitute themselves, reflectively or unreflectively, but, in varying ways and degrees, project an image or paradigm of a world, whether natural or social, external to themselves, in which they are situated. The criterion of this 'world' is not something which meta-practices can unilaterally and authoritatively adjudicate, since it is, in effect, a discursive residue of first-order practice.

Since the phenomena encountered by the social sciences and other second-order practices are conventional and artefactual, they are not, in the first instance, functions of or constituted by social scientific interpretation. They are discursively autonomous and *pre-constituted* and, in an important sense, as Wittgenstein said about forms of life, 'given'. This fact has significant implications, one of which is that, unlike first-order discourses and practices, their subject matter always, so to speak, exceeds its theoretical domain. While it would make little sense to speak about the difference between nature and natural science's conception of nature without resorting to the paradigm of another first-order discourse, it is always necessary to distinguish, for example, between politics and second-order accounts of politics.

The position at the core of the theoretical and taxonomic nexus that I am defending is what I will call *conventional realism*. Although, for many, the concept of convention implies something ephemeral, if not ultimately subjective, conventions, as such, are not only theoretical entities (as real as atoms, DNA, etc.) but irreducible and incommensurable. Conventions are not only, as such, theoretically real objects but, pragmatically encountered, have an objective public existence, a 'givenness', in a manner that natural objects do not. While many theorists have been adamant about distinguishing between natural and social science and stressing the conventional character of the subject matter of the latter, they nevertheless, as in the case of individuals such as Habermas and Taylor, predicated the distinction on a latent positivist assumption regarding the unique givenness of natural objects.

When we talk, from a philosophical or second-order perspective, about the relationship between a first-order practice such as natural science and its object of knowledge, that is, 'reality' or the 'natural world', we are talking about a grammatical, or discursive, internal relationship. This claim is not a defence of metaphysical idealism but only a recognition of the fact that 'nature' has no meaning independent of its formulation in natural science or some other first-order discourse – any more than philosophers of religion can talk about god, and the relationship between religion and god, apart from how it appears in the discursive universe of religious practice. Unlike the 'world' constituted in the discourse of natural science, the object of second-order enquiry is not, in the first instance, the discursive residue of second-order theoretical practice. The relationship between social science and its object is not merely 'grammatical'. That object is itself a discursive realm with its indigenous theoretical vision of itself and the world. What, then, are we to make of a whole range of contemporary second-order claims, in both the philosophy of social science and political theory, that suggest that second-order discourses either possess some form of epistemic privilege or inhabit a position of reflective transpectivity which allows their perspicuous understanding and account of the 'other' to supersede the latter's self-image and view of reality? And what are the implications for democratic commitments?

We might say that there is, for example, a sense in which the philosophy of natural science understands science, that is, its logic and epistemology, better than science understands itself. After all, science is more interested in the world than in self-reflection. Similarly, we might conclude that, in principle, social science is in a better position to understand social practices than the practices themselves. All this would assume a large degree of simultaneous disinterestedness and intense engagement, but images of a critical social science go considerably further. Like psychiatrists, they claim to know the 'world' constituted by first-order practices in a more authoritative and true manner than the inhabitants of those practices and to be able to relate to it therapeutically. Once this kind of claim is made there is no longer simply a *cognitive* issue but a *practical* one, since social science presents its truth in competition with society. Second-order knowing, that is, enquiry directed toward conventional objects, involves a theoretical and practical confrontation between two discursive realms.

The character of first-order discourses, and the discursive constitution of reality, have implications for thinking about democracy which will be more fully elaborated at a later point, but two promissory remarks are in order. Such discourses are, in the last analysis, incomparable both in the lateral sense of their relationship to each other and from the perspective of second-order commentary. Any pre-eminence in the relationship between first-order discourses – let us say, between natural science and religion or between natural science and politics – must be conventional, that is, it has no neutral epistemic or ontological basis. Similarly, the claims of second-order discourse regarding these realms constitutes unajudicable theoretical, descriptive, and normative challenges whose resolution must ultimately, as in the case of the relationship between first-order discourses, be a practical matter. In the modern world, however, the only basis on which second-order practices can make a practical claim on first-order practices is via the authority of knowledge. Political theory, for example, usually has no political authority, any more, or less, than the philosophy of science has scientific authority. This is the reason for the consistent worry, even obsession, within second-order practices, including the philosophy of science and political theory, about relativism and which creates uneasiness about conventionality. It is actually less a reflection of concern about the loss of criteria of judgement in the practices that it studies than a repressed fear about the vulnerability of its own cognitive, and consequently practical, authority. This is still the dream of second-order discourse – to find a basis of its epistemic authority and one that is guaranteed by the very nature of the subject matter.

One implication of conventional realism is that there cannot, literally, be a theory of politics, since politics is only a historically limited form of conventionality. The only universality attaching to politics is either historical continuity or a certain definitional or functional universality such as when we identify politics with some characteristic attribute such as power or the authoritative allocation of values. This also means that even less can there be any such thing as a general theory of democracy – any more, for example, than there can be a theory of chess. Democratic theory is, so to speak, a recommendation about how to play the game of politics, and to argue that the game, by its very nature, or the nature of games as such, demands that it must be played according to a certain strategy or must represent a certain form is untenable. So, once again, the issue is whether there is a connection between democracy and conventionality, but it is clear that the connection cannot, strictly speaking, be *theoretical* even though there may be theoretically grounded reasons for choosing democracy.

Glaucon, in Plato's *Republic*, posed the question of whether forms of political order and standards of justice are based on anything more than convention and agreement, and although the question was not answered definitively by Socrates, or by Plato in the work as a whole, it was unambiguous that, however ultimately achieved and justified, they are in practice *always* based on human action and opinion. This was part of the radicalness of Plato's work, that is, the severance of politics from nature, and the problem was that, once so disjoined, were there any extraconventional criteria or grounds for either constraining or vindicating particular forms of politics? There was, however, a problem with the very formulation of this issue – one which, I would suggest, Plato was very aware of and which in large measure subtly structured the dialogue. The problem was that all claims about extraconventional phenomena (nature, God, etc.) are, themselves, conventionally constituted. As Wittgenstein noted, it is 'impossible to describe the fact which corresponds to . . . a sentence, without simply repeating the sentence' (1980: 10). The real issue involved in asking whether there are extraconventional criteria for evaluating and judging political convention is the status of the claim of one order of discourse to epistemic, and practical, authority over another. The attempt to ground democracy in language is in part an attempt to circumvent the dilemma of second-order discourse at a time when the authority of such discourse based on traditional foundationalist meta-narratives has been called into question. The problem with such a move is that, despite the arguments of Habermas and others, it is impossible to extrapolate from the fact of conventionality a prescription for the substantive form it should take. But although democracy is not vouchsafed by the nature of language, there are good reasons that may be adduced for arguing that conventionality points toward, provides defensible reasons for, a choice of democracy.

It is in the work of Wittgenstein that we find the most direct and influential account of human activity as linguistic and conventional and the most detailed exploration of the relationship between first and second-order discourses. The attempt to link Wittgenstein with political theory has, however, been frustrating and disappointing. Hanna Pitkin, for example, has explored extensively the question of the manner in which there might be a Wittgensteinian political theory and how Wittgenstein's work might have applications for political theorising. Pitkin focused on a variety of things such as Wittgenstein's concern with the particular and ordinary; the manner in which politics consists of and is revealed in language; the implications of his work for an analytical treatment of political concepts and argument; the manner in which his ideas provide an epistemology for understanding political action and institutions; and the sense in which his work could show how people 'entrap' themselves yet find 'democratic ways' of escaping. She avows 'that Wittgenstein has sustained both my stubbornly persistent democratic hopes', but two decades after the initial publication of her book the exact connection between Wittgenstein, political theory, and democracy seems difficult to articulate (Pitkin 1972/1993: xvii–xviii). And what persists in Pitkin's analysis is what would seem to be a latent very 'unWittgensteinian' attachment to the essentiality of 'the political' as well as a continuing concern with establishing a basis for the epistemic authority of political theory *vis-à-vis* politics.

More recently, Mouffe has also turned explicitly to Wittgenstein for a corroboration of her pluralist vision and her image of critical theorising. His vision of reality as an 'ensemble of language games', she suggests, challenges the model of rational argumentation characteristic of the 'universalising and homogenising mode' associated with individuals such as Habermas and Rawls and offers 'a *new way of theorising about the political*' which both escapes the paradox of choosing between universality and difference and bridges the gap between philosophical and political discourse (Mouffe 2000). As in the case of Pitkin, a paradox in Mouffe's use of Wittgenstein is that it continues to ontologise politics and to assert the epistemic privilege of second-order discourses. Nigel Pleasants, however, has sought to demonstrate at length how Wittgenstein's work points up the 'incoherence and impotence of critical social theory', as it has been advanced by many contemporary academic theorists, as well as its anti-democratic implications and its failure to confront the epistemological and practical distance between second and first-order discourses such as social science and politics (1999). Much of philosophy and social theory, despite its initial infatuation with conventionality, seeks, in the end, for transconventional standards and for a basis of second-order superiority.[5]

Alice Crary, in an extensive survey of attempts to bring Wittgenstein's work to bear on political thought, has focused on the striking convergence of left and right-wing criticisms of Wittgenstein for what they take to be the manner in which he relativised discourses and held them 'immune to external criticism'. She rejects these 'inviolability interpretations' and the attempt to locate his work within the 'logical space' defined by the poles of use theories of meaning and theories based on external fixed criteria, but she suggests that Wittgenstein offers a view of immanent rational critique. Much like Rorty, she sees in his work an 'edifying' potential and suggests that 'the contribution Wittgenstein's philosophy makes to political thought is a function of what it teaches us . . . about how the exercise of rational responsibility requires a distinctly human form of activity in language', and 'that this lesson is one which we would find reflected in forms of social life that embody the ideals of liberal democracy' (2000: 120, 140–1). Such notions of social pluralism, epistemic diversity, and the like are, indeed, implicit in Wittgenstein's work, but there are yet more radical democratic implications.

Wittgenstein directs our attention more deeply than any previous philosopher to the autonomy of the 'ordinary', that is, the conventionality of social life, and this, in turn, reminds us that there is no authority and right other than the conventional. The real point is not, any more than it was for the original contract theorists, that the individual (or self or subject) is primordial and inviolable but, in some ways quite the opposite, that the self is in the end a conventional, and public, entity. Individual cognitive capacities are not the source of meaning and value, and consciousness itself is a public phenomenon. And what some earlier theorists, such as John Stuart Mill, may have referred to as the inevitable fallibility of human choice can be rephrased in Wittgensteinian terms as the impossibility of transcending conventions. Knowledge is, in the end, grounded in mutual acknowledgement and in criteria relative to what Wittgenstein called a 'form of life'. If there are no transconventional standards of judgement, immanent or transcendental, then it would seem that the 'logic of democracy' is persuasive, that is, the logic of popular sovereignty and equal participation. This kind of argument for democracy had its heyday in the 1930s but fell out of favour with the advent of a felt need to find a basis for an absolutist condemnation of totalitarian practices (Gunnell 1993: chapter 6). The persistent idea, however, that events such as the Holocaust are the consequence of the loss, or infiltration, of some philosophical idea is a distinctly academic affectation. Fear of relativism, however, is a distinctly meta-practical anxiety which emanates less from a concern about intellectual and political anarchy in first-order realms such as science and politics than from the problematics of second-order discourses. What is often construed as the source of relativism is precisely what I have termed conventional realism, but which, I would urge, is actually is less an invitation to nihilism than a reason to embrace democracy.

In the end, it is difficult to link Wittgenstein with concrete exemplars of contemporary democratic theory, despite the emphasis on discourse and pluralism in a wide range of current literature. It is difficult to escape the residue of elitism in social scientific images of democratic practice (Etzioni-Halevy 1993, 1999), and while the democratic implications of conventionalism for what we might think of as the 'horizontal' dimensions of social interaction might be viewed as quite obvious and acceptable to many, the implications for the 'vertical' relationship between second-order discourses and practices, such as philosophy and political theory, and their object of analysis are more contentious. The conjunction of democracy and the ordinary finds its most distinct expression in the theory of governance as democracy from below (Bang and Sørensen 1999; Bang and Dyrberg 2001; Rhodes 1997), but, despite their allegiance to some abstract vision of democracy, most political theorists find it difficult to accept the kind of tolerance of the 'ordinary' and conventional that Wittgenstein's work entails.

Although it has often been pointed out that in Wittgenstein's work there is nothing that we can call, in the traditional sense, a theory of either language or conventions, we might reasonably suggest that it represents, or exemplifies, a kind of phenomenology or natural history of conventional practices which supports certain generalisations regarding these matters and presents, as Peter Winch suggested so long ago, an 'idea of a social science' (Winch 1958). If we assume that the subject matter of the human and social sciences is action and institutions, then Wittgenstein's work illuminates this terrain. And this idea of a social science included calling into question any natural superiority and universality regarding the status of second-order practices. Wittgenstein consistently rejected what he called 'theory', by which he meant a universal reductive answer to questions such as 'What is meaning and understanding?' and 'How can language represent?' One implication of his work is that we should not seek a second-order theory of politics (Gunnell 1998: chapters 1–2), or even a theory of democracy, since politics, despite what we may understand to be the universality of its principal attributes and functions (power, interest, order, etc.), is only a historically contingent genus of practice, and democracy is only a species of that practice. The political theorist is continually seduced into essentialising 'the political', and Wittgenstein helps to show us the way out of this trap as well as how we may have been seduced into it.

The dilemma that lies at the heart of contemporary democratic theory, however, is still the question of how we can valorise both conventionality and democracy, on the one hand, along with the rejection of second-order claims to transcendent reason that they both seem to entail, and still cling to the possibility of some form of critical judgement that exceeds that of 'normal' (in a Kuhnian sense) first-order claims. One way of posing this issue is to think about the constant tension in Wittgenstein's work between the descriptive and therapeutic attitudes, that is, the claim that, on one hand, what must be accepted is the forms of life, that philosophy leaves everything as it is, and that the task of philosophy is descriptive rather than explanatory and normative, and, on the other hand, the image of philosophy as a critical activity that seeks to release us from the pictures that hold us captive and to show us the way out of the 'fly bottle'. How can the philosopher, the second-order commentator, mediate between what Wittgenstein referred to as the 'ice' and the 'rough ground', that is, stay focused on the 'ordinary' and stop language from going on holiday and at the same time map and clarify that ground? One commentator has suggested what she calls the situation of 'privileged marginality' (Scheman 1996).

Naomi Scheman recognises that the issue 'of where one can stand to obtain a perspective on a set of practices that is simultaneously informed and critical is a deep and central question for political theory'. If the criterion of judgement is found in conventional practices, how is it possible to find a basis for disapproving of a form of life without being drawn toward an external realm that causes us to slip and ignore the complexities of the world in which real decisions must be made? 'How can we make intelligible that depth and extent of dissatisfaction with the rough ground of our forms of life without invoking transcendent standards?' Scheman contends that, first of all, we must reject Manichaean readings of Wittgenstein revolving around poles of conservatism, moral realism, or political acquiescence, on the one hand, and critical deconstruction on the other hand. Scheman argues that, despite Wittgenstein's personal inhibitions regarding practical involvement, 'we' professional philosophers and academicians potentially occupy 'social locations' that are 'privileged *as marginal*' and which at once make it possible to 'politicise' such locations and 'give what we say and do a claim to legitimacy'. Like 'diasporic Jews', philosophers can have an idea of home which is neither any existing place nor a utopia without friction. In modern societies, the philosopher is neither 'native' nor 'stranger' and may engage in critical transformative work (1996: 390–1, 394, 399, 403). All this may sound attractive, but there are at least three basic problems that are elided in Scheman's discussion.

First of all, she does not deal with the actual situation of the philosopher's relationship to politics in any specific society. Second, she still assumes that philosophy has some inherent capacity for perspicuity that transcends the practices about which it speaks. And, finally, she does not consider the implications of 'privilege' – marginal or otherwise – for democratic practices and principles. It would seem that, to be true to conventionality as the 'stuff' of social reality as well as to democracy, the philosopher must either descend into the 'cave' and enter the first-order forms of life or engage those forms on some basis other than even the attenuated form of epistemic privilege that Scheman suggests. When Wittgenstein made statements to the effect that philosophy must accept the forms of life as given and that philosophy left everything as it is, his point, I would suggest, was both that the activity of philosophy, and of second-order practices in general, did not, as such, transform its subject matter and that the criterion of truth and knowledge in such practices was neither grounded in nor disestablished by philosophical analysis. This in no way prohibited a practical therapeutic relationship between first and second-order discourses, but it did suggest that the relationship could not be conducted on the presumption of the inherent authority of the latter, that second-order discourses would have to enter the conversation of humankind on a level playing field.

Conventionality entails that the relationship between theory and practice should also be a democratic relationship, since there are no hierarchical grounds on which it can be based. The question of how second-order discourses can at once recognise conventionality and seek critical purchase is predicated on the false premise that there is some general answer. As long as political theory holds on to an image of even 'privileged marginality' as its home, it will find that, in fact, 'there is no place like home' and that its commitment to democracy is ultimately fraught with paradox. Scheman suggests that we may take heart from the story of the Wizard of Oz, who turned out to be just another person without any special powers but yet, because of the status he was accorded, enabled others to realise their true selves. There is, however, no need to persist in the myth of social theory as wizardry and the contradictions in democratic commitment that it involves.

## Notes

1 An overview of the relationship between language and politics, Dallmayr (1984), is typically inconclusive, as is the broader discussion of language and norms Dallmayr and Benhabib (1991).
2 See, for example, Ricoeur (1971) and, for a broader survey, Shapiro (1981).
3 For a consideration of the theoretical underpinning that is missing in this kind of account see Bloor (1997).
4 For a fuller treatment of conventions and the relationship between forms of discourse and practice see Gunnell (1998).
5 See, for example, Bernstein (1976), Hollis and Lukes (1982) and Searle (1995). For a criticism of this kind of literature see Gunnell (1998).

## References

Bang, H. P., and Dyrberg, T. B. (2001), 'Governance, self-representation and the democratic imagination', in M. Saward (ed.), *Democratic Innovation: Deliberation, Representation and Association* (London: Routledge).

Bang, H. P., and Sørensen, E. (1999), 'The everyday maker: a new challenge to democratic governance', *Administrative Theory and Praxis* 21: 325–41.

Bernstein, R. (1976), *The Restructuring of Social and Political Thought* (New York: Harcourt Brace).

Bloor, D. (1997), *Wittgenstein, Rules and Institutions* (London: Routledge).

Crary, A. (2000), 'Wittgenstein's philosophy in relation to political thought', in A. Crary and R. Read (eds), *The New Wittgenstein* (London: Routledge).

Dallmayr, F. (1984), *Language and Politics* (Notre Dame IN: University of Notre Dame Press).

Dallmayr, F., and Benhabib, S., eds (1991), *The Communicative Ethics Controversy* (Cambridge MA: MIT Press).

Etzioni-Halevy, E. (1993), *The Elite Connection* (Cambridge: Polity Press).

Etzioni-Halevy, E. (1999), 'Elites, inequality and the quality of democracy in ultra-modern society', *International Review of Sociology – Revue internationale de sociologie* 9 (2): 239–50.

Gunnell, J. G. (1993), *The Descent of Political Theory: The Genealogy of an American Vocation* (Chicago: University of Chicago Press).

Gunnell, J. G. (1998), *The Orders of Discourse: Philosophy, Social Science, and Politics* (Lanham MD: Rowman & Littlefield).

Habermas, J. (1984), *The Theory of Communicative Action I, Reason and the Rationalization of Society* (Boston MA: Beacon Press).

Habermas, J. (1996), *Between Facts and Norms* (Cambridge MA: MIT Press).

Hollis, M., and Lukes, S., eds (1982), *Rationality and Relativism* (Cambridge MA: MIT Press).

Laclau, E., and Mouffe, C. (1985), *Hegemony and Socialist Strategy: Towards a Radical Democratic Politics* (London: Verso).

March, J. G., and Olsen, J. P. (1989), *Rediscovering Institutions: The Organizational Basis of Politics* (New York: Free Press).

March, J. G., and Olsen, J. P. (1995), *Democratic Governance* (New York: Free Press).

Mouffe, C. (1992), 'Democratic citizenship and the political community', in C. Mouffe (ed.), *Dimensions of Radical Democracy: Pluralism, Citizenship, and Community* (London: Verso).

Mouffe, C. (1993), *The Return of the Political* (London: Verso).

Mouffe, C. (1996), 'Contesting the boundaries of the political', in S. Benhabib (ed.), *Democracy and Difference* (Princeton NJ: Princeton University Press).

Mouffe, C. (2000), *The Democratic Paradox* (New York: Verso).

Oakeshott, M. (1962), *Rationalism in Politics and other Essays* (New York: Basic Books).

Pitkin, H. F. (1972, 1993), *Wittgenstein and Justice* (BerkeleyCA: University of California Press).

Pleasants, N. (1999), *Wittgenstein and the Idea of a Critical Social Theory* (New York: Routledge).

Rawls, J. (1971), *A Theory of Justice* (Cambridge MA: Harvard University Press).

Rhodes, R. A. W. (1997), *Understanding Governance: Policy Networks, Governance, Reflexivity and Accountability* (Buckingham: Open University Press).

Ricoeur, P. (1971), 'The model of the text', *Social Research* 38: 529–62.

Rorty, R. (1979), *Philosophy and the Mirror of Nature* (Princeton NJ: Princeton University Press).

Scheman, N. (1996), 'Forms of life: mapping the rough ground', in H. Sluga and D. G. Stern (eds), *The Cambridge Companion to Wittgenstein* (Cambridge: Cambridge University Press).

Searle, J. (1995), *The Construction of Social Reality* (New York: Free Press).

Shapiro, M. (1981), *Language and Political Understanding: The Politics of Discursive Practices* (New Haven CT: Yale University Press).

Taylor, C. (1964), *The Explanation of Behaviour* (London: Routledge).

Taylor, C. (1970), 'The explanation of purposive behaviour', in R. Borger and F. Cioffi (eds), *Explanations in Behavioural Science* (Cambridge: Cambridge University Press).

Taylor, C. (1971), 'Interpretation and the sciences of man', *Review of Metaphysics* 65: 3–51.

Taylor, C. (1983), 'Political theory and practice', in C. Lloyd (ed.), *Social Theory and Political Practice* (Oxford: Clarendon Press).

Taylor, C. (1984), 'Philosophy and its history', in R. Rorty, J. B. Schneewind and Q. Skinner (eds), *Philosophy in History* (Cambridge: Cambridge University Press).

Taylor, C. (1985), *Human Agency and Language* (Cambridge: Cambridge University Press).

Taylor, C. (1992), 'The politics of recognition', in A. Gutmann (ed.), *Multiculturalism* (Princeton NJ: Princeton University Press).

Taylor, C. (1995), *Philosophical Argument* (Cambridge MA: Harvard University Press).

Winch, P. (1958), *The Idea of a Social Science* (London: Routledge).

Wittgenstein, L. (1980), *Culture and Value* (Oxford: Blackwell).

# 10
## Contingency and the limits of contract

Tracy B. Strong

> The new development for our age cannot be political, for politics is a dialec-
> tical relationship between the individual and the community in the *represen-*
> *tative* individual; but in our times the individual is in the process of becoming
> far too reflective to be able to be satisfied with being merely *represented*.
> (Kierkegaard, *Journals*, 1846)
>     Briefly put – Alas! – this will for a long time be kept silent about: What will
> not (henceforth) be built any more, cannot be built any more is – a society in
> the old sense of that word. To build this building everything is lacking, above
> all the material. *All of us are no longer material for a society*; this is a truth
> for which the time has come. (Nietzsche, *The Gay Science*, No. 356)

These two citations describe modernity as lacking or failing in some manner
having to do with the relations of individuals to one another. The intent of
this chapter is to explore what it is that Kierkegaard and Nietzsche think
humans to be missing and to make some preliminary determinations as to
what the consequences for politics as a form of human interaction might
be. I argue that the standard – we may call it 'liberal' – model for understanding the relations of individuals to each other in modern society has
been that of the contract and that this model is no longer suitable for understanding a system in which ordinary human capacities for self-governance
must play an increasingly important role.

### The contract as a form of absolutism

We tend to think of the purpose of the idea of a social contract to be the
limitation of the power of government. However, this is not necessarily true
and certainly was not always the case. The idea that the legitimation of
some or all parts of political society rests on a contract has a long history.
In the Christian West it was first used to justify the absolute authority of
one ruler over against the contingent authority of another. Thus medieval
papal theorists had argued that the emperor held power only by virtue of
a *de facto* contract with the people. If the emperor were to break into the

exercise of tyranny, 'without any breach of faith or loss of piety no fidelity or reverence should be paid' to him, declares Manegold of Lautenbach (Lewis 1971: 165). While such a limitation served at first to justify the absolute power of the pope, it was not long till the other side deployed the contract metaphor. William of Occam and Marsilius of Padua soon extended the concept to the *final* power of a council to limit that of the Pope.

When Protestants took over the metaphor in the sixteenth century, the metaphor of the covenant or contract was again used to justify the right-eous punishment of God of his people, once they had broken the covenant. Here again the *absolute* power of God is justified by the contractual rela-tion of Adam to God – a contract that paradoxically could not but be broken, as we also know.

The arguments for a contractual basis of government were in tension with those who attributed the legitimacy of government to its historical antiq-uity. In the seventeenth century, groups such as the Levellers and the Diggers denied the legitimacy of the English state on the grounds that conquest gave no right to govern. For such, history had not settled anything. 'We may have been conquered,' they said in effect, 'but that means nothing, for one day we will conquer the conquerors.' The English revolution gave substance to the potential of this claim: it required a justification of governance on a basis other than that of conquest or inheritance – categories that had received their early modern formulation in Machiavelli. It fell to Hobbes to rouse thought from its historical slumber and found modern political philosophy by uniting contract with sovereignty. To the warring partners of the Civil War, Hobbes said in effect that conquest or no conquest – no matter who the winners and losers of the historical war were – it mattered not. The state that would be established by the contractual elaboration of sovereignty was, Hobbes argued, what each, whether in victory or in defeat, actually wanted (Foucault 1997: 21–100). Only by making the state *our* state, he saw, could its stability and legitimacy be assured.

## Hobbes and the contract as legitimation of power

Hobbes deployed two central arguments to demonstrate his claim that the sovereign was, in the end, or rather at the beginning, what each of us con-sidered as a representation of what lay in each of our hearts. The first argu-ment was a claim that he (or someone like him) could see better than we did how it was with each of us. In the *Elements of Law* Hobbes's intention is explicitly 'to put men in mind of what they know already, or may know by their own experience'.[1] In the preface to *De Cive* he sets down as a 'prin-ciple known to all men and denied by none' that every man 'will distrust and dread in each other'. He goes on to ask what is one to make of those who would deny such a principle. Note that for Hobbes the political problem comes from the fact that humans *deny that which they know*. His answer, paralleled by a famous passage in *Leviathan*, chapter 13,[2] is that their actions will belie their claims and that the philosopher's task is to bring their words and actions together. In the Appendix to the Latin edition of *Leviathan* he writes:

> Natural law is eternal, divine and inscribed only in human hearts. *But there are very few men who know how to examine their own heart and read what is written there.* Thus it is from written laws [i.e. from laws which have authority behind them] that men know what they must do or avoid.[3] (Our italics)

The internal writing that is in each of our hearts is hard to read: we have not ordinarily the ability to know ourselves. Humans thus need external written laws, set down by one who can read the human heart, in order to know what it is in their hearts to do. But the laws thus written are laws that are in each heart. For Hobbes, human use will and can teach us the meaning; however, a sovereign must be constructed so as to embody it.

The second element to Hobbes's construction is that of representation. The reason that one cannot complain against the sovereign is that the sovereign represents one's *own* will as one would understand it except for the fact that we deny ourselves knowledge of ourselves. The grounds for this are set in the famous chapter 16 of *Leviathan*, a chapter with no parallel in *De Cive* and that Hobbes added to the English version of *Leviathan*. There he argues that representation is a species of ownership, whereby those who authorise the sovereign own the actions of the sovereign. The sovereign is, so to speak a me that I have constructed and whose actions are mine, for I am their sole owner. Artificial persons have nothing of their own. (So, for instance, William the Conqueror is said never to have owned anything as sovereign, the fields and forests 'being reserved to him in his private capacity'.) Although that which is owned are those of my actions that I would sooner give up in most circumstances (because it is hard for me to read my heart, because I do not like what is in my heart), I am bound to those actions in an irredeemable manner.

That which represents me is thus, for Hobbes, a me over which I can have no control, because control is contradictory to the terms of the representation. We should obey an authority, even and perhaps especially one that we have authorised. Yet this authority is ourselves as our own fathers or super-egos: we have met the king and he is us.[4] Revolt becomes a form of violence to the self, perhaps of suicide.

The argument against revolt in fact parallels arguments against suicide: it is self-contradictory to put an end to oneself. Kant was to pick up on this understanding and, as is well known, was to give strong arguments against suicide. In doing so, Kant also showed why it was that the human encounter with morality must always take place in the form of a command, an imperative. Nietzsche, always nasty about this, wrote that the categorical imperative 'riecht nach Grausamkeit'. Within two centuries, the tension inherent in this arrangement proves impossible to sustain.

Hobbes in effect takes over the early Protestant use of contract and makes it human, makes me my own master. Just as I have no right to resist (or even complain about) God's punishment if I have broken my contract with Him, so also have I no right to resist myself, or more accurately the self that I might refuse to admit is myself. It is important to realise that in Hobbes the need for governance arises not from trust or mistrust but from the fact that, since I cannot accept life in the uncertainty of the state of nature, I will misread what I in fact know about myself. (Hobbes translates *gnosce teipsum* as 'read thyself'.)[5] The sovereign is to set me right about myself.

There is thus an absolute quality to the idea of the contract – it is designed to give me something against which I cannot legitimately complain: myself. More precisely, it is to make sure that what counts as an infringement of an agreement is perfectly clear, clear in the way that moving the bishops on the medians is an infringement of the rules to which one has agreed when one sits down to play chess.

## Rawls and rules

Have things changed much in our time? Let us look briefly here at what Rawls has to say about these matters.[6] In an early essay, 'Two Concepts of Rules' (1955: 2–32), Rawls argues that some rules are constitutive in that they define what something is; other rules tell you what to do when. Only the second are instrumental or utilitarian in nature. The task he set for himself in that essay was to find a set of rules of politics and ethics that would correspond to the first kind.

This is the foundation of the project in *A Theory of Justice* (1971). This latter book is based on the notion that under certain conditions humans can be understood to come rationally to agreement on the 'principles of justice for the basic structure of society' (1971: 11). These conditions require such judgements to be made in an 'original position' behind a 'veil of ignorance' where one will not know precisely how the rules agreed to will affect oneself (i.e. one's position in society). When we have such principles we will be able to 'say to one another' about any institution that corresponds to those principles that we are 'co-operating on terms to which [we] would agree if [we] were free and equal persons . . .' (1971: 13). Note that by resting compliance and the legitimisation of governance on conversation ('we can say to one another') Rawls seems to avoid resting the state on the avoidance of violence.

Now Rawls establishes – conclusively, as far as I can determine – that no natural difference between you and me is adequate grounds for you having domination over me. The point – one of the points – of the original position is that I would be unwilling to agree to the rule of the best (strongest, wisest, most beautiful, with the most ancient traceable ancestry) given, first, that I cannot know who in particular (what actual being) might have such

qualities, and, more important, secondly, that the values which the members
of any society might seek to pursue are multiple and not necessarily of a
piece. The first limit is a limit on our knowledge; the second limit is historical. Let us call this second factor the historical actuality of pluralism,
or rather the reality of life after the death of God. In somewhat more European terms, Max Weber phrased this as the:

> one fundamental fact, that so long as life remains immanent and is interpreted
> in its own terms, it knows only of an unceasing struggle of these gods with
> one another. Or, speaking directly [Weber continues], the ultimate possible atti-
> tudes towards life are irreconcilable, and hence their struggle can never be
> brought to a final conclusion. (1961: 152)

A premise of modern liberalism is therefore the recognition that, in
Alaisdair MacIntyre's words, there is a 'range of goods . . . accompanied by
a recognition of a range of compartmentalised spheres within each of which
some good is pursued: political, economic, familial, artistic, athletic, scientific' (1988: 337). More important, to be educated to liberalism – that is,
to live in our ['our' designates people such as those who may read this text]
century – is thus to pursue a variety of goods. (One does not have to live
in one's own century: Wittgenstein, one might say, did not; Nietzsche,
famously, claimed to be born posthumously). The important thing about
this pluralism is that every individual will find him or herself in the situation of wanting to pursue more goods than he or she can possibly do. (Is
it the dream of a perfected liberalism which Marx parodies in the *German
Ideology*, the dream of hunting in the morning, fishing in the afternoon and
criticising after dinner, all the while without *becoming* a hunter, a fisher-
man or a 'critical critic'?)[7]

There are two possible implications to the fact and desirability of pluralism, and I will argue that in the end they are not compatible. The first
establishes the need for a social union, given that no one can be all that
there is to be. This is the direction that John Rawls takes: 'it is through the
social union founded on the needs and potentials of its members that each
person can participate in the total sum of the realized natural assets of each
other' (1971: 523). From this we get the familiar division of private and
public, self-regarding and other-regarding acts, and so forth. The point of
political philosophy here is to elaborate the claims that the social union can
make on the individual. I do not think that this is wrong – society is in
some sense in our interest; I do not think that we want to give up the notion
of rights – but I do not think that it can stand alone.

There is a second possible and different implication of pluralism, to the
effect that there is no single thing that I am, or rather that I am *in potentia* everything and everyone. This position is elaborated most fully in the
great American philosophers of the last century – Emerson, Thoreau and
Whitman – as well, I have argued, as in Rousseau and Nietzsche. A contemporary exponent is the Princeton political theorist George Kateb. In a

discussion of Whitman as the greatest theorist of democratic individuality, he argues:

> All the personalities that I encounter, I am already: that is to say, I could become or have been something like what others are. . . . I am potentially all personalities and we equally are infinite potentialities.[8]

This position is not that of Rawlsian liberalism. Here the self for democratic politics is not thin but, I might say, transparent, without historical givenness. Its being is becoming. Note that this is not a claim that I can be anything I want to be, but merely the claim that whatever anyone is, has been, and might be, has to do with me. In such a political theory one must use theory to *restrict* the claims of politics and community: these are the appeals of the Cave, of what Emerson calls, in the poem he places as epigraph to his great essay 'Experience', the 'Lords of Life'. The vision of politics here is that of Emerson:

> The world is awakening to the idea of union, and these experiments show what it is thinking of. It is and will be magic . . . But this union must be inward, and not one of covenants . . . The union is only perfect when all the uniters are isolated. It is the union of friends who live in different streets or towns. (Emerson 1983: 599)

The contract here serves to keep or separate one from the other as much as possible in relation to politics. All communities, be they of interest, or of election, or even of accident and contingency, are to be refused. What interests me here is that, in both visions, contingency is rejected, much as it was in Rawls and Hobbes, on, to use Emerson's term, 'reverse' reasons. From a very different path – an importantly different one – each arrives at a kind of non-contingent claim on persons.

## What is wrong with rules in politics?

I have here tried to establish a number of principles that constitute the grammar of a society in which the legitimisation of governance rests on the idea of a contract.

1 First is the recognition that no human being can be privileged in his (and, as time moves on, in her) access to whatever is the most important for the legitimisation of governance, be it God, power, or knowledge.
2 Second, the qualities which are required for one to be able to be participant in a contract must be, in principle, available to all. In Rawls and in Hobbes they are fairly limited: in Hobbes, the willingness to avoid subjecting one's life to the random possibility of violence by placing it under the certainty of violence; in Rawls, the ability to view human arrangements as meeting certain requirements. Whether or not this simplicity is a gain or a loss we shall see later.

The aim in Rawls and Hobbes is to establish principles that may not be rationally disputed by those who subject themselves to them, nor indeed would it be rational not to subject oneself to them. In both Rawls and Hobbes (and in most social contract theorists *per se*) the claim is that, if certain conditions are met, one *is* a legitimate subject. And the choice one's voice is given is either exit or loyalty. The purpose of the social contract as a mode of thought is to establish a line which marks an inside and an outside, and marks them in such a way that refusal of them is denial of one's self. What was not the case in these theorists is that the contract had always to have the quality of contingency. It is for this reason that the contract, while justifying limited government, nonetheless gives an absolute justification to that government. It is instructive here to return to the example of chess and Rawls's early essay on rules. If you want to play chess, you must play by the rules; not to do so is not to play chess. Likewise, for Rawls, the claim is that if you want justice in a society such as ours, you must rationally accept *these* principles; not to do so will be to be other than just. In both cases it is also presumed clear what it means to infringe the rules.

And this – that one knows what it means to break the rules – is the nub of a serious problem. As Stanley Cavell and, following him, Hanna F. Pitkin and others have pointed out, this is problematic (Pitkin 1973; Cavell 1979). If you pick up your bishop and move it sideways I know that you have broken a rule on which, I can assume, we agree. However, much of the time, in the society in which we live, we do not know whether an action actually 'breaks the rules'. Even assuming we live in a moderately just society (one that has justice as at least a central aim), it is not always clear what it means to act outside – or within – the norms of justice.

Contrary to what liberals such as Hobbes or Rawls think, what is important here seems to me to be the fact that this condition is not a fault but a strength of a just political society. We cannot grasp the nature of political justice without understanding that it always appears to us with the quality of contingency. But to claim this requires one to introduce the idea of contingency into the very bedrock of the pursuit of political justice. Where and how might contingency come into these matters?

Contingency is whatever it is that keeps me from being assured that the present must be like the future. I want to argue that it is a good thing, in that it constantly calls to mind the essence or nature of what one is doing. Thus marriage is made more valuable – made more our own – by the existence of divorce. Or, more accurately, the existence of divorce makes more valuable what it actually means to be married. Compare the claims in Hobbes with those advanced some years earlier by Milton in his tract on divorce. 'There is,' says Milton:

> no place in Heaven or Earth, except Hell, where Charity may not enter: yet Marriage, the Ordinance of our Solace and Contentment, the Remedy of our Loneliness, will not admit now either of Charity or Mercy, to come in and

mediate, or pacify the fierceness of this gentle Ordinance, the unremedied Loneliness of this Remedy. Advise ye well, supreme Senate, if Charity be thus excluded and expulst, how ye will defend the untainted Honour of your own Actions and Proceedings. He who marries, intends as little to conspire his own ruin, as he that swears Allegiance: and as a whole People is in proportion to an ill Government, so is one Man to an ill Marriage. If they, against any Authority, Covenant, or Statute, may by the sovereign Edict of Charity, save not only their Lives, but honest Liberties from unworthy Bondage, as well may he against any private Covenant, which he never enter'd to his mischief, redeem himself from unsupportable Disturbances to honest Peace, and just Contentment:[9]

Milton goes on to say that the state owes the individual the possibility of release from harm of a 'mute and spiritless mate', without which the life of its citizens cannot be 'spiritful and orderly'. Milton is making (at least) two points. First, if 'charity' be not part of the institution of marriage (and of society), that is, if marriage and society rest only on 'authority, covenant, statute', it will then lack some humanly significant element. Secondly, if we cannot call marriage into question, we cannot know what it is. Likewise, he suggests, for government. What are the implications here for our understanding of citizenship?[10]

We see, I think, a limitation of the idea of contract as it is given to us in Hobbes and Rawls. In Hobbes, we might say, there is no chance of divorce from oneself. The I that I would deny is in effect to be placed in charge of the I that denies. Hence representation is absolutely necessary for governance in Hobbes. To pursue these matters further, we must keep the question of the ultimacy of representation up in the air for a while.

In Rawls, the matter is similar and a bit different. Rawls is clearly aware that he has given standards, one might say a utopia of justice, and that any given system will diverge to some degree or another from the various principles that he lays down – among them the priority of the right over the good (as above), as well as the principle that any inequality must be justified in relation to the least favoured in a society. Rawls continues his elaboration of the conversation of justice with the claim that a rational person is 'not subject to envy', meaning by that that rationally I am not to be envious of a change in what you have and in what I have, as long as that change does not make me worse off in relation to what I was before.

## Why politics is not like basketball

Attractive as the prohibition on envy is – the addition of Michael Jordan to the Chicago Bulls basketball team makes no one worse off, despite his enormous salary – Rawls's prohibition masks another set of considerations. Consider this story from Marx, who writes in *Wage Labour and Capital*:

A house may be large or small: as long as the surrounding houses are equally small it satisfies all social demands for dwelling. But let a palace arise beside the little house and it shrinks from a little house into a hut. The little house shows that its owner has only very slight or no demands to make; and however high it may shoot up in the course of civilization, if the neighboring palace grows to an equal or even greater extent, the occupant of the relatively small house will feel more and more uncomfortable, dissatisfied and cramped within its four walls . . . Our desires and pleasures spring from society; we measure them therefore by society and not by the objects which serve for their satisfaction. Because they are of a social nature, they are of a relative nature. (Marx 1981: 84–5)

The point of this story is that my wants are not precisely my wants, if by 'my' one means an agent in some sort of autonomous independence from others. More precisely, what will need recasting is the picture of the individual and society as ultimately separate. On the other hand, it will not do simply to move the individual into society, to construct him or her 'thickly', as, say, Michael Sandel argues.

In any case, it is important to realise that neither the Marxian nor the Soviet case responds well to Rawls's discussion of envy. The conditions that encourage an outbreak of envy, says Rawls, are (1) lack of confidence in self; (2) a lowered estimation of self; (3) having no constructive alternative (Rawls 1971: 535). Marx is arguing that the concepts of desire and interest make no sense apart from the structure of society and thus that the distinction between institutional structure and psychology that Rawls invokes (1971: 536) is misleading. Rawls could perhaps respond here that in a well ordered society we would all live in development-project houses and that the problem would not arise. The second case, however, poses a greater problem. It might be that I simply do not want to see my neighbour advantaged even if I should benefit absolutely by it. As Rawls pursues this matter he finds that envy is not a rational sentiment in a reasonably just society and that, to the degree that it is present, envy derives from 'primitive . . . moral notions' such as those in children (1971: 540). It would seem that it is not only simply irrational to be envious, but also politically dangerous and destabilising.

## Ways of suffering injustice

One could say much more about the problematic status of envy in Rawls;[11] however, Rawls argues that envy is not a moral feeling and is thus only improperly part of the conversation of justice. He distinguishes it from resentment, which is a moral feeling. Most important, he argues that those who have a complaint about a given distribution of goods must be able to formulate their complaint in terms of how they have been injured. How so?
    He writes:

If we resent our having less than others, it must be because we think that their being better off is the result of unjust institutions, or wrongful conduct on their

part. Those who express resentment must be prepared to show why certain
institutions are unjust or how others have injured them. (1971: 533)

In other words, if you make an accusation against some act of mine and
cannot show what it is that I have done or what it is that I have participated in doing that has, with reference to a principle of justice, injured you,
I may, in that case, hold myself to be 'above criticism' (1971: 422). We have
here, then, a situation that is less different from that which we saw in
Hobbes than might first appear. If I can relate my action to a principle on
which we have agreed, I am invulnerable to any claim of justice by you.
My human skin is, so to speak, impenetrable. This is the process that Rawls
calls *reflective equilibrium*. To this one must ask first: to whom or what
must I be prepared to show what specific injustice has been done to me?
Secondly, what constitutes showing?

When Marx pushed these matters to the extreme he wrote that German
emancipation depended on the 'formation of a class with radical chains
... a sphere which ... claims no particular right because no particular
wrong but wrong in general is perpetrated against it'.[12] His claim here is
that revolution will occur only when a particular class conceives of itself as
being wronged not in a particular way, but in general. One might imagine
a similar moment in literature, the moment when, at the end of *A Doll's
House*, Thorvald questions Nora as to what is wrong with her situation.
As the interrogation proceeds, we find that there is no particular thing that
Nora can identify as wrong. She goes to her room – Thorvald thinks, to
bed. She comes downstairs in different clothes.

*Thorvald.* What's this? Not in bed? You've changed your clothes.
*Nora.* Yes, Thorvald. I've changed my clothes.[13]

And, as her clothes, so also herself. As the subsequent exchange with
Thorvald reveals, she is or needs to be 'before everything else' a human
being, or at least she can/should 'try to become one'. Attaining this explicitly means, in the world in which she lives, rejecting marriage, parenthood,
religion. Only if the unimaginable happens to Thorvald can he be saved,
can she be saved with him. And she leaves; the door slams behind her.

The point of these two examples is that for neither Marx nor Ibsen can
a claim to injustice be referenced to rules or principles.[14] What are we to
make of these judgements and what is their relation to the problem of
governmentality?

The above cases, especially that of Nora, might appear to legitimate the
solitary voice crying in the wilderness, the individual against society (as
embodied, say, by Thorvald). One line that might come out of this is
Deleuze's emphasis on 'nomad thought' (Deleuze 1977) – an elevation, not
unfair nor without reason, of what Durkheim had seen as pathology (here
*anomie*) to the possibility of philosophy. (One remembers Wittgenstein's
statement that the philosopher has no country.)

This, however, is not the case. The question that is, rather, posed for me concerns what relationship Nora craves with Thorvald and which he – in his Rawlsian understanding of justice, shall we say – cannot find in him to allow her. To do this is to raise the question of the place of contingency in governance, and more especially to raise the question of what might be democratic about democratic governance. We want to say that there is injustice between them, but it is hard to say what kind of injustice it is. Is her being human *dependent* on Thorvald? That hardly makes it possible. Who is to say what being human is, if not her? Can she not simply proclaim it? More important, is there a political theoretical understanding by and from which one might raise the question of what the self's duties to itself are, and of how and why this might be considered a matter for politics and political theory? In other words, how are we to think about justice in the political world without relying upon a foundation that we have made unassailable?

## What might be a source of political authority then?

In *Between Past and Future* Hannah Arendt, speaking of Marx, Kierkegaard and Nietzsche, wrote that 'The greatness of these . . . thinkers . . . lies in the fact that they perceived their world as one invaded by new problems and perplexities which our tradition of thought was unable to cope with. . . . They were the first who dared to think without the guidance of any authority whatsoever' (1968: 27–8). Thinking without authority, or, as she phrased it elsewhere, without a banister, means that thinking must be action and can no longer be separate from activity. Perhaps the best place to examine the questions that arise is in Kierkegaard's *Authority and Revelation*. He writes:

> A clergyman who is entirely correct in eloquence must speak thus, introducing a word of Christ: 'This word was spoken by Him to whom, according to his own statement, all power hath been given in heaven and earth. Now, thou, my hearer, must consider by thyself whether thou wilt bow to his authority or no, receive it and believe it or no. But if thou wilt not do so, then for heaven's sake (!!) do not go off and accept the word because it is clever and profound or wondrously beautiful, for this is blasphemy, it is wanting to treat God like an aesthetic critic. For so soon as the dominant note of authority, of the specific paradoxical authority, is heard, then this sort of appropriation, which otherwise is permissible and desirable, is a crime and presumption. (1966: 117)

In the 'Postscript' to this book Kierkegaard suggests that the religious situation is of the same sort as the political situation that now confronts us, only more so. In the third preface to the book, written in response to the events of 1848, Kierkegaard remarks that 'Throughout Europe people have in a worldly way, with ever increasing velocity of passion, lost themselves in problems which can be solved only in a godly way' (1966: lvii). I take him to mean here that our mode of discourse in relation to politics is fundamentally religious and that the required concept of authority has disappeared in the modern.

Kierkegaard continues: 'how can an apostle prove that he has authority? ... He has no other proof than his own assertion.' We have moved from a minister to one who makes a claim by him/herself on and for society. Suppose we now take this as paradigmatic of Nora's problem, or more generally, with Marx, of anyone who is a victim of society. What kind of response would acknowledge Nora's act? I take it that a human response would not be one of pity, nor would it be a threat (implicit or not), or one of more or less enlightened self-interest.

A warning against a natural confusion furthers the argument. The Marx/Ibsen examples seem to point us towards the poor, the downtrodden and the obviously oppressed. I don't actually think that this is in fact what Marx and Ibsen meant to draw our attention to, and I certainly do not want to think that it is what I am doing. This is rather a question of self-enslavement. What is the problem of governance when the self governs the self? There is a famous passage in the first chapter of Thoreau's *Walden* where he writes:

> I sometimes wonder that we can be so frivolous, I may almost say, as to attend to the gross but somewhat foreign form of servitude called Negro Slavery. There are so many keen and subtle masters that enslave both north and south. (1966: 4)[15]

Thoreau – who had gone to jail so as not to pay a tax to a 'state which buys and sells men, women and children' (1966: 115) – is not here in defence of chattel slavery but is rather calling our attention to the fact that we (those of moderate means, people like those who may read this text) are self-enslaved. And we are self-enslaved because we do not acknowledge the fact and implications of our inalterable membership in this society to which we are not aware of committing our self. In *Civil Disobedience* Thoreau relates that he once gave the town clerk a statement to the effect that he did not wish 'to be regarded as a member of any incorporated society which [he] had not joined' (1966: 235). Thoreau then says that he would sign off from all societies to which he had never signed on but that he could not find the list. So his very separation implies his membership: this is what most do not understand and is the source of the self-enslavement.

Thoreau has here reposed *the* central question of political thought as it confronts us in modern times: what does it mean for me to be a member of a society to which I am not aware of having committed my self and in which I nevertheless find myself implicated, that is, to which I am not originally bound by any contract whatsoever? Hume has argued that the idea of a contract as the legitimating basis of a society was empty, in that it presupposed the very thing that it hoped to establish. Famously: 'In vain we are asked in what record the chapter of our liberties is registered. It is not written on parchment, nor yet on the leaves or bark of trees.' While Hume is perfectly willing to say that humans consent to (in the sense of accept) the government they have; but he cannot say that they have voluntarily contracted to establish it. Hume thought that for a society to rest on a contract it would have to be a society of philosophers – that is, of experts – and was fully aware that a just society could not rest on the dominance of experts and professionals.

There are problems with Hume's thought here: a confusion between knowing what another means with having the same thoughts as the other. I have investigated them in some detail elsewhere. But the point is that Hume was right about the idea of a social contract. It does not serve to establish a society. And the fact that brings into our presence – requires from us the acknowledgement of – is the actuality that we are both of and not of political society; the failure to recognise this, to require that this ecstatic doubling be available to ourselves, is the source of the self-enslavement that Thoreau decried.

## The acknowledgement of contingency: Rousseau

I call the recognition that we are both members and not members of political society the acknowledgement of contingency. A key to the maintenance of this contingency may be found in Rousseau. He insists on contingency as a limitation on what can be represented. To recall: Rousseau makes a distinction between sovereignty and government. Sovereignty has to do with the matters of the general will, that is, with what humans have in common. What we have in common is for Rousseau the way in which I am exactly the same as you – one might call it the acknowledgement of the fact that you are human (and that I am also). (I think this is what Marx was trying later to get at with the idea of *Gattungswesen*.) Government, on the other hand, has to do with the adjudication of the particularities of each of us and of their relation to each other. He calls this *administration*.

The first thing to recall is that for Rousseau sovereignty does not exist and cannot exist over time. It is pure presence. Each moment of sovereignty – what Rousseau calls 'law' – is 'absolute, independent of the preceding, and never does the sovereign act because he willed (past tense) but only because he wills (present tense)'.[16] This thought, given formulation in several places in Rousseau's drafts as he worked on the *Social Contract*, appears in final form in the extraordinary claim that 'yesterday's law carries no obligations today'.[17] And Rousseau makes no concession to the pragmatism of politics by his immediate recognition that 'consent is presumed from silence'. Rather he is saying that our very act of saying nothing about a law is a recognition of our complicity in it. Sovereignty and the very being of political society are held to exist solely in the present tense. Not only can the future not be tied down, but it cannot be rightly named without sin. There is not 'any kind of obligatory fundamental law for the body of the people, not even the social contract'. Not that this means that, whether or not obligation is an important component of a political society, politics and society cannot be properly conceived of as resting on obligation. For I cannot be obliged without some form of representation. In politics (at least), the dancers can only be told from the dance. Sovereignty is here the source of a new authority that will take the place of that which Kierkegaard had found wanting.

Let me note in passing that this is *not* a description of what has come to be called participatory democracy. Rousseau does include as a logical Aristotelian category government – that is, administration – by all. He has no hostility, however, to representation on the level of government – only as to sovereignty. Whatever the arguments are for or against participatory democracy – along the lines of, say, Benjamin Barber's work – they are of a different matter from what I am trying to discuss here today.

From what does the authority of this contingent sovereignty derive? The second thing to recall is the centrality of Rousseau's idea of the 'common' to his reconceptualisation of sovereignty as a contingent relation. Sovereignty in Rousseau's understanding is made possible by virtue of our apprehension and acknowledgement of our commonalty with others. The word 'common' as Rousseau uses it always has a double meaning: that which we share, have in common, and that which is ordinary and everyday. The common is for Rousseau the object of the General Will and designates precisely and only that in which I am exactly as are you. A society (that is, truly human society) will have, famously, the quality that results when each of us puts in common his or her person and when we receive that common person in and as our self.[18] Rousseau's 'contract' is thus not at all a contract in the manner of Hobbes or Rawls: it is a contract between the self of mine and the self of you that are exactly the same. It establishes and acknowledges our commonalty, our sharing the same time and space.

I have now argued the following points.

1 The notion of a just society as resting on a contract, as that idea has been formulated in thought from Hobbes to Rawls, still partakes in the desire to rest political society on a ground from and to which there can be no appeal. One of the consequences of this grounding was that claims to injustice must rest on the ability to make reference to specific appeals as to how an act or an institution has, in particular fact, harmed me.

2 I suggested that there is much in this that denies the reality of the experience of finding oneself – in the word I used from Thoreau – 'enslaved'.

3 I then suggested that we recast the idea of a contract so as to foreground our inevitable doubleness in relation to society: that we are always both of it and not of it. (This is not the public–private distinction.) This quality, which I named *contingency*, leads us to constantly ask our self what something *is* – my aesthetics are modernist, if you will – the better to know what it means to be part of something.

4 I finally argued that Rousseau's understanding of sovereignty as a
    contingency relation, always called into question, establishes a relation
    between human beings the acknowledgement of which forms that which
    we then have in common and of which we have a share.

Well, you might ask, what has been gained by the acknowledgement of such
contingency? Let me sketch out an answer. When Nora leaves, we might
say that she has started on a journey by rejecting society as she has lived it
in the name of some further, more human, society and self. The notion of
a journey here does not imply some final point: only that we have reasons
for desiring any state of self and society and are also at risk of remaining
attached to any conception. It implies, however, the possibility of a way of
being human and of acknowledging others as human that is not just rational and reasonable. (Rawls, I might add, limits the human qualities of political justice to the rational and reasonable.) This question is, for me, best
approached by a slightly circuitous route. Here I draw upon work that has
appeared in a number of venues, most specifically Stanley Cavell, James
Conant, Stephen Mulhall, and some of my own.[19]


### Acknowledgement and democracy

Is this, in any sense of the word, at all democratic? Clearly, not at all, if
by democracy one means something like what, say, John Rawls means.
Furthermore, it is a human experience that like Rousseau's conception of
sovereignty is denied to us by liberal notions of the proper role of governance or of the private and the public. Where does this leave us? I have
argued for a reconceptualisation of the idea of contract as a foundation of
political society so as to include in it the constant presence of contingency.
It requires that I acknowledge the other as *my* other. The danger here – it
was explored by Nietzsche in his early writings[20] – is that one will be
tempted to fix the voice of others as the voice of *the* other, that is, as the
voice against which one defines oneself, a way of replacing contingency with
dialectic. Such will be the burden of his explorations of slave morality in
the *Genealogy of Morals*. In closing, I want briefly to explore this question.
It is of direct political significance in any society where the other is readily
available.

Jean-Luc Nancy, in an essay called 'La comparution/compearance', concludes as follows:

> community . . . always excludes and on principle. . . . At the bottom, that
> which the community wants to exclude is that which does not let itself be iden-
> tified in it. We call it the 'other'. Community excludes its own foundation. . .
> . But to exclude, exclusion must designate: it names, identifies, gives form. 'The
> other' is for us a figure imposed on the unpresentable (infigurable). Thus we
> have for us – to go to a heart of the matter – the 'Jew' or the 'Arab', figures
> whose closeness, that is, their in-common with 'us', is no accident. (1992: 392)

'Us' here reflects that Nancy speaks as a Frenchman and a member of the French 'community'. The problem of 'the other', as he goes on to clearly recognise, will be specifically different for other communities, but not structurally so. The double question is always 'How to exclude without fixing (figurer)?' and 'How to fix without excluding?' (1992: 393).

The answer to Nancy's question is difficult. I think it would go something like this.[21] Let us consider the problem of the outsider – for Nancy here the 'Arab', but for others the 'Turk' or the 'Mexican' or the 'Black'. I clearly know that he is in some sense different from me – not to admit this would be to deny the actuality of our presence to each other. (It follows from this, for instance, that 'race' cannot be relegated to the private world in the conversation of justice: part of what justice requires is not denying that an other is what that other is to me.)[22] I think I also have to say, following the analysis in Stanley Cavell's *The Claim of Reason*, that I cannot fall back on the (Rawlsian) claim that the other and I could or do have common understandings of primary goods. I may claim precisely that we do not, that the other is not (really, fully) human ('I just can't stand their smell . . .' 'They're not like us, you know'). When I say something like that about the other, what is it that I am missing about them, or what is it that I want to miss? Cavell: 'What [a man who sees certain others as slaves] is missing is not something about slaves exactly and not exactly about human beings. He is missing something about himself, or rather something about his connection with these people, his internal relation with them, so to speak' (1979: 377). Cavell goes on to point out that my actions show that I cannot mean in fact that the other is not human, or is less than human.

> When he wants to be served at table by a black hand, he would not be satisfied to be served by a black paw. When he rapes a slave, or takes her as a concubine, he does not feel that he has, by that fact itself, embraced sodomy. When he tips a black taxi driver . . . it does not occur to him that he might more appropriately have patted the creature fondly on the side of the neck. (1979: 377)

No matter what the slave owner, or the Frenchman in Nancy's essay, can claim (and assert that he truly believes) his actions show that he holds to something quite different. He can allow that the others have qualities (their cuisine or their music, say) but what he cannot allow is for them to see themselves as he sees them. For then he would see himself as they see him. His power consists in requiring that the others have no existence for him except as he allows it. Montesquieu saw this as the central quality of tyranny in *The Persian Letters*.

What is missing is an acknowledgement of the other. It is not simply a matter of knowing (all there might be to know) something about the other, but acknowledgement. Cavell again:

> acknowledgment goes beyond knowledge not in the order, or as a feat, of cognition, but in the call upon me to express the knowledge at its core, to recog-

nize what I know, to do something in the light of it, apart from which this knowledge remains without expression, hence perhaps without possession . . . acknowledgment of the other calls for recognition of the other's specific relation to oneself, and that this entails the revelation of oneself as having denied or distorted that relationship. (1979: 428)

To allow the other a voice is to recognise something about one's relation to the other – that there is the relation of being human – and to recognise one's constant temptation to deny that relation. My existence as human depends on theirs, and this in turn on the acknowledgement that no one's soul or self or body is his or her own. Indeed, this may be what Montesquieu was trying to capture in his telling of the undoing of the Troglodyte community. Letter 11 of *The Persian Letters* concludes with the words of a doctor from a neighbouring country who has been wronged by the Troglodytes:

'Away with you!' he said, 'for you are unjust. In your souls is a poison deadlier than that for which you want a cure. You do not deserve to have a place on earth, because you have no humanity, and the rules of equity are unknown to you.' (Montesquieu 1973)[23]

We verge here on territory that is only beginning to be explored; I hope that this book takes us further down that path. Acknowledgement in the case of the reconstitution of the self along the lines of this journey both introduces contingency in any conception of justice (there may be a first word, but there is never a last) and makes impossible the 'core–periphery' conception of a just political society so dear to the hearts of liberals. It also introduces a whole new set of questions and problems for a truly democratic theory for our modern, postmodern, Western times.

## Notes

1  Thomas Hobbes (1962), *English Works* I, *Elements of Law*, Part 1, chapter 1, section 2.
2  'It may seem strange, to some man that has not well weighed these things, that nature should thus dissociate, and render men apt to invade and destroy one another. And he may, therefore, not trusting to this inference made from the passions, *desire perhaps to have the same confirmed by experience*' (my italics).
3  'Appendix to Latin *Leviathan*' in Hobbes (1989: 760). For a more extensive discussion of these matters see Strong (1993). See also Miller and Strong (1997).
4  Thus were one to follow Foucault and cry 'Off with his head' it would be our own that fell. This merely points at how complex the Foucault move is. For further reflection on one's own head falling see Hawthorne (1983).
5  For a full exploration of this see Strong (1993).
6  I am helped here by S. Cavell (1993: 101 ff.); see also Stephen Mulhall and Stanley Cavell (1994: 258–82).
7  See the illuminating discussion in Terrell Carver (1988: 129–36).
8  Kateb (1992: 247); see Strong (1996).

9  John Milton, *The Doctrine and Discipline of Divorce* (Milton Society on the Internet), p. 4; also partially cited in Cavell (1993: x), to which I owe the thought to use this passage.
10  I draw here upon Cavell (1991, 1993: 104–5).
11  See the discussion in Wolff (1977: 187–91), from which I have learned much.
12  Marx (1981: 186). I am indebted in what follows here to Cavell (1993: 49–54) and Conant (2001). See also Strong (1975: chapters 6 and 10, 1990, 1996) and Mulhall (1994).
13  Ibsen (1976: Act 3, p. 224). I take the example from Cavell (1993) without any sense of theft.
14  Thus in Marx (1967) he responded to Proudhon's claim that 'property was theft' with the response that it was no such thing.
15  I am, throughout, indebted to Cavell (1972).
16  *Fragments politiques*, in Rousseau (1966 III: 485).
17  *Social Contract* III, section 11, in Rousseau (1966 III: 424).
18  This is the formulation of the social compact (*Social Contract* I, section 6, in Rousseau 1966 III: 361). See the extended discussion in Strong (2002: chapter III).
19  See the material listed in note 12.
20  See Strong (1996).
21  I am importantly indebted here to Cavell (1979), as well as to e-mail exchanges with Utz Lars McKnight (University of Lund) and Linda Zerilli (Northwestern University).
22  See here McKnight (1996: chapter one).
23  This passage is also a striking prefiguring of the closing paragraph of Hannah Arendt's *Eichmann in Jerusalem* (1994). Compare the above with the terms in which Arendt imagines the judgement might have been worded, were justice to have been done: 'And just as you supported and carried out a policy of not wanting to share the earth with the Jewish people and the people of a number of other nations – as though you and your superiors had any right to determine who should and should not inhabit the world – we find that no one, that is, no member of the human race, can be expected to want to share the earth with you.' See Smith (n.d.). for an analysis of the relationship between these passages.

## References

Arendt, H. (1968), *Between Past and Future* (New York: Viking Press).
Arendt, H. (1994), *Eichmann in Jerusalem* (London: Penguin Books).
Carver, T. (1988), 'Communism for critical critics? A new look at the German ideology', *History of Political Thought* 9 (1).
Cavell, S. (1972), *The Senses of Walden* (New York: Viking).
Cavell, S. (1979), *The Claim of Reason* (Oxford: Oxford University Press).
Cavell, S. (1991), *Pursuits of Happiness: The Comedy of Remarriage* (Cambridge MA: Harvard University Press).
Cavell, S. (1993), *Conditions Handsome and Unhandsome* (Chicago: University of Chicago Press).
Conant, J. (2001), 'Schopenhauer as educator and exemplars', in R. Schacht (ed.), *Nietzsche's Postmoralism: Essays on Nietzsche's Prelude to Philosophy's Future* (Cambridge: Cambridge University Press).

Emerson, R. W. (1983) ('Experience', in *Essays and Lectures* (New York Library of America).

Foucault, M. (1997), *Il faut défendre la société* (Paris: Gallimard).

Hawthorne, N. (1983), 'The custom house', in *The Scarlet Letter* (New York: Library of America).

Hobbes, T. (1962), *English Works* I, ed. W. Molesworth, *Elements of Law*, Part 1, chapter 1, section 2 (Aalen: Scientia Press).

Hobbes, T. (1989), *Leviathan*, ed. François Tricaud (Paris: Sirey).

Ibsen, H. (1976), *A Doll's House* (London: Penguin Books).

Kateb, G. (1992), *The Inner Ocean: Individualism and Democratic Culture* (Ithaca NY: Cornell University Press).

Kierkegaard, S. (1966), *Authority and Revelation* (New York: Harper).

Lewis, E. (1971), *Medieval Political Ideas* II (Chatham: Cooper Square).

MacIntyre, A. (1988), *Whose Justice? Whose Liberalism?* (Notre Dame IN: University of Notre Dame Press).

Marx, K. (1967), *The Poverty of Philosophy* (New York: International Publishers).

Marx, K. (1981), 'Introduction to the Contribution to a Critique of Hegel's Philosophy of Right', *Collected Works* III (New York. International Publishers).

Marx, K. (1981), 'Wage Labor and Capital', in *Karl Marx and Friedrich Engels: Selected Works* (New York: International Publishers).

McKnight, U. L. (1996), *Race and Political Liberalism* (Lund: University of Lund).

Miller, T., and Strong, T. B. (1997), 'Meanings and contexts: Mr Skinner's Hobbes and the English mode of political theory', *Critical Inquiry*, fall.

Montesquieu, C. L. de S. (1973), *The Persian Letters* (London: Penguin Books).

Mulhall, S. (1994), 'Perfectionism, politics, and the social contract', *Journal of Political Philosophy* 2 (3): 222–39.

Mulhall, S., and Cavell, S. (1994), *Philosophy's Recounting of the Ordinary* (Oxford: Oxford University Press).

Nancy, J.-L. (1992), 'La comparution compearance', *Political Theory*, August.

Pitkin, H. F. (1973), *Wittgenstein and Justice* (Berkeley CA: University of California Press).

Rawls, J. (1955), 'Two concepts of rules', *Philosophical Review*, 64, 1 January.

Rawls, J. (1971), *A Theory of Justice* (Cambridge MA: Harvard University Press).

Rousseau, J.-J. (1966), *Oeuvres complètes* (Paris: Gallimard).

Smith, V. (n.d.), 'Liberty's Grammar': Of Sovereigns, Subjects, and the Concept of Constitutionalism', unpublished dissertation Ms on file with the author.

Strong, T. B. (1975, 1988), *Friedrich Nietzsche and the Politics of Transfiguration* (Berkeley CA and Los Angeles: University of California Press).

Strong, T. B. (1990), 'The political misappropriations of Nietzsche', in K. Higgins and B. Magnus (eds), *The Cambridge Companion to Nietzsche* (Cambridge: Cambridge University Press).

Strong, T. B. (1990), 'The political misappropriations of Nietzsche', in K. Higgins and B. Magnus (eds), *The Cambridge Companion to Nietzsche* (Cambridge: Cambridge University Press).

Strong, T. B. (1993), 'How to write scripture: Hobbes on words and authority', *Critical Inquiry*, November.

Strong, T. B. (1996), 'Politics and transparency', in D. Villa and A. Sarat (eds), *Liberal Modernism and Democratic Individuality* (Princeton NJ: Princeton University Press), pp. 97–111.

Strong, T. B. (1996), 'The song in the self', *New Nietzsche Studies*, I$^1$/$_2$.

Strong, T. B. (2002), *Jean-Jacques Rousseau: The Politics of the Ordinary* (Lanham MD: Rowman & Littlefield).

Thoreau, H. D. (1966), *Walden* and *Civil Disobedience* (New York: Norton).

Weber, M. (1961), 'Science as a vocation', in H. H. Gerth and C. Wright Mills (eds), *From Max Weber* (New York: Oxford University Press).

Wolff, R. P. (1977), *Understanding Rawls* (Princeton NJ: Princeton University Press).

# 11

# A decentred theory of governance

Mark Bevir

In 1992 the World Bank introduced the concept of *good governance* as part of its criteria for lending to developing countries (World Bank 1992). 'Governance' referred to changes in the public sector associated with the New Public Management and marketisation. The bank suggested that the introduction of neo-liberal reforms led to greater efficiency in public services. In contrast, the Local Government and Whitehall Programmes organised by the British Economic and Social Research Council used 'governance' to refer to a new pattern of relations between state and civil society (Stoker 1999, 2000; Rhodes 2000). Governance consisted of networks rather than hierarchies or markets. The political scientists involved in these programmes used 'governance' to refer to what they saw as the unintended consequences of the New Public Management and marketisation. The introduction of neo-liberal reforms, they implied, had led to a public sector very different from that envisaged by the World Bank.

Obviously 'governance' means different things to different people. Despite some overlaps, it has one meaning for the economists of the World Bank and another for the political scientists of the Local Government and Whitehall Programmes. The reasons are not hard to find. The two groups understand governance differently because they constructed it from within different narratives. A narrative is a form of explanation that unpacks human actions in terms of the beliefs and desires of actors. Narratives embody particular theories about rationality, institutional embeddedness, and agency, as well as a historical story. The varied theories at work in different narratives prompt their adherents to take different views of changes in government, society, and the economy.

If we take concepts such as narrative seriously, we will allow that the world is not given to people as pure perception; rather, different people perceive the world differently because they hold different theories. This insight, in turn, might lead us to a decentred analysis of governance at odds with those upheld by the economists of the World Bank and the political scientists of the Local Government and Whitehall Programmes. Before we explore a decentred analysis of governance, we should examine more fully existing narratives of governance. In doing so, we will highlight the theoretical role of rational choice theory and institutionalism, thereby opening a space in which to push and pull these theories in an interpretative direction. Only then will we develop a decentred analysis of governance. Next we will expand on this analysis by indicating the distinct answers it might give to questions that surround the concept of governance. Finally we consider the implications of a decentred analysis for policy making and democracy.

## Narratives of governance

The current fascination with governance derives in large part from the reforms of the public sector promoted by neo-liberal governments in Britain and the United States during the 1980s. The neo-liberal narrative that inspired those reforms now informs a global policy agenda that incorporates one concept of governance. The Organisation for Economic Cooperation and Development, like the World Bank, appeals to a neo-liberal concept of governance to describe desirable changes in the nature of public services (OECD 1995, 1996). It understands governance in terms of the increased efficiency in the public sector allegedly ensured by measures such as marketisation, contracting out, new management techniques, staff cuts, and stricter budgeting.

Governance, on many accounts, has a profound relationship to a neo-liberal narrative that emphasises the inefficiencies of bureaucracy, the burden of excessive taxation, the mobility of capital, and competition between states. A hierarchic model of the provision of public services is condemned as inherently inefficient. The state reasonably might make policy decisions, but instead of delivering services itself it should promote an entrepreneurial system based on competition and markets – 'less government' and 'more governance' (Osborne and Baebler 1992). Neo-liberals, of course, believe states should turn to markets because they are inherently efficient. In addition, they often suggest that we now live in a global age in which the increased mobility of technology, trade, and finance capital has created a world market that underpins an almost Darwinian selection process such that states must liberalise their economies and their public sectors or perish (Ohmae 1990; Porter 1990; Reinecke 1994). According to neo-liberals, the mobility of finance means that states characterised by large, inefficient bureaucracies, high rates of taxation, and onerous regulations on the corporate sector will inevitably suffer capital flight and ultimately impoverishment. The global market has produced an inexorable process of imitation and catch-up in which neo-liberal measures are sweeping across the globe. For neo-liberals, the hidden hand of globalisation explains and guarantees the spread of governance – the minimal state, marketisation, and the New Public Management.

The neo-liberal narrative of governance has a complementary relationship with rational choice theory. Both of them draw on neo-classical economics, which explores human affairs using an analytic approach located
at the micro-level to derive formal models from assumptions about rationality, utility, and profit maximisation. While the neo-liberal narrative of
governance deploys a similar approach to promote reforms such as the New
Public Management, rational choice theorists attempt to extend it from economic matters to political activity. Rational choice theorists seek to construct theoretical models as deductions from a few elementary assumptions.
The economic approach to politics, as it is also known, presupposes that
actors choose a particular action or course of actions because they believe
it to be the most efficient way of realising a given end, where the ends an
actor has are supposedly given by his utility function (Becker 1976; Elster
1986; Monroe 1991).

The most prominent alternative to the neo-liberal narrative of governance
comes from political scientists who define governance in terms of networks
conceived as the unintended consequences of neo-liberal policies.[1] For these
institutionalists, neo-liberal reforms fragmented service delivery and weak-
ened central control without establishing proper markets: they created networks as opposed to markets and hierarchies. The Local Government and
Whitehall Programmes, for example, suggest that the neo-liberal reforms of
the 1980s undermined the capacity of the state to act while failing to establish anything like the neo-liberal vision. The state now acts, they imply, as
one of several organisations that come together in diverse networks to
deliver services. Often the state can no longer command others: it must rely
instead on limited steering mechanisms and diplomacy. All the organisations in any given network depend on others for some of their resources
and to attain their goals. Often the boundaries between different organisations, let alone their respective roles, have become blurred. Governance
is characterised by power-dependent organisations that form semi-
autonomous and sometimes self-governing networks.

Just as the neo-liberal narrative utilises rational choice theory, so the narrative of governance as networks draws on institutionalism.[2] Its proponents
typically accept that pressures such as globalisation, inflation, and state
overload brought about neo-liberal reforms, only then to emphasise that
embedded institutional patterns and inertia were such that the reforms did
not operate as neo-liberals hoped. Institutions, they argue, create a space
between policy intentions and unintended consequences: institutions
explain the difference between the dream of governance promulgated by
neo-liberals and the reality of governance as networks. A concern with institutions unites advocates of governance as networks with other critics of the
neo-liberal narrative.[3] Institutionalism emphasises the diverse national,
organisational, and cultural contexts in which capitalism operates (Zysman
1996; Hay 2000). It shifts our attention from an allegedly inexorable
process fuelled by the pressures of globalisation, capital mobility, and com-

petition between states to the ways in which inherited institutions generate diverse responses to these pressures. Although states are experiencing much the same disruptive forces, the speed and intensity with which they do so depends on the stability of their institutions. Some institutionalists even argue that common pressures or inputs need not lead to common consequences or outputs, since the pressures and the reforms associated with them impact on states differently. Institutions are thus said to generate diverse responses to global pressures and so diverse national trajectories.

Currently the dominant narratives of governance are the neo-liberal one and that of governance as networks. The neo-liberal one has a symbiotic relationship with rational choice theory. It postulates global pressures such as inflation, bureaucratic overload, and the mobility of finance capital, all of which are to be explained through micro-economic analysis based on utility functions and profit maximisation. The narrative of governance as networks has symbiotic ties with institutionalism. It too postulates global pressures, but it insists states respond to these pressures in diverse ways, depending on their historical and institutional trajectories.

## Theoretical reflections

No one path runs straight through what I want to say; there is no starting point from which all else follows. One way of beginning, though, is to explore the relationship of institutionalism and rational choice theory to those concepts – narrative, episteme, and paradigm – that imply our perceptions of the world vary in part with the theories we bring to bear on them. Contrary to positivism, perceptions always incorporate theories – even everyday accounts of experiences embody numerous realist assumptions, including things such as that objects exist independently of our perceiving them, objects persist through time, other people can perceive the same objects we perceive, and objects sometimes act causally upon one another. The place of our theories within perception does not mean our categories determine what experiences we have: rather, objects force sensations on us. However, it does mean our categories influence the way we experience the sensations we have: we make sense of the sensations objects force upon us only in relation to our theoretical categories.

Although positivism was subjected to forceful philosophical criticism as early as the 1950s, and although few political scientists today would describe themselves as positivists, both institutionalism and rational choice theory often fail to take seriously what follows from rejecting the positivist belief in pure experience.[4] More particularly, they cling tenaciously at times to the positivist belief that we can understand or explain human behaviour adequately in terms of allegedly objective social facts about people. In doing so, they seek largely to dismiss the interpretation of beliefs and meanings from their visions of political science. A lingering positivism leads many political scientists to neglect interpretation in favour of attempts to explain actions solely by reference to such things as institutional location or economic interest.

When political scientists repudiate positivism, they are usually distancing themselves from the idea of pure experience without intending thereby to repudiate the goal of a political science that eschews interpretation. Typically political scientists try to avoid direct appeals to beliefs by reducing them to intervening variables between social facts – class or institutional location – and actions – voting or bureau shaping. Instead of explaining why people voted for the British Labour Party by reference to their beliefs, for example, a political scientist might do so by saying they were working-class. Similarly, the anomaly this explanation creates out of workers who vote for the Conservative Party is one that a political scientist might deal with, not by examining beliefs, but by reference to something such as religious affiliation, gender, or housing occupancy. Few political scientists would want to claim that social class and the like generate actions without passing through human consciousness. Rather, the correlation between social class and a particular action allegedly allows us to bypass beliefs. The implication is that belonging to a particular class gives one a set of beliefs and desires such that one acts in a given way. To be working-class, for example, is allegedly to recognise that one has an interest in, and so a desire for, the redistributive policies historically associated with the Labour Party.

I want to suggest, in contrast, that once we accept there are no pure experiences we can no longer adhere to the positivist dismissal of the interpretation of beliefs. A rejection of pure experience implies we cannot reduce beliefs and meanings to mere intervening variables. When we say that someone X in a position Y has given interests Z, we necessarily bring our particular theories to bear in order to derive their interests from their position and even to identify their position. Thus someone with a different set of theories might believe either that someone in position Y has different interests or that X is not in position Y. The important point here is that how the people we study actually see their position and their interests inevitably depends on their theories, which might differ significantly from our theories. X might possess theories that lead him to see his position as A, rather than Y, or to see his interests as B rather than Z. For example, some working-class voters might consider themselves to be middle-class, with an interest in preventing further redistributive measures, whilst others might consider themselves working-class but believe redistributive measures are contrary to the true interests of the workers. Similarly, we cannot reduce people's beliefs about their social class or their interests to something such as their religious affiliation, gender, or housing occupancy. We cannot do so because the beliefs and desires associated with things such as religious affiliation are not simply given to people but rather are again things they construct using their theories.

To explain people's actions, we implicitly or explicitly invoke their beliefs and desires. A rejection of positivism implies that we cannot properly do so by appealing to allegedly objective social facts about them. Instead, we must explore the theories and meanings through which they construct their world, including the ways they understand their location, the norms that affect them, their interests, and their desires more generally. Because people cannot have pure experiences, their beliefs and desires are saturated with contingent theories. Thus political scientists cannot read off beliefs and desires from things such as social class. They have instead to interpret them by relating them to other theories and meanings.

Of course, institutionalists and rational choice theorists have grappled with some of the issues raised here. Although some of them seem to remain wedded to the dismissal of any interpretation that rests on positivism, others do not. What I want to suggest, though, is that the more they disentangle themselves from positivism the further they depart from the principles that typically give their approaches their content. Political scientists can avoid the problems that derive from entanglement with positivism only by allowing considerable latitude for interpretation – so much latitude, indeed, it is unclear that what remains can helpfully be described as institutionalism or rational choice.

Institutionalists typically attempt to explain actions and trajectories by reference to entrenched institutions, whether within different states or at other geographical levels. The implication is that formal institutions, understood in terms of rules or norms, explain, and perhaps determine, behaviour. March and Olsen, for example, define institutions as 'collections of standard operating procedures and structures that define and defend interest', thereby both explaining the political actions of individuals and constituting 'political actors in their own right' (1984, 1989). Yet there remains considerable ambiguity about how we should conceive of institutions. On the one hand, institutions often seem to be being given an unacceptably reified form in a way that enables political scientists to take them for granted: they are defined as allegedly fixed operating procedures or rules that limit, and arguably even determine, the actions of those subjects within them. On the other hand, institutions are sometimes opened up to include cultural factors or meanings in a way that suggests they do not fix such meanings nor thus the actions of the subjects within them. If we open up institutions in this way, however, we cannot treat them as if they were given. We have to ask instead how meanings and so actions are created, recreated, and changed so as to produce and modify institutions.

By and large, institutionalists like to take institutions for granted; they treat them as if the people within them are bound to follow the relevant procedures or rules; they treat these rules, rather than contingent agency, as the source of something akin to path dependence. Yet to treat institutions as given in this way appears to be to adopt the positivist eschewal of interpretation we have been challenging. Institutionalism, so conceived, assumes that allegedly objective procedures or rules prescribe or cause behaviour so that someone in a position X who is thereby subject to a rule

Y will behave in a manner Z. The problem with this assumption is not just that people can wilfully choose to disobey a norm or rule, but also, as we have seen, that we cannot read off people's beliefs and desires from their social location. People who are in a position X might not grasp that they fall under rule Y, or they might understand the implications of rule Y differently from us, and in these circumstances they might not act in a manner Z even if they intend to follow the rule.[5]

Faced with such considerations, institutionalists might decide to open up the concept of an institution so as to incorporate meanings; they might conceive of an institution as a product of actions informed by the varied and contingent beliefs and desires of the relevant people. We should welcome such an opening up, or decentring, of institutionalism. Even while we do so, however, we might wonder whether or not we should still think of the approach as, in any significant sense, institutionalist. All the explanatory work would now be done, not by allegedly given rules or procedures, but by the multiple, diverse ways in which people understood such rules and reacted to them. An appeal to an institution would thus represent slightly misleading shorthand for the conclusions of explorations into and interpretations of the beliefs and desires of the people who acted so as to maintain and modify that institution in the way they did.

We might rephrase this commentary on institutionalism to say simply that the rejection of positivism leaves it desperately needing a micro-theory. Institutionalists can avoid engaging with beliefs and preferences only if they assume we can read these things off from people's social location, but, of course, that is exactly what the rejection of positivism suggests we cannot do. The lack of a micro-theory in a post-positivist world does much, I believe, to explain the vulnerability of institutionalism to the challenge of rational choice theory. Similarly, the fact that rational choice theory constitutes a micro-theory does much to explain the ways in which various political scientists have sought to bring it together with institutionalism (Grafstein 1991; Ostrom 1991; Dowding and King 1995). When we now turn to rational choice, however, we find that it too confronts a choice between an unacceptable positivism and a decentred approach.

Because rational choice theory conceptualises actions as rational strategies for realising the preferences of the actor, there is a sense in which it seems to reduce the motives of political actors to self-interest. Yet, as most rational choice theorists would recognise, we have no valid grounds for privileging self-interest as a motive.[6] Even if an action happens to have beneficial consequences for the actor, we cannot from that fact alone conclude that the actor acted in order to bring about those beneficial consequences, let alone that he did so solely for that reason. Besides, a theory predicated solely on self-interest cannot properly make sense of altruistic actions. These obvious problems with exclusive reliance on self-interest have led rational choice theorists to expand their notion of preference: they have moved towards a 'thin' analysis of preferences that does not examine the motives for actions but requires them only to be consistent (Elster 1983: 1). The problem with thus reducing all motives to an expanded concept of preference is that it is either false or valid but of limited value. If we use an expanded notion of preference merely as a cloak under which to smuggle back in a naive view of self-interest, it is false. If we extend our concept of a preference to cover any motive for any action, we leave the concept devoid of content.

A valid concept of preference is one pretty much devoid of all content. The problem for rational choice theorists thus becomes how to fill out the concept of a preference on any given occasion. At times, of course, rational choice theorists in effect fill it out by reference to a quasi-analytic notion of self-interest, even if they also pay lip service to the problems of doing so. More often, however, they attempt to fill it out by reference to what they suggest are more or less self-evidently the 'natural', 'obvious', or 'presumed' preferences of people in a certain position. For example, bureaucrats want the increased power that standardly comes from increasing the size of their fiefdoms. Typically, as in this example, the relevant preferences are made to appear 'natural' or 'obvious' by loose reference to self-interest in the context of a particular institutional framework. Obviously, however, this way of filling out the concept of preference falls prey to the criticism of positivism that has run through our theoretical reflections. Even if we assume that the dominant motivation of most bureaucrats is to increase their power – a difficult assumption, as many of them probably also value things such as time with their family and interesting work – we cannot blithely assume that bureaucrats understand and judge their institutional context as we do.

Faced with such considerations, rational choice theorists might decide to return to a largely empty notion of preference, that is, to conceive of people's actions as products of their beliefs and desires without saying anything substantive about what these might be (Mitchell 1993; Vicchaeri 1993: 221–4). Once again, we should welcome such a decentring of rational choice theory. However, we also might wonder whether or not we should still think of the approach as, in any significant sense, rational choice. All the explanatory work would now be done not by deductions based on assumptions of self-interest, but by appeals to the multiple and diverse beliefs and desires that motivated the actors. The types of formal model developed by many rational choice theorists would thus be mere heuristics unless, on some rare occasions, empirical interpretations of the beliefs and preferences of the various actors showed they corresponded to those informing the model.

The purpose of these theoretical reflections is not to undermine all appeals to institutions, rules, and norms, nor is it to preclude appeals to self-interest and the use of deductive models, nor yet is it to deny that quantitative techniques or formal models have a role in political science. To reject any of these things outright would be far too hasty, partly because none of

the relevant approaches or techniques is monolithic, with a fixed content –
rather, some institutionalists and some rational choice theorists have tried
to push their approach in an interpretative direction – and partly because
political scientists inspired by such an approach often do work that manages
to overcome the limitations of the theories to which they explicitly appeal.
Our theoretical reflections suggest only that we need to think about, and
tailor our use of, institutions, rationality, statistics, and models to a recognition that political science is an interpretative discipline within which most
explanations work through the ascription of contingent beliefs and desires
to the relevant actors.

The overlapping nature of approaches to political science opens up at
least three ways of locating the decentred analysis of governance to which
we will now move. In the first place, we might take a decentred analysis to
be the development of a rational choice theory that remains truly agnostic
as to the preferences at work in any given case and so aware of the need
to interpret the beliefs and desires of the relevant actors. Alternatively, we
might take it to be the development of an institutional theory that takes the
contingent nature of institutions seriously and so treats them as products
of human agency informed by diverse sets of beliefs and desires. Finally, we
might suggest that a decentred theory offers such a radical challenge to the
dominant concepts of 'preference' and 'institution' that we should think of
it as an alternative approach to political science – an interpretative approach
based on a hermeneutic philosophy rather than a lingering positivism.[7] It
matters little how we locate a decentred analysis. The important thing is
that we begin to think of governance as the contingent product of political
struggles embodying competing sets of beliefs.

## Understanding governance

Our theoretical reflections suggest that an adequate account of governance
should eschew any lingering positivism for the task of interpretation. In
doing so, we question both the neo-liberal and the network narratives of
governance in ways that parallel difficulties we found in rational choice
theory and institutionalism.

The neo-liberal narrative, with its overlap with rational choice theory by
way of neo-classical economics, defines governance in terms of policies proposed on the basis of a particular reading of neo-classical theory together
with the consequences this theory suggests these policies will have. Governance consists of a revitalised and efficient public sector based on markets,
competition, and management techniques imported from the private sector.
Behind such definitions lurk neo-classical ideas of preference formation,
utility, rationality, and profit maximisation. Because social democracy, with
its Keynesianism and bureaucratic hierarchies, did not allow for such ideas,
it allegedly ran aground on problems of inflation and overload. Neo-liberal
reforms are thus needed to restructure the state in accord with these ideas.

Within the neo-liberal narrative of governance we often find difficulties with the concepts of preference, utility, and rationality that mirror those within rational choice theory. Typically neo-liberals rely more or less explicitly on a fairly naive view of self-interest to treat preferences, utility, and rationality as unproblematic. Only by doing so can they conclude that reforms such as the New Public Management will lead to greater efficiency without regard for the particular circumstances in which they are introduced. It is just possible that neo-liberals might try to deploy a richer notion of self-interest so as to allow that people have all sorts of motivations, based on their particular and contingent beliefs. Surely, however, if they did so, they would have to allow such particularity and contingency to appear in both the workings of hierarchies and the consequences of neo-liberal reforms, and to do that they would have to tell a far more complex story of governance; they would have to decentre governance by unpacking it in terms of actual and contingent beliefs and preferences.

Institutionalists often define governance more or less stipulatively as something like self-organising, inter-organisational networks. Behind these definitions lurks the idea that the growth of governance reflects a process of functional and institutional specialisation and differentiation that is characteristic of advanced industrial societies. Entrenched institutional patterns or trajectories ensure that neo-liberal reforms actually lead not to markets but to the further differentiation of policy networks in an increasingly hollow state. Within the narrative of governance as networks, we thus find an ambiguity that mirrors that within institutionalist theory. On the one hand, differentiation can evoke recognition of differences, or the specialist parts of a whole, based on function. When advocates of governance as networks understand differentiation in this way, they move toward a positivist account of governance; they think of governance as a complex set of institutions and institutional linkages defined by their social role or function in a way that renders otiose appeals to the contingent beliefs and preferences of agents. On the other hand, differentiation can evoke recognition of differences and contingent patterns based on meaning. If advocates of governance as networks understood differentiation in this way, they would move toward a decentred account of governance; they would unpack the institutions of governance through a study of the various contingent meanings that inform the actions of the relevant individuals.

Most current accounts of governance as networks take a loosely positivist direction apparent in their focus on the objective characteristics of policy networks and the oligopoly of the political market place. A decentred analysis of governance, in contrast, would focus on the social construction of networks through the ability of individuals to create meanings. It would thus extend aspects of the institutionalist critique of neo-liberalism to institutionalism itself – institutions no more have natural or given forms that render certain developments or trajectories inevitable than does capitalism, the global market, or competition between states.

In contrast to the positivism lingering within many existing narratives of governance, a decentred approach would encourage us to examine the ways our social life, institutions, and policies are created, sustained, and modified by subjects acting upon beliefs that are not given by either an objective self-interest or by the institution itself but rather arise from a process within which these subjects modify traditions in response to dilemmas.[8] Because we cannot read off people's beliefs from knowledge of objective social facts about them, we have to explore both how traditions prompt them to adopt certain meanings and how dilemmas prompt them to modify these traditions. A tradition is a set of theories, narratives, and associated practices that people inherit, and that then forms the background against which they hold beliefs and perform actions. A dilemma arises for people when a new belief, often itself an interpretation of an experience, stands in opposition to their existing ones, thereby forcing a reconsideration of the latter. Once we thus unpack governance in relation to various traditions and the ways they inspire diverse responses to dilemmas, we will problematise the notion that it arose from given inputs, pressures, and policies just as much as that the relevant policies necessarily had the outcomes expected by neo-liberals. State actors construct their understanding of the pressures or dilemmas, and also the policies they adopt in response to them, in different ways, depending on the traditions against which they do so. Institutionalists emphasise the unintended consequences of neo-liberal reforms. A decentred approach would add to this recognition of how the reforms and the responses to them reflect contests of meaning between actors inspired by different traditions. Allegedly given pressures are merely the constructions of the particular narratives that currently happen to dominate political debate.[9]

A decentred approach highlights the importance of dilemmas, traditions, and political contests for the study of governance. Any existing pattern of government will have some failings, although different people typically ascribe different content to those failings. When people's perception of a failing is such that it stands at odds with their existing beliefs, it poses a dilemma that pushes them to reconsider their beliefs and so the tradition that informs those beliefs. Because people confront these dilemmas within diverse traditions, there arises a political contest over what constitutes the nature of the failings and so what should be done about them. Exponents of rival political positions seek to promote their particular sets of theories and policies in the context of certain laws and norms that prescribe how they might legitimately do so. This political contest leads to a reform of government – a reform that thus stands as the contingent product of a contest over meanings whose content reflects different traditions and dilemmas.

The pattern of government established by this complex process will exhibit new failings, pose new dilemmas, and be the subject of competing proposals for reform. There thus arises a further contest over meanings, a contest in which the dilemmas are often significantly different, a contest in which the traditions have usually been modified as a result of accommodating the previous dilemmas, and a contest in which the relevant laws and norms have sometimes changed as a result of simultaneous political contests over their content. Moreover, although we can distinguish analytically between a pattern of government and a political contest over its reform, we rarely can do so temporally: rather, the activity of governing continues during most political contests, and most contests occur partly within local practices of governing. What we have, therefore, is a complex and continuous process of interpretation, conflict, and activity that generates an ever-changing pattern of government. We can begin to explain a mode of governance by taking an abstract snapshot of this process and relating it to the varied dilemmas and traditions that inform it.

A decentred analysis of governance would shift the emphasis of our attempts to understand governance at the global, national, and local levels. We might begin, for example, by examining how diverse state traditions have led to different interpretations and practices of governance. We could ask whether the Danish emphasis on local government and popular participation has highlighted efforts to keep changing, and perhaps multiplying, markets and networks under democratic control. Similarly, we could ask whether the Germanic tradition, with its emphasis on the importance of a legal framework to official action, has encouraged particular ways of controlling markets and networks at one level while remaining highly tolerant of their diversity at other levels. When we find continuities of the sort here suggested, moreover, we would not assume we could explain them by some vague appeal to institutional patterns within the relevant state. Instead, we would recognise the importance of unpacking them by reference to political conflicts and compromises between groups inspired by diverse beliefs. In the German case, for example, we might explore the alternative interpretations of the country's post-war development offered by, say, a liberal tradition, a tradition of social partnership, and a radical democratic and environmentalist tradition.[10]

## Questions and answers

A decentred analysis of governance departs from both the neo-liberal narrative and that of governance as networks. It encourages us to understand governance in terms of a political contest resting on competing webs of belief and to explain these beliefs by reference to traditions and dilemmas. In shifting attention to such things, moreover, it points us toward novel perspectives on many of the questions that recur in discussions of governance, especially among political scientists interested in governance as networks. Thus we can expand on our decentred analysis by bringing it to bear on these questions.

*Is governance new?*
Positivist political scientists sometimes suggest the emergence of markets
or networks in the public sector is a new phenomenon characterising a new
epoch. Their sceptical critics, in contrast, argue that markets and networks
are not new, even that governance is no different from government. In reply
to such sceptics, proponents of governance have allowed that neither
markets nor networks are new while still insisting that both of them are
now noticeably more common than they used to be (Rhodes 1997: chapter
3). The difficulty with current approaches to this question, of course, is that
the issue of continuity gets reduced to the facile, scholastic, and probably
impossible task of counting markets and networks in the past and in the
present.
   A decentred approach to governance casts a new light on this facile
debate. For a start, it encourages us to treat hierarchies, markets, and networks alike as meaningful practices created and constantly recreated
through contingent actions informed by diverse webs of belief. Governance
is not new, then, in that it is an integral part of social and political life. We
find the main characteristics of networks in hierarchies and markets as well
as in governance. For example, the rules and commands of a bureaucracy
do not have a fixed form but rather are constantly interpreted and made
afresh through the creative activity of individuals as they come across
always slightly novel circumstances. Likewise, the operation of competition
in markets depends on the contingent beliefs and interactions of interdependent producers and consumers who rely on trust and diplomacy, as well
as economic rationality, to make decisions. Once we stop reifying hierarchies and markets, we find that many of the characteristics allegedly associated with networks are ubiquitous aspects of political practices. In
addition, however, a decentred approach encourages a shift of focus from
reified networks, now recognised as an integral part of political life, to the
beliefs held by political actors and the stories told by political scientists.
Governance is new, then, in that it marks and inspires a significant change
in these beliefs and stories. Governance as decentred networks provides a
different story from both institutional and economic rationality.

*Is governance a vague metaphor?*
Sceptics who say governance is nothing new often go on to denounce the
concept as uninformative and inelegant. Peter Riddell has said, for example,
'every time I see the word "governance" I have to think again what it means
and how it is not the same as government'. He complains, 'terms such as
"core executive", "differentiated polity" and "hollowed out executive"
have become almost a private patois of political science' (Riddell n.d.).
   Presumably we should defend concepts on the grounds that they provide
a more accurate and fruitful way of discussing the world. Riddle, however,
appears to reject the language of governance not because he thinks it inac-
curate but because it lacks clarity. To respond to such concerns we have to

ask, what gives a concept clarity? Many interpretative approaches hold that a concept derives its meaning in large part from its place in a body of concepts. All concepts are thus vague when taken on their own. Just as the concept of governance gains clarity only by being filled out through ideas such as networks, the hollow state, and the core executive, so the elder concepts associated with the Westminster system gained clarity only in relation to others such as the unitary state and Cabinet government. No doubt people who are unfamiliar with concepts such as the hollow state will benefit from having them explicitly related to processes such as the erosion of state authority by new regional and international links. Equally, however, people who are unfamiliar with the concept of a unitary state might benefit from having it explicitly related to the fusion of a single transnational authority or the contrast provided by federal systems. Although the terminology of governance can sound metaphorical, we need not worry about that. It is metaphorical only in that it applies novel names, such as the hollow state, to processes and practices we can unpack in more literal terms, such as the erosion of the authority of the state. What is more, all concepts begin as metaphors in just this sense: they begin as novel names, such as loyal opposition, that we apply to more literal processes and practices, and only later do they acquire a familiarity such that they no longer have the unsettling effect they once did. One day the now unfamiliar language of governance may become as much a part of our everyday political discourse as are many of the concepts that define the Westminster system.

### Is governance uniform?

Neo-liberals portray governance as composed of policies, such as marketisation and the New Public Management, which are allegedly the inevitable outcomes of global economic pressures. Institutionalists argue that these neo-liberal policies do not have uniform consequences but rather effects that vary across states according to the content and strength of established practices. A decentred analysis suggests, in addition, that the pressures are not given as brute facts, but constructed as somewhat different dilemmas from within various traditions. Hence it suggests that the policies a state adopts are not necessary responses to given pressures, but a set of perceived solutions to one particular conception of them. A decentred approach would have us concern ourselves with the contests through which patterns of governance are created, instead of postulating some sort of inevitable process that renders such a concern otiose. Our emphasis should no longer fall upon an abstract model of natural selection in the context of capital mobility and competition between states. On the contrary, we should highlight the political contests, complete with the coercion contained therein, that surround the selection and implementation of policy.

By raising the possibility of continuing diversity of inputs and policies as well as of outputs, a decentred approach might even prompt us to wonder again about the value of the concept of governance. Governance typically refers to a set of shared inputs, policies, and outputs tied to economic and technological developments since about 1970. Once we challenge the necessity, and so commonality, not only of the outputs, as do the institutionalists, but also of the inputs and policies, we should be wary not only of any straightforward dichotomy between governance and government, but also of any attempt to use the abstract idea of governance to account for more particular developments within various states. The relevance of a concept of governance will depend upon empirical studies that explore the ways in which different states have constructed their public sectors. How similar have been their conceptions of the relevant dilemmas, the policies they have adopted, and the consequences of these policies? How far have different state traditions fed through into diverse inputs, policies, and outputs?

### How does governance change?
The question of how governance changes is far more difficult for network theorists to answer than it is for neo-liberals. Neo-liberals can unpack change in terms of the economic self-interest of the key actors. Network theorists, in contrast, often deploy an institutionalism that remains ambiguous about the nature of change. In order to avoid the need to interpret beliefs and desires institutionalists often reduce individual behaviour to a matter of following the rules or norms that govern the institution and the role of the relevant individual therein – but, of course, if individuals merely follow rules, they cannot be the causes of change. In order to explain change, therefore, institutionalists often appeal to external factors that might appear to avoid the need to unpack the beliefs and desires of individuals – but, of course, external factors will bring about changes in an institution only if they lead individuals to modify established patterns of behaviour, where we can understand how individuals do this only by interpreting their beliefs and desires.

Network theorists, like institutionalists more generally, typically try to explain change by reference to external causes. Marsh and Rhodes, for example, effectively dismiss the way in which individuals constantly create and recreate the networks of which they are a part by emphasising that networks create routines for policy making.[11] They identify four categories of change – economic, ideological, knowledge, and institutional – all of which they define as external to the network. A decentred analysis, in contrast, draws our attention to the fact that such external factors influence networks and governance only through the ways in which they are understood by the relevant actors. Although change can be of varying magnitude, a decentred analysis portrays it as continuous in the sense of being built into the very nature of political life. Change occurs as individuals interpret their environment in ways that lead them constantly to modify their actions or even to act in dramatically new ways. We can explain change, then, as was suggested earlier, by reference to the contingent responses of individuals to dilemmas, many of which will be produced by new circumstances such as those created by the actions of others.

*Is governance failure inevitable?*
The neo-liberal narrative of governance relies heavily on the idea that hierarchy has failed: the problems of inefficiency and overload justify calls for the New Public Management and marketisation. Likewise, the narrative of governance as networks relies on the idea that the neo-liberal reforms have failed: the reforms ignored the need for trust, diplomacy, and accountability in the public sector. Some advocates of governance as networks present networks as the solution to the failings of bureaucracy and markets.[12] Others argue that networks typically create problems of their own: they are, for example closed to outsiders, unrepresentative, and relatively unaccountable, and they can serve private interests as well as being difficult to steer and inefficient (Rhodes 1997: chapter 3). The implication of such analyses appears to be that no governing structure works for all services in all conditions. Governance failure is inevitable.

A decentred analysis complements and challenges aspects of this emerging account of governance failure. A focus on contingent meanings provides us with one way of understanding why all ways of providing public services fail. The workings of a policy or institution depend on the ways various actors interpret the relevant directives. Because these responses are inherently diverse and contingent, reflecting the traditions and agency of the relevant individuals, the centre cannot have prior knowledge of the way any policy or institution will operate. Hence the unexpected pervades political life: all policies are subject to unintended consequences that prevent them from perfectly fulfilling their alleged purpose.

A decentred approach also draws our attention to the diverse beliefs and preferences of actors within a network. By doing so, it should make us aware of the way in which positivist debates on governance failure blithely take government intentions as their yardstick. Positivist studies typically aim to improve the chances of a policy's success in terms defined by the state. Yet civil servants and citizens can deliberately attempt to prevent policies having the effects the state intends. From their standpoint, policy failure may be a success.

## Implications for policy and democracy

Once we take seriously the implications of rejecting positivism, we will move toward the need to decentre governance. While our focus so far has been on the study of governance, a decentred analysis also has implications for our thinking about policy and democracy. By resisting the teleological accounts of neo-liberals, and to a lesser extent the apolitical ones of institutionalists, we create a space within which to think creativity about different ways of understanding our contemporary situation and so different ways of responding to it – we encourage political imagination.

Most of the policy-oriented work on governance seeks to improve the ability of the state to manage the markets, quasi-markets, and networks that have flourished since the 1980s. Typically this work exhibits a positivist tendency in that it treats networks as more or less objectified structures that governments can manipulate using appropriate tools and techniques. There appear to be three main approaches to the issue of how the state can manage networks and governance in general – the instrumental, the interactive, and the institutional (Kickert *et al.* 1997). The instrumental approach adopts a top-down stance toward the management of governance: its exponents recognise the existence of new restrictions on the state's ability to steer markets and networks, while still proposing it to do so using fairly traditional strategies – the state can still devise and impose tools to integrate new patterns of governance and thus realise its objectives. The interaction approach to the management of governance focuses on organisations developing shared and appropriate goals and strategies through processes of mutual learning: its exponents advise the state to manage by means of negotiation and diplomacy and thereby foster trust and mutual understanding within networks. Finally, the institutional approach concentrates on the formal and informal context of laws, rules, and norms within which governing structures operate: its exponents encourage the state to concentrate on changing things such as the relationship between actors, the distribution of resources, and the rules of the game.

Our decentred analysis suggests a compatible but rather different way of thinking about the management of governance. It insists that all forms of organisation are conceived as products of the contingent actions of the various participants. In doing so, it prompts us to reject the very idea of a set of techniques or strategies for managing governance: if governance is constructed differently, contingently, and continuously, we cannot have a toolkit for managing it. Instead of looking for techniques or strategies of management, a decentred approach encourages us to learn by telling and listening to stories. While statistics, models, and claims to expertise all have a place within such stories, we should not become too preoccupied with them. On the contrary, we should recognise that they too are narratives or guesses about how people have acted or will react, given their beliefs and desires, where we can try to gauge their beliefs and desires only from their actions and utterances. No matter what rigour or expertise we bring to bear, all we can do is tell a story and judge what the future may bring. One important lesson of taking this view of expertise derives from the diversity and contingency of traditions.[13] The fate of policies depends on the ways civil servants, citizens, and others understand them and respond to them from within all sorts of traditions. If policy makers kept this firmly in mind, they still would not be able to predict the consequences of their policies but they might at least forestall some of their unintended consequences. More generally, they might allow that the management of networks is in large part about trying to understand, and respond suitably to, the beliefs, traditions, and practices of those they hope to influence.

To recognise how providers and customers of services impact upon policies is also to prompt a shift of focus away from the state. Positivist debates on the management of governance typically focus on the problems confronted by managers rather than lower-level civil servants or citizens. In contrast, a decentred analysis reminds us that there are various participants in markets and networks, all of whom can seek to manage them for diverse purposes. By reminding us of the significance of political participation in this way, a decentred theory of governance also raises issues about democracy. Whereas positivist accounts of governance often concentrate on the problems the state has steering it, a decentred theory locates this problem in the context of democratic participation and accountability. To emphasise the extent to which we make our patterns of governance through political contests is to encourage us to think creatively about how we might conceive of and respond to the relevant issues. One aspect of this creative thinking is the impetus given to policy makers to reflect on their activity. Another is the opportunity to reimagine democracy.

A greater interest in markets and networks, it appears to me, suggests we might reflect on how we can best steer a course between diverse forms of devolution and participation, on the one hand, and central control and formal accountability on the other. Although it would be presumptuous to suppose we can resolve the tension between these different demands, we might perhaps indicate how they appear from the view of a decentred theory of governance. Markets and networks allow citizens to express more nuanced preferences in a more continuous way than they can when restricted to electing representatives. Governance opens up new possibilities of participation and devolution in democracy. Because positivist accounts of governance reduce the actions of the people involved to objective rationality or the objective characteristics of a network, they typically neglect these possibilities. A decentred theory, in contrast, emphasises agency, and so the fact that people are expressing their particular and contingent beliefs and preferences through their activity (Bang and Sørensen 1999). An emphasis on agency suggests that while the central state legitimately might seek to influence the operation of markets and networks, we should typically be wary of its attempting to impose outcomes upon them. The state might attempt to persuade citizens to act in a particular manner, but it must then allow them to reflect on the relevant arguments – with a greater or lesser degree of conscious concentration – and choose to do as they decide. Equally, however, we should remain aware of the ways in which markets and networks often embed inequalities and impose identities upon people in a way that then might require the state to act as a guarantor of effective agency and difference. Still, we might look to a time when states will be less concerned to control through laws and regulations and more concerned to persuade through all sorts of interactions with groups and individuals. Such a shift toward persuasion, of course, would fit well alongside an understanding of policy making that highlights contingency and diversity – telling stories and listening to them – rather than certainty and expertise – devising rules designed to have a definite outcome.

Governance might provide more active and continuous opportunities for political involvement to citizens. Yet, as many political scientists have pointed out, the forms of devolution and participation offered by markets and networks raise special problems of political control and accountability. As we have seen, an emphasis on agency might lead the state to rely more on influence than imposition. In a similar fashion, the state might seek to steer markets and networks more by looking to set a framework for their conduct than by relying on rigid rules. The relative power of the state might even make us wary of the danger that its attempts to influence will be so heavyhanded they will in effect undermine participation and agency. Equally, however, we should not forget that markets and networks respond primarily to levels of wealth and organisation in ways that can undermine the equality and fellowship characteristic of a democratic community. A growth in the use of markets and networks to manage and deliver public services surely should be accompanied, therefore, by the development of suitable lines of political accountability. Still, we might look to a time when the state will rely less on moral rules that impose requirements and restrictions and more on an ethic of conduct that constitutes a practice through which citizens negotiate their own relationship to such requirements and restrictions. Once again, of course, an emphasis on conduct would fit well alongside an understanding of policy making that highlights contingency and diversity – a sensitivity to agency informed by various traditions – rather than certainty and expertise – rules that require or prohibit certain behaviour.

A decentred theory of governance highlights not only the difficulties managers face in controlling markets and networks but also the possibilities and dangers markets and networks pose for democracy. It encourages us to treat governance as an opportunity to redefine democracy. It prompts us to search for patterns of devolution, participation, control, and accountability that better reflect our capacity for agency, the contingency of our identities, the importance of moral conduct as well as moral rules, and an aspiration to an open community.

## Notes

1 OECD (1995, 1996), Ansell (2000), Rhodes (1997), particularly chapters 1 and 3, and, for an emphasis on the place of regulation within neo-liberalism itself, Vogel (1996), particularly pp. 1–9.
2 Both Rod Rhodes and Gerry Stoker, respectively the directors of the Whitehall and Local Governance Programmes, evoke institutionalism and unintended consequences in this way (Rhodes 1997: chapter 4; Stoker 1999: introduction).

3 The classic account of institutional economics is Shonfield (1965). A more recent example is Hodgson (1993).

4 The main criticism of positivism of relevance to what follows is a semantic holism that implies our beliefs encounter the world only as a whole so that theory plays an ineluctable role in perception. See Quine (1961: 20–46).

5 Wittgenstein's analysis of rule-following (1972: 143–242) suggests interpretation is inevitable, since rules can never fix their own application.

6 Early exponents of rational choice theory sometimes privileged self-interest in this way (Downs 1957: 27–8).

7 Other varieties of interpretative theory include culturalism and post-structuralism, for examples of which see respectively Scott (1998) and Barry *et al.* (1996).

8 On interpretation and a decentred approach see Bevir (1999a, b: 345–59) and Bevir and Rhodes (2002).

9 On the establishment of dominant narratives in the context of a crisis composed of various dilemmas see Hay (1996) and, for competing narratives of such dilemmas, Bevir and Rhodes (1999). The emphasis on beliefs, ideas and meanings in these essays contrasts with the more standard institutionalism of Rhodes (2000).

10 Nick Ziegler is exploring developments in corporate governance in Germany in this way. For an early example of his work see Ziegler (2000).

11 Marsh and Rhodes (1992: 261). For an interpretative theory of policy networks see Bevir and Rhodes (forthcoming).

12 Attempts to specify the conditions under which networks thrive include Powell (1991) and Lowndes and Skelcher (1998).

13 That a 'high modernism' which forgets this can lead to catastrophe is the principal moral of Scott (1998).

## References

Ansell, C. (2000), 'The networked polity', *Governance* 13: 303–33.

Bang, H. P., and Sørensen, E. (1999), 'The everyday maker: a new challenge to democratic governance', *Administrative Theory and Praxis* 21: 325–41.

Barry, A., Osborne, T., and Rose, N., eds (1996), *Foucault and Political Reason: Liberalism, Neo-liberalism and Rationalities of Government* (London: UCL Press).

Becker, G. (1976), *The Economic Approach to Human Behaviour* (Chicago: University of Chicago Press).

Bevir, M. (1999a), *The Logic of the History of Ideas* (Cambridge: Cambridge University Press).

Bevir, M. (1999b), 'Foucault, power, and institutions', *Political Studies* 47: 345–59.

Bevir, M., and Rhodes, R. (1999), 'Narratives of Thatcherism', *West European Politics* 21: 97–119.

Bevir, M., and Rhodes, R. (2002), 'Interpretative theory', in D. Marsh and G. Stoker (eds), *Theory and Methods in Political Science* (London: Palgrave).

Bevir, M., and Rhodes, R. (forthcoming), 'Analysing networks: from typologies of institutions to narratives of belief', *Revue française d'administration publique*.

Dowding, K., and King, D., eds (1995), *Preferences, Institutions, and Rational Choice* (Oxford: Oxford University Press).

Downs, A. (1957), *An Economic Theory of Democracy* (New York: Harper & Row).

Elster, J. (1983), *Sour Grapes: Studies in the Subversion of Rationality* (Cambridge: Cambridge University Press).

Elster, J., ed. (1986), *Rational Choice* (Buffalo NY: New York University Press).

Grafstein, R. (1991), 'Rational choice: theory and institutions', in K. Monroe (ed.), *The Economic Approach to Politics* (New York: Harper Collins), pp. 237–50.

Hay, C. (1996), 'Narrating crisis: the discursive construction of the winter of discontent', *Sociology* 30: 253–77.

Hay, C. (2000), 'Contemporary capitalism, globalization, regionalization and the persistence of national variation', *Review of International Studies* 26: 509–32.

Hodgson, G. (1993), *The Economics of Institutions* (Aldershot: Edward Elgar).

Kickert, W. J. M., Klijn, E-H., and Koppenjan, J. F. M., eds (1997), *Managing Complex Networks: Strategies for the Public Sector* (London: Sage).

Lowndes, V., and Skelcher, C. (1998), 'The dynamics of multi-organisational partnerships: an analysis of changing modes of governance', *Public Administration* 76: 313–33.

March, J. G., and Olsen, J. P. (1984), 'The new institutionalism: organisational factors in political life', *American Political Science Review* 78: 738–49.

March, J. G., and Olsen, J. P. (1989), *Rediscovering Institutions: The Organizational Basis of Politics* (New York: Free Press).

Marsh, D., and Rhodes, R., eds (1992), *Policy Networks in British Government* (Oxford: Clarendon Press).

Mitchell, W. (1993), 'The shape of public choice to come: some predictions and advice', *Public Choice* 77: 133–44.

Monroe, K., ed. (1991), *The Economic Approach to Politics* (New York: Harper Collins).

OECD (1995), *Governance in Transition: Public Management in OECD Countries* (Paris: OECD/PUMA).

OECD (1996), *Ministerial Symposium on the Future of the Public Services* (Paris: OECD).

Ohmae, K. (1990), *The Borderless World: Power and Strategy in the Interlinked Economy* (London: Collins).

Osborne, D., and Baebler T. (1992), *Reinventing Government: How the Entrepreneurial Spirit is Transforming the Public Sector* (Reading MA: Addison-Wesley).

Ostrom, E. (1991), 'Rational choice theory and institutional analysis: towards complementarity', *American Political Science Review* 85: 237–50.

Porter, M. (1990), *The Competitive Advantage of Nations* (London: Macmillan).

Powell, W. W. (1991), 'Neither market nor hierarchy: networks of organisation', in G. Thompson, J. Frances, R. Levacic and J. Mitchell (eds), *Markets, Hierarchies, and Networks: The Coordination of Social Life* (London: Sage), pp. 265–76.

Quine, W. (1961), 'Two dogmas of empiricism', in *From a Logical Point of View* (Cambridge MA: Harvard University Press), pp. 20–46.

Reinecke, W. (1994), *Global Public Policy: Governing without Government?* (Washington DC: Brookings Institution).

Rhodes, M. (2000), 'Desperately seeking a solution: social democracy, Thatcherism, and the 'third way' in British welfare', *West European Politics* 23: 161–82.

Rhodes, R. A. W. (1997), *Understanding Governance: Policy Networks, Governance, Reflexivity and Accountability* (Buckingham: Open University Press).

Rhodes, R. A. W., ed. (2000), *Transforming British Government*, 2 vols (London: Macmillan).

Riddell, P. (n.d.), 'Portrait of the Whitehall Programme', unpublished Ms.

Scott, J. (1998), *Seeing like a State: How Certain Schemes to Improve the Human Condition have Failed* (New Haven CT: Yale University Press).

Shonfield, A. (1965), *Modern Capitalism* (London: Oxford University Press).

Stoker, G., ed. (1999), *The New Management of British Local Governance* (London: Macmillan).

Stoker, G., ed. (2000), *The New Politics of British Local Governance* (London: Macmillan).

Wittgenstein, L. (1972), *Philosophical Investigations* (Oxford: Blackwell).

World Bank (1992), *Governance and Development* (Washington DC: World Bank).

Ziegler, J. (2000), 'Corporate governance and the politics of property rights in Germany', *Politics and Society* 28: 195–221.

Zysman, J. (1996), 'The myths of a "global economy": enduring national foundations and emerging regional realities', *New Political Economy* 1: 157–84.

# 12

## Governing at close range: demo-elites and lay people

Henrik P. Bang and Torben Bech Dyrberg

### From pluralism and elitism to demo-elitism

Pluralism and elitism are usually presented as opposites. Pluralists have been eager to distance themselves from elitism, which is associated with auto-cratic rule by the few over the many and with a dichotomy between elites and masses. In the wake of industrial society, and with the emergence of what could be called network society, elites and lay actors grow ever more interdependent of each other in new boundary-crossing issue and policy net-works, private–public partnerships and social projects. By displacing old axioms and oppositions these ways of governing society present major chal-lenges to how we can conceive of democratic governance.

Etzioni-Halevy has tried to bridge the pluralist argument, 'that there is a multiplicity of power centres and elites in Western democracies', and the elitist one, 'that there are elites of elites – some elites which are signifi-cantly more powerful than other elites' (1993: 76). Her demo-elitism differs from pluralism, because it 'looks not primarily at interest groups or 'civil' society . . . but at elites and sub-elites' (1993: 5). She dissociates herself from Dahl's view that elite power is inherently undemocratic and that elite autonomy, though an important condition for the stabilisation of democ-racy, is harmful to it as an inherently oppressive power (Dahl 1982: 32–6). Demo-elitism goes further than even the most democratic version of tra-ditional forms of elitism, holding that relative elite autonomy is a meta-principle for the emergence, stabilisation and development of democracy. But this is only the case in so far as this principle is made public and rep-resentative and is accepted as valid by the elites themselves (Etzioni-Halevy 1993: 115–21).

Governing the complexity, uncertainty and pace of change of network society requires elites to facilitate democratic processes, as their autonomy depends on the active involvement of lay actors in governance networks as responsible subjects. Coupling interweaves the principle of elite autonomy 'not merely with liberalism, but with the explicit electoral and other principles of democracy' (1993: 120). Etzioni-Halevy can thus insist on demo-elitism being more democratic than pluralism by not presuming that responsiveness and collaboration on the part of elites operate on the background of a normative consensus in civil society, as the early Dahl (1956) would have it. Elite autonomy and coupling are contingent on conflict and consensus, which means that one must take note of 'the possibility of the subjugation and collusion of elites even in a democracy', and that one must appreciate that 'although the relative autonomy of elites, in itself cannot ensure public participation, it is nonetheless necessary for it' (Etzioni-Halevy 1993: 120, 78).

Demo-elitism advances beyond elitism and pluralism by extending the realm of politics beyond the domains of a dominant power bloc or a dispersed public power. It does not situate interest groups, social movements and voluntary organisations outside the political realm but expands the latter to include the self-sustaining powers of a plurality of forces and sub-elites in the political culture of a society. Elite autonomy is a condition of living in a democratic political culture that potentially extends into every social relation. Demo-elitism does not only break with the tendency that sees politics as derived from economic and social forces and interests. It also dissociates itself from the tendency to identify the terrain of legitimate political decision and action with behaviour and activities that take place within the public realm of a democratic regime. Thus elite theory takes an explicit political stance by stating that politics is dictated neither by market forces nor by community norms, but by 'how elites go about gaining, exercising, and maintaining power' (Dye and Zeigler 1997: 159).

However, demo-elitism is still elitist in assuming that lay actors would fall into despair and anarchy without elites being able to steer and provide them with ideas and visions of good governance. In what follows we argue that self- and co-governance on the part of lay actors in their everyday practices is a key to fulfil the need for wholeness and coherence in expert systems upon which the relative autonomy of elites depends. We refer to this as culture governance which focuses on the problems of coupling 'system' and 'life world'. The problem with demo-elitism is that it has no conception of lay actors as capable, knowledgeable and responsible individuals who can supply politics with something different from elites, and by extension that it lacks a notion of everyday life as constituting a political community.

In a network society, it is as much the elites that would fall into despair without lay actors as the other way round. Hence the notions of elite autonomy and coupling would gain more relevance and utility if they were tied to a two-way definition of autonomy and coupling as relating to both experts and ordinary individuals, and as involving much more than formal political representation. The discussion of culture governance will set out to do just that.

## Democratic governance in the light of tensions between demo-elitism and ordinary politics

There are two issues in demo-elitism that are intrinsic to understanding politics. First, the notion of relative elite autonomy as 'independence of resources' in decision-making processes (Etzioni-Halevy 1993: 98–9) and, second, the idea of elite desertion or uncoupling, as 'the process whereby elites abandon the disadvantaged – promotes socio-economic inequality and detracts from the quality of democracy' (1999: 242). Relative autonomy places a claim upon pluralism by communicating that it is not 'the *plurality* of power groups' but the 'self-sustaining power of even a few such groups [which is] the main mechanism sustaining democracy' (1993: 78). This principle challenges elitism in arguing that self-sustainment is not merely an expression of struggle for power but of democratic inclusion and recognition, since 'in order to defend their own autonomy, elites must defend the meta-principle of autonomy' (1993: 79). This combined attack on pluralism and elitism gives way to a normative critique. Etzioni-Halevy (2000: 2) states that the 'distancing of . . . elites from the less well-to-do classes of the public means that the shapers of policy are not attuned to, and do not promote the concerns and interests of, those that most need their intervention. This exacerbates inequalities, at the same time that it creates problems for democracy.'

Demo-elitism stimulates a new empirical and normative approach to understanding democratic coupling at all levels, from local to global contexts, and it raises two major challenges to contemporary political theory and research.

1 Demo-elitism shifts the political focus from democratic government to democratic governance (Rosenau 1997; McGinnis 1999; Pierre 2000). The latter expands the domains of politics and democracy to comprise the personal, the social and the global. It makes politics appear as multi-level networks populated by many different types of agents that operate below and above, inside and outside the state (Pierre and Peters 2000: chapter 4). These agents typically show mutual respect of difference within their own networks, share competences and responsibilities across the spheres of the private, public and voluntary, and possess a relative autonomy *vis-à-vis* one another (Bang *et al.* 2000: chapters 2, 12).

2 With regard to coupling and uncoupling, demo-elitism substitutes a political logic of appropriateness for the exogenous logics of consequentiality and normative integration (March and Olsen 1989: 160–2), which is to say that it focuses on political community instead of market and civil society. The central question is no longer how to balance effectiveness and solidarity by bridging the gap between 'rational man' and 'irrational society', as has been characteristic of the behaviourist era in political science. The question is rather how to cope with trends that uncouple elites from lay actors at all levels of politics.

The notion of democratic governance allows for a substantial and not simply a procedural view of pluralism, which refers to the distinction between pluralisation and pluralism (Connolly 1995). Pluralisation stresses that pluralism is measured not only by the number of access channels to the democratic regime but also by the scope and extent to which actors recognise and accept each other in a political community. The logic of appropriateness that relates to the problem of coupling provides a political logic, which signals that 'coupling entails a reciprocal relationship, whereby elites or would-be elites promote the interests of certain parts of the public, who in turn generate those elites and endow them with their elite positions, or else support them when they already wield power' (Etzioni-Halevy 2000: 2). In this way reciprocal relations of power-knowledge in a political community become a condition for market forces as well as for establishing social solidarities. However, there are two problems.

1 In demo-elitism relative autonomy covers elites only, which means that the responsibility for appropriate coupling lies upon them. Only by being representative of and responsive to lay actors and publics is it possible for elites to assert their power without losing credibility when defending the principle of autonomy. However, there is no reason why relative autonomy and processes of pluralisation have to be narrowed down to comprise elites only. It may be that lay actors would fall into despair without elites, but from this it does not follow that lay actors cannot make a difference *as* lay actors. On the contrary, it is difficult to see how elites could have relative autonomy and live up to their responsibility of coupling unless lay actors possessed the relevant knowledge and ability to assert and communicate the problems that elites are called upon to solve. After all, without lay actors elites would simply be ghosts in the machine. Yet demo-elitism tends to treat lay actors as 'docile bodies' or as objects of knowledge upon which elites place their imprints. A two-way model of relative autonomy is needed according to which elites could not honour their own principle unless lay actors were able and ready to recognise and accept their significance for democracy.

2 Demo-elitism lacks a notion of political community in which relative autonomy can be grounded. It emphasises that 'in the notion of civil society – as in the notion of interest groups – the distinction between elites, sub-elites and the public is blurred, and the focal role of the autonomy of elites is, once again, relegated to the back of the stage' (Etzioni-Halevy 1993: 81). The principle of relative elite autonomy is substantial, but there is no reason to assume that it is 'only the independence of the processes in which elites and sub-elites are involved [which] can organise and defend that of all other micro-processes of interaction – without which the formal procedures of democracy would have little value' (1993: 81). This is an empirical question. Rather than reassessing civil society as 'a distinction between the elite and public component' (1993: 81), relative autonomy should be based on a notion of *political* community as comprising a division of labour between

elites and non-elites for articulating and implementing collectively binding decisions (Easton 1965: chapter 13). In this way the perspective would change from elite politics, with its emphasis on efficient governance, to the processes in which elites and lay people interact.

Relative autonomy in a political community *also* depends on the active and reasonable involvement of lay people. The recognition and reciprocity of power on the part of elites and lay actors in the political community distinguish the principle of autonomy from the formal principles and norms that protect the free and equal access of pressure groups and power holders to the regime (pluralism). Pluralisation through micro-politics thus challenges proceduralist views of democracy, indicating that the universalisation of rights with regard to democratic norms of plurality, participation and equality derives from the particularities of co-operation and autonomisation between agents in a political community (Connolly 1999; Bang *et al.* 2000).

We will conceive of political autonomy and democratic coupling in a dialogue with demo-elitism, which in the first place requires discussion of what is involved in speaking of governance. What is the political significance of the growing stress on governance as opposed to government, how does it affect our understanding of democracy and what does a governance-managed network society do to political representation, which is the central mechanism of coupling in government discourses? Second, we will use the discussion of governance, and culture governance in particular, to connect the notion of political regime with that of political community as mutual relations of autonomy and dependence between lay actors and elites. The reason is that one should distinguish the authoritative description of democracy that unfolds under the constitution from conventional views of democracy making up a political community as an ensemble of reflexive practices (Giddens 1993; Pedersen 1998; Bang and Dyrberg 2000: 154–7). Etzioni-Halevy's demo-elitism should be discussed in the light of this distinction. Is her version of elite rule in a democracy the most adequate way to cash in on the values of liberal democracy: liberty and equality? Or is it the case that her elitism prevents her from doing just that? We will argue that the latter is the case. The third point is then to focus on the blind spot of elitism, namely the micro-politics of lay actors involved in common concerns. No matter how 'demo' elitism is, it remains antithetical to democracy as long as it does not recognise and accept the relative autonomy of lay actors in a political community.

Demo-elitism is entangled in the dilemma of reconciling two assumptions. On the one hand, it is argued that the meta-principle of democracy consists of the relative autonomy of elites from each other as well as from those they represent. On the other, elite autonomy depends on coupling elites and non-elites, which is to say that the former depends on and accounts to the latter (Etzioni-Halevy 1993, 1999). She is right to point at the political problem of articulating elite autonomy and coupling, but by turning relative elite autonomy into *the* meta-principle of democracy the autonomy of lay actors has no place in her view of democracy. This is not only a democratic problem, but also a problem of being able to articulate democracy and governance in a way that can meet the challenges of present-day politics where lay people are individuated and reflexive as opposed to being part of an anonymous mass.

## From distant governing to governing at close range

One of the major threats facing democracy is that global–local alliances lead to uncouple elites from non-elites. Etzioni-Halevy has aptly phrased it 'elite desertion', which she sees as a key problem for democracy. By this she means that 'elites forge a close "elite connection" among themselves', which 'leads them to uncouple from the disadvantaged' (1999: 242). The new private–public–voluntary partnerships sometimes fit her description in tending to uncouple organised elites from the groups they represent. However, she limits the range and scope of the risks that elite desertion implies for democracy by hanging on to the government conception where 'the term democracy denotes a regime in which the authority to govern derives from the consent of the majority of the people' (1997: xxiii). What this argument neglects is the political problem of commonality. Access to and recognition within the regime do not automatically give access to and recognition within the political community.

In demo-elitism, only elites have political existence and they alone can safeguard the cohesion of the political community. Just because one is not a political authority or engaged in power struggles between elites, it does not follow that one does not know how to 'go on' politically or is unable to make a difference in the political division of labour. Relations between elites and lay people are marked by relations of autonomy and dependence, which restrict the power of hegemonic authorities to define the political terrain and to bind the political community to the regime. Demo-elitism partly accepts this by arguing that it 'is practically forced by its inner logic to deal with movement generated change. For by defining elites and sub-elites *inter alia* on the basis of personal resources such as those of charisma and energy, it must include in its analysis leaders and activists of social movements' (1993: 201). But by focusing on the opposition between key elites in the state (authorities in the shape of politicians, administrators, dominant interest organisations, the media, etc.) and sub-elites in civil society (leaders of voluntary associations, social movements, etc.), demo-elitism gives a reductionist account of both governance and democratic politics.

When studying coupling and uncoupling in relation to democracy, it is necessary to distinguish between elites and non-elites *vis-à-vis* state and government, on the one hand, and network and governance on the other (Bang 2000: 292; see table 12.1). If a democratic regime is to sustain and renew

**Table 12.1**  *The coupling problem*

|            | *State and government*       | *Network and governance*          |
|------------|------------------------------|-----------------------------------|
| *Elites*     | Protect and serve            | Care and facilitate               |
| *Lay actors* | Accept the rules of the game | Recognise and accept differences  |

itself over time, elites have to protect and serve non-elites, while non-elites have to be willing to accept the autonomy of elites. Just as lay actors have to recognise that everyone is able to act politically, so elites have to demonstrate that they are ready to facilitate lay actors' potential for governing themselves and others. This is required for the persistence of a political community and for its democratic cohesion.

The framework of democratic government is relatively blind to the community angle of the elite/lay actor connection. If elites protect and serve in line with democratic standards and if lay actors accept the rules of the game there can be no steering and legitimation problems. Demo-elitism illustrates that this conclusion can be too hasty. The elite connection and consensus between private and public interests within elite discourses push in the direction of elite desertion and inequality and weaken the disadvantaged. 'For the weakness of the disadvantaged makes it more difficult for elites to organise them for the promotion of their interest. And this makes it easier for governments to pursue policies that disadvantage the disadvantaged even further, and exacerbate inequalities' (Etzioni-Halevy 1999: 245).

What we see here is an alternative idea of elite steering as facilitating, being attentive to and showing care of the needs and interests of others. Demo-elitism explicitly formulates an egalitarian perspective via the notions of relative elite autonomy and coupling. Its critique of new links among elites and the consensus they foster does not primarily concern the issues of rights and who are authorised to get access to decision making in a democratic regime. The criticism is primarily concerned with the vicious circle of inequality which destabilises political order and weakens democracy. Yet demo-elitism sticks to the authoritative view of liberal democracy as protected by the state. It never goes beyond the abstract politics of ideas provided by the left/right opposition, which is about how individuals, groups or classes are supposed to be organised by political representation based on common interests within each segment. No regime, the arguments goes, can grant its members direct access to authoritative decision and action. This prerogative is reserved for what Dahl calls 'the political stratum' (1961: chapter 8).

What culture governance points at is that lay people are included in the political division of labour as capable and knowledgeable agents, as this tends to improve political steering and strengthen democratic concerns and traditions. Having a sense of difference and common destiny means recognising and accepting the equal value of everybody making up the political capital of everyday life (Rawls 1993: 54). This is unacceptable to elite theory because it does not recognise the difference non-elites make to the structuring and functioning of democracy. This also holds for 'demo' versions of elitism, as elites may be protective, representative and egalitarian yet lack the respect of lay persons that is all-important for a democratic political community. Elitism is not concerned with connecting strategies of steering by facilitating and empowering with the various ways of solving problems in common that are inherent to the political traditions of a democratic society. The reason for this lack of concern lies in the meaning of coupling. Coupling is not a set of relations of reciprocal autonomy–dependence, but a way of organising popular consent or support to regime structures. When coupling is for all practical purposes defined as support it is, obviously, also defined from the perspective of elites. Demo-elitism is here strictly opposed to democracy, and it cannot grasp the political importance of forms of governance that aim to improve both the efficiency and the legitimacy of political decisions *and* facilitate the development of the governance powers of lay people.

## The dilemma of demo-elitism

According to Etzioni-Halevy (1993: 103), 'the autonomy of elites forms an overarching meta-principle' of democracy, whereupon 'the relative autonomy of elites forms a large part of what the principles of democracy are really about'. Elite rule and democracy reinforce each other in that only the former can cash in on the principles and values of the latter. In this attempt to square the circle Etzioni-Halevy presents an up-to-date elitism. Gone is the earlier explicit contempt for democracy, its impossibility and undesirability; gone is also the cynical view of the political immaturity of citizens as exemplified in Schumpeter's (1976: 262) assertion that 'the typical citizen drops down to a lower level of mental performance as soon as he enters the political field . . . He becomes a primitive again.' This does not mean that ordinary people play no role in politics, but their role is defined as support of the regime, that is, of different elites which sort things out among themselves. It is with this mandate of support that they can become legitimate political players.

With demo-elitism things are somewhat different because the public plays a more prominent role and because relations between elites, sub-elites and lay people is less rigid. Demo-elitism endorses democracy; it values open-mindedness, flexibility, mobility, and it bridges the dual concerns of liberal democracy: liberty and equality. But it is still elitist in maintaining that politics has to be the business of elites, which can easily fit into a governance perspective of loosely coupled and informal networks. Citizens do not have what it takes to engage in politics. They tend to be ignorant, emotional,

inflexible and moved by short-term interests as opposed to being knowledgeable, reasonable, flexible and able to consider long-term interests. It is
in this respect that lay people are seen as politically 'disadvantaged'. This
also holds for Etzioni-Halevy (1993: 204), for whom 'One of the most
important developments in Western democracies has been the governing
elites' gradual *shift from strategies of repression to such strategies of
absorption*' (our emphasis). This shift accounts for the endorsement of a
form of democracy in which 'strategies of absorption' play a central role
for elites' ability to govern effectively and legitimately.

The strategic shift could also be seen in the light of the development of
governance structures. A governance strategy of absorption with regard to
social movements would diverge from an oppressive strategy for two
reasons. 'It does not involve coercion directly' and 'The aim and/or result
of the mechanism is not to eliminate the movement and its activities, or
even to alter it completely, but rather to *let it persist while dissipating its
threat*' (Etzioni-Halevy 1993: 204, our emphasis). Every type of public–
voluntary partnership in a governance context could be studied in the light
of elitist strategies of dissipation and stabilisation. But they might also be
analysed from the vantage point of ordinary politics: public–voluntary relations could be seen as multiple political tactics to forge connections with
elites whilst at the same time evading their attempts to dissipate threats and
ensure stability by creating holes, ruptures and ambiguities into conserving
strategies of absorption (Certeau 1984).

The quality of governance relations in the political community has a
bearing on escalating socio-economic inequalities and social fragmentation.
Because elites 'derive their power and influence from promoting their [dis-
advantaged groups' and classes'] interests', which 'helps decrease socio-
economic inequalities and works in favour of democracy' (Etzioni-Halevy
1999: 242; see also 1997: 314), it follows that governance jeopardises representative government by disconnecting elites and non-elites. If inequalities are aggravated it is because elites are not responsive to those they
represent. Political representation is the major mechanism of coupling elites
and non-elites, which makes it possible to defend equality *and* to ensure
elite competition in an orderly and competent manner. Such a 'government'
assumption is problematic from a democratic point of view because it
allows for one coupling mechanism only, which is defined at the regime
level and controlled by elites. The problem is that non-elites are seen in
reactive terms as disadvantaged. Hence the concern for equality is social
and economic rather than political.

However, elite desertion and consensus also depend on lay people's
attempts to gain autonomy by uncoupling themselves from the 'big' political problems in favour of a variety of 'small' projects of local involvement.
They can also turn their back on democratic procedures in favour of assert-
ing their relative autonomy in relation to elites in globalising processes,
whether on the Internet or in new glocal movements (like Attac).

The democratic problem in 'ultra-modern society' is that it 'creates increasing prosperity and new liberties', whilst it at the same time 'producing increasing inequalities, and thereby detracting from the quality of liberal democracy' (Etzioni-Halevy 1999: 239). Three paradoxes mark this type of society, which have been accentuated by elite desertion and consensus (1999: 240–1; see also 1997: 319–24): economic growth *and* growing inequality, increased inequality *and* its decreased visibility, and dissipation of classes *and* the growth of inequality (1999: 240–1; see also 1997: 319–24).

Non-elites are ill equipped to deal with these paradoxes. Those who are disadvantaged can hope to improve their lot only by either forging strong ties with the elites representing them or 'generat[ing] their own elites' (Etzioni-Halevy 1999: 244). Thus uncoupling is a threat to democracy that elites alone can prevent. If they do not, uncoupling becomes a threat to relative elite autonomy too, because it undercuts what conditions it in the first place. Uncoupling is not only a problem for disadvantaged groups, then; it also weakens the ability of representative political institutions to govern effectively, just as it derogates from the legitimacy of political representation.

If this is the case, it challenges stable political governance as well as liberal democratic values of liberty and equality. Here it is important to look at the relation between (1) relative elite autonomy viewed in terms of the continuum between the autonomy of, and co-operation among, elites (Etzioni-Halevy 1993: 109–13); and (2) elites and the groups they represent viewed in terms of the continuum between coupling and uncoupling at the level of representation (1997, 1999). The question is whether the relative autonomy of elites and the uncoupling of elites and lay people are antithetic or imply each other. Etzioni-Halevy goes for the former, thereby ruling out that relative elite autonomy could trigger uncoupling. This is not surprising, as it would be a problem if the two traits of demo-elitism –relative elite autonomy and coupling – worked against each other. However, it is difficult to see how this can be avoided.

1 Although Etzioni-Halevy is justified in emphasising both the horizontal and the vertical dimension, it remains a problem that she ignores the possibility that there might be a tension between them. It cannot be ruled out in advance that the relative autonomy of elites is one of the factors triggering uncoupling. It seems more likely that they are two sides of the same coin which reinforce each other.

2 Although uncoupling is undoubtedly a prevalent feature of present-day politics, it would be unwarranted to conclude that it signals the decay of democracy and the increase of inequality. Even though uncoupling does produce effects on these lines, it also points to the possibility of creating forms of politics that are uncoupled from elites. Thus whilst uncoupling presents a problem for some elites by restructuring the power relations among them, it might have a liberating effect on non-elites.

For elites to be relatively autonomous, they have to be autonomous not only in relation to each other, but also in relation to those they represent. Some degree of elite cohesion is a necessary component of what it means to speak of relative elite autonomy, and this implies that institutional mechanisms of uncoupling are not only unavoidable but also necessary for a democratic regime. When elites represent groups they are relatively autonomous *vis-à-vis* these groups. The question is, of course, what 'relatively' means, that is, how far can elite autonomy go and still claim to represent people? The demo-elitist meta-principle of democracy is caught in the dilemma that the principle that should uphold democracy – the trade-off between elite co-operation and autonomy – relies on what negates it, because elite autonomy entails uncoupling and thus releases a tension in the democratic meta-principle. If democratic effectiveness relies on elites' ability to govern at a distance, uncoupling becomes a measure for sustaining democratic regimes. The problem is that what conditions democracy (relative elite autonomy: pluralism) also triggers its impossibility (uncoupling: elitism). Etzioni-Halevy inherits this problem from elite pluralism. For people like Schumpeter, Dahl and numerous others democratic government is about governing this distance in situations of polyarchy.

## The political relation between elites and ordinary people

For Etzioni-Halevy two types of relations have an impact on how elites interact. The first could be called *a semi-external relation between elites and lay people*, which is that of representation viewed in terms of coupling and uncoupling. Groups are organised by a political leadership whose power and legitimacy are based on its ability to shape and serve the common interests defining groups. Coupling means that representatives are accountable to their groups and promote their interests, because their power derives from the persistence of the groups they represent. Uncoupling refers not only to representatives being independent of those they represent, but also to the fact that that this political independence is used against the interests of those they represent.

In speaking of uncoupling as a threat to democracy Etzioni-Halevy refers to lay people as playing a necessary role in how elites interact. Each elite has to have a strong group behind it to position itself in relation to other elites. People play much the same role as they do in elite pluralism: as political non-beings whose role is instrumental in producing strong government, whereby the only political role assigned to civic men is that of being buffers between political men. This is also the reason why people are at a loss when they have no political leadership to represent them and defend their interests. The patronising concern for the 'disadvantaged' goes hand in hand with the real threat of uncoupling, that it disturbs power relations among elites and that it slackens the means to control lay people by, for instance, 'strategies of absorption'.

This brings us to the second influence on the relations among elites, which could be termed *an external influence on the politics conducted among elites*. It concerns the relations among people and how they interact politically as lay persons. This is strictly speaking a non-issue for elitism because there cannot and must not be politics among citizens that is not controlled by elites. If politics occurs among them without elite mediation it is, by definition, less organised, more anarchic, more *ad hoc*, and hence less informed, less qualified and so on. This is a strategy to control politics by locating it in 'the political stratum' (Dahl 1961: 90–4) and assigning its task as that of generating support and exercising social control (figure 12.1).

*The upper horizontal dimension (E–E)*. State and non-state elites are relatively autonomous in relation to each other (cf. Durkheim's relation between the state and intermediary levels or corporatism). Politics is located at this level and democracy is the balancing of the cohesion and fragmentation of elite interaction. This is Etzioni-Halevy's meta-principle of democracy, which defines the political terrain: elites struggling for power and resisting being dominated, and democracy as a set of values and principles governing elite interaction.

*The vertical dimension (E–G)*. Groups are represented by elites. Democracy depends on a high degree of coupling of elites and the groups they represent. This works both ways: those who represent exercise authoritative political power over those who are represented, who in return are being taken care of in a mixture of welfare and social control. Uncoupling, by contrast, threatens democracy by disturbing *E–G*, which affects both *E–E* and *G–G*. With the undermining of the relations of representation between elites and non-elites – which characterises the shift from government to governance – the balance of power within each group will be destabilised and political identifications more unpredictable and hence perhaps threatening.

*The lower horizontal dimension (G–G)*. This is a political non-issue in elite theory, as groups only interact politically *vis-à-vis* elites. Lay people can and indeed must play a political role only when they are staged by the elites representing them. This role can take many forms. For Schumpeter it

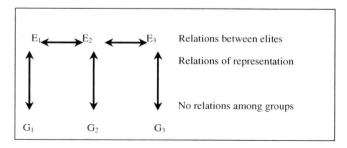

Figure 12.1  *The relations between elites and lay people. E elites, G groups*

is curtailed to a bare minimum as people are assigned the role as voters exclusively so as to function as buffers between elites. For Etzioni-Halevy the political role of lay persons has been augmented owing to her emphasis on the public and the more open nature of elites. But it goes for both of them that politics is the business of elites and sub-elites. It is a defining feature of elitism that lay people are excluded from politics, that politics is defined in terms of this exclusion and that democracy is conceptualised on the basis of this exclusion.

Elitism can then be defined as an ensemble of strategies to control G–G through E–G so as to monopolise political power and the means of social control in E–E. Against this background, it is the *political* uncoupling that defines elitism, which can coexist with economic and cultural coupling. In the latter half of the twentieth century elitism was developed in close connection with pluralism, as in Dahl and others. Attentiveness, accountability, responsiveness, openness and so on were worked into the elitist vocabulary. Seen in this light, uncoupling is not a problem only for the disadvantaged because they tend to get worse off. It is also a problem for elites if relations of representation (E–G) erode, as that impairs the means to absorb criticism and to dissipate threats. But it should also be noted that uncoupling can give way to a *political* empowerment of lay people.

## Micro-politics and culture governance

Bang and Sørensen's (2001) discussion of 'everyday makers' is among other things a critique of the reductionist accounts of democratic politics provided by various forms of elitism. Everyday makers are largely uncoupled from elite politics when engaging in local politics on an *ad hoc* basis. They challenge demo-elitism with their small micro-politics of becoming (Connolly 1999; Philips 1999) according to which you should do as in table 12.2.

Everyday making takes place at the level of G–G and couples itself to the E–E level in a way the latter might have difficulty in controlling. This is emphasised by the resistance on the part of everyday makers to both steering from above and being contained by elite governance in networks, which shows a practical alternative to demo-elitism. Though everyday makers vote and keep themselves informed about the 'high politics' at governmental level, they do not primarily gain their political identities from being citizens but from being engaged in networks and locales for political governance. Collective ideological images play a minor role in political identity. Everyday makers are more geared to enhancing their personal and common capacities for self- and co-governance where they are than to submitting to abstract social norms or modes of citizenship. They prefer a 'thin' democratic political community that allows for the reciprocal recognition and acceptance of differences; and they consider 'strong', effective and responsive government from above to be a threat to their political engagement.

**Table 12.2**  *Micro-politics and culture governance*

| Micro-politics | Culture governance |
| --- | --- |
| Do it yourself | Facilitate and moderate the empowerment of individuals and groups |
| Do it where you are | Connect with the spaces, institutions, practices, communities and projects of everyday life |
| Do it for fun but also because you find it necessary | Develop competences and make room for self-realisation but |
| Do it *ad hoc* or part-time | Enable overlapping and limited engagement in partnerships and projects |
| Do it concretely instead of ideologically | Allow a voice to the concerns of civil society and make room to involve citizens in producing effective and relevant services that meet their actual needs |
| Do it confidently and with self-esteem | Show trust in the practical knowledge and ability of lay actors to construct their own identities |
| Do it with respect for others | Create space to develop critical responsiveness and critical publics |
| Do it with experts and elites if need be | Build public confidence in the way policy makers use expert advice |

Everyday makers posit themselves in relation to the new elite connection, and they are more geared to the new global–local relations than to the state. In contrast to demo-elitism their criticism is not coined in terms of political effectiveness and social responsibility, but is ordinary prudential action to be found everywhere. They do not posses the rationalised means to be players in power struggles among elites, and they hardly make up groups. They engage within the fields of vision of others – in local institutions, social movements or voluntary associations. Everyday makers do not have the option of planning general strategy and viewing the situation as a whole. Their interventions are particular, on and off, seizing the opportunities for self-and co-governance that are on offer at any given moment (Certeau 1984: 37). Everyday makers use the cracks that particular conjunctions open in the political community: 'It poaches in them. It creates surprises in them. It can be where it is least expected. It is a guileful ruse' (1984: 37).

Everyday makers challenge demo-elitism by showing that democracy is not only a matter of strategic calculations within expert networks. They insist on the irreducibility of their own narratives and logics of appropriateness as conventional modes of political intervention in terms of 'what everyone knows' about how to go on in the daily routines of a political community (Giddens 1987). The 'hit and run' politics of everyday makers illustrates that it is elites that have a problem with uncoupling, as they have difficulty attracting, organising and representing people. Uncoupling refers to the dual phenomena of elite collusion and desertion, which destabilise government, undercut democracy and fragment the citizenry. This is a problem, granted that politics must be controlled by elites, and that in the absence of elite rule people become primitives again, fit for fight in a Hobbesian state of nature. But things might not work out that way unless hierarchy/anarchy is the only political choice on offer.

## Forging a dialogue between micro-politics and culture governance

To break out of the demo-elitist dilemma it is necessary to forge a dialogue between democracy and governance. This requires, on the one hand, acknowledging the autonomy of political community as 'our common human world' consisting of 'equals in basic matters' (Rawls 1993: 54), and on the other that governance is not an autopoietic systems logic but a conglomerate of practices which among other things incorporate everyday politics and identity politics. The point is that elites neither can nor ought to control ordinary politics, and that elite autonomy has to take into account the links between elites and autonomous lay actors.

It is in this respect that uncoupling should be seen as also having liberating effects on non-elites by slackening control mechanisms, and by accepting that non-elites develop political means of making a difference to the political structuring of their everyday life. Elite autonomy is not only a power over resources and subjects, but also a power to make a difference to the political division of labour with non-elites. Democratic politics requires that elites recognise the political autonomy of non-elites, and that this is the legitimate basis for elites to exercise authoritative political power, whether as political authorities or as members of a political community.

Democratic culture governance implies that elites are willing to facilitate self- and co-governance for solving common concerns and to draw upon a fund of ordinary knowledge and power. This requires replacing the old elite/mass dichotomy with an articulation of individuality/commonality that is able to take account of reflexivity, individuality and flexibility, and hence acknowledging that authoritative decisions could not be made and implemented by elites unless non-elites took responsibility for outcomes too. Lay people could not play a political role unless they were able to make a difference to the political constitution of their daily life, whether in their capacity of political consumers, users or citizens.

Political autonomy goes both ways. Often elites merely formulate and rationalise what non-elites have been doing all along on the basis of a conventional knowledge of how to go on in a democratic political culture (Giddens 1987). Ordinary power-knowledge does not degrade the differences made by elites. Most non-elites would probably recognise 'that the survival of democratic values – individual dignity, limited government, equality of opportunity, private property, freedom of speech and press, religious tolerance, and due process of law – depends on enlightened elites' (Dye and Zeigler 1997: 157). But they would insist that there is more to democracy than a regime's authoritative description such as conventional and imaginable practices in a democratic political community based on the recognition and acceptance of differences.

Dye and Zeigler (1997: 157) also hold that the 'masses respond to the ideas and actions of elites. When elites abandon democratic principles, or the masses lose confidence in elites, democracy is in peril.' But the argument could also be turned round. The problem for democracy arises when elites have no confidence in people and when the latter do not recognise and accept differences. This presents a crisis for both regime and community, which uncouples elites from non-elites and destabilises politics.

Discussing coupling/uncoupling of elites and non-elites calls for a culture governance approach in which elites communicate with non-elites on an ongoing basis and where the relationship between them is one of reciprocal autonomy and dependence. Elites have to be responsible not only in relation to their political results, but also in relation to the daily concerns of lay people. Political leadership should not present itself in terms of technocratic and elitist policies, but should make non-elites gain confidence in their own skills and possibilities, which obliges elites to let go of some control to make room for ordinary politics. Only through such action can governance network avoid the dangers of uncoupling and be able to cope with changes, challenges and threats.

Culture governance is geared to the many new norms and values that are developing in the shifts from government to governance. These place concerns for individuality and networking capacities at the forefront. March and Olsen (1995: 167–81) have looked at the democratic norms and values they consider valid for governance conditions. They argue that networks and institutions ought to partake in developing democratic identities of citizens, politicians and administrators; add to the growth of political resources and competences of citizens and other political actors; be democratically responsive and responsible; and create possibilities for democratic learning and experiments.

These values constitute new rules for the democratic interaction of elites and non-elites under conditions of governance, and they rely on the appearance of new political identities such as micro-elites and everyday makers to be carried out in practice. If this is to succeed both elites and non-elites have to pay attention to the problem of coupling/uncoupling. Demo-elitism is not able to deal effectively and democratically with this political division of labour because it refuses to relate to ordinary politics. Another take on the challenges facing democracy is needed, which emphasises two important dimensions of democratic politics. First the vertical one in which both

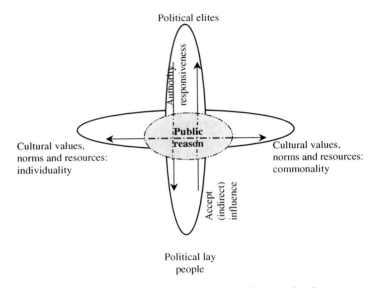

Figure 12.2   *Elites and lay people in relation to politics and culture*

elites and non-elites have to realise that political freedom and equality come from their mutual recognition and acceptance of the difference they make to the political constitution of society both as elites and as non-elites (Rawls 1997). The second dimension is the horizontal one which looks at how lay people interact in the political community, that is, how the relations between the individuality and commonality are structured, and the extent to which people recognise and accept each other. The two dimensions are illustrated in figure 12.2.

Public reason takes shape in the intersection between the two types of relations – elites/lay people and individuality/commonality – making up the political community. This gives full weight to what Rawls (1993: 157) terms 'political capital', which 'depends not only on existing political and social institutions . . . but also on citizens' experience as a whole and their knowledge of the past'. From a democratic point of view, then, political co-operation and hence the virtues of reasonableness and fairness cannot be guaranteed by elites or the regime alone, but rely equally on lay actors. Virtues and rights are not simply a constitutional matter. They are practical and ordinary, and cannot be stronger than the willingness to defend them. Liberty, as Foucault (1984: 245) stresses, 'is never assured by the institutions and laws that are intended to guarantee them. This is why almost all of these laws and institutions are quite capable of being turned around. Not because they are ambiguous, but simply because "liberty" is what must be exercised'.

## References

Bang, H. P. (2000), 'Dansk republikanisme på en skillevej', in H. P. Bang, A. D. Hansen and J. Hoff (eds), *Demokrati fra neden. Casestudier fra en dansk kommune* (Copenhagen: Jurist- & Økonomforbundets Forlag), pp. 275–307.

Bang, H. P., and Dyrberg, T. B. (2001), 'Governance, self-representation and the democratic imagination', in M. Saward (ed.), *Democratic Innovation: Deliberation, Representation and Association* (London: Routledge), pp. 146–61.

Bang, H. P., and Sørensen, E. (2001), 'The everyday maker: building political rather than social capital', in P. Dekker and E. M. Uslaner (eds), *Social Capital and Participation in Everyday Life* (London: Routledge), pp. 148–62.

Bang, H. P., Hansen, A. D., and Hoff, J., eds (2000), *Demokrati fra neden. Casestudier fra en dansk kommune* (Copenhagen: Jurist- & Økonomforbundets Forlag).

Certeau, M. de (1984), *The Practice of Everyday Life* (Berkeley CA: University of California Press).

Connolly, W. E. (1995), *The Ethos of Pluralization* (Minneapolis MN: University of Minnesota Press).

Connolly, W. E. (1999), *Why I am not a Secularist* (Minneapolis MN: University of Minnesota Press).

Dahl, R. A. (1956), *A Preface to Democratic Theory* (Chicago: University of Chicago Press).

Dahl, R. A. (1961), *Who Governs?* (New Haven CT: Yale University Press).

Dahl, R. A. (1982), *Dilemmas of Pluralist Democracy: Autonomy vs. Control* (New Haven CT: Yale University Press).

Dye, T. R., and Zeigler, L. H. (1997), 'The irony of democracy', in E. Etzioni-Halevy (ed.), *Classes and Elites in Democracy and Democratization: A Collection of Readings* (New York and London: Garland), pp. 155–60.

Easton, D. (1965), *A Systems Analysis of Political Life* (New York: Wiley).

Etzioni-Halevy, E. (1993), *The Elite Connection* (Cambridge: Polity Press).

Etzioni-Halevy, E. (1997), *Classes and Elites in Democracy and Democratization: A Collection of Readings* (New York and London: Garland).

Etzioni-Halevy, E. (1999), 'Elites, inequality and the quality of democracy in ultra-modern society', *International Review of Sociology – Revue internationale de sociologie* 9 (2): 239–50.

Etzioni-Halevy, E. (2000), 'Linkage Deficits in Transnational Politics', paper presented to the World Congress of the International Political Science Association, Quebec City, Canada.

Foucault, Michel (1984), 'What is enlightenment?' in P. Rabinow (ed.), *The Foucault Reader*, Harmondsworth: Penguin Books.

Giddens, A. (1987), *Social Theory and Modern Sociology* (Cambridge: Polity Press).

Giddens, A. (1993), *New Rules of Sociological Method*, 2nd edn (Stanford CA: Stanford University Press).

March, J. G., and Olsen, J. P. (1989), *Rediscovering Institutions: The Organizational Basis of Politics* (New York: Free Press).

March, J. G., and Olsen, J. P. (1995), *Democratic Governance* (New York: Free Press).

McGinnis, M. D. (1999), *Polycentric Governance and Development* (Ann Arbor MI: University of Michigan Press).

Pedersen, O. K. (1998), 'Interesseorganisationerne og den parlamentariske styre-form', in K. Ronit (ed.), *Interesseorganisationer i dansk politik* (Copenhagen: Jurist- & Økonomforbundets Forlag), pp. 197–232.

Philips, A. (1999), *Which Equalities Matter?* (Oxford: Blackwell).

Pierre, J., ed. (2000), *Debating Governance: Authority, Steering and Democracy* (Oxford: Oxford University Press).

Pierre, J., and Peters, B. G. (2000), *Governance, Politics and the State* (London: Sage).

Rawls, J. (1993), *Political Liberalism* (New York: Columbia University Press).

Rawls, J. (1997), 'The Idea of Public Reason revisited', *University of Chicago Law Review* 64 (3): 765–807.

Rosenau, J. N. (1997), *Along the Domestic–Foreign Frontier: Exploring Governance in a Turbulent World* (Cambridge: Cambridge University Press).

Schumpeter, J. A. (1976), *Capitalism, Socialism, Democracy*, 5th edn (London: Allen & Unwin).

# 13

# A new ruler meeting a new citizen: culture governance and everyday making

Henrik P. Bang

Governance as political communication may be claimed to rearticulate the relationship between political authorities and lay people as one between (1) strategic communication oriented towards attaining influence and success by involving and partnering with individuals and groups in the political community, and (2) tactical communication oriented towards the buildings of reflexive communities where individuals and groups can feel engaged and practise their freedoms in their mutual recognition of difference. One example of this new relationship is what we call *culture governance* and *everyday making*. Both concepts have their basis in the output side of political processes, and picture the emergence of a new relationship between political authorities and lay people in the political community in the shape of a highly politicised and culturally oriented new management and administration and a strongly individualised and consumption-oriented new citizen.

Both culture governors and everyday makers are extremely sceptical of democratic government. They want to 'modernise' and transform it so that it can stand up to the challenges of self-reference and complexity and at the same time provide spaces for the exercise of self-governance from below in the solving of concrete everyday problems. I shall provide two concrete examples of this new mode of rule and citizenship in the shape of the EU White Paper on good governance and an in-depth interview with a young woman, Eve, in a small town in Denmark. Together these two cases indicate how democratic rule and participation are going increasingly 'glocal' (local in the global) and thereby are tending to undermine the conventional and strong relationship between the state and the nation. At the same time they also bear witness to a new kind of political reasoning, which dismisses the old ditch between state and civil society in order to consider the political regime both a medium and the outcome of the situated interaction between political authorities (formal or informal) and lay people in the political community.

## The unsettled relation between government and governance

A basic task for high modern social and political theory should be to draw new boundaries for both government and governance so that they do not undermine and counteract each other. We must not forget that democratic government presumes exactly what democratic governance does its utmost to erode, namely a clear distinction between system and life world, the rational and the ordinary, the programmatic and the everyday, etc. Liberal democracy ideally builds on a very strict separation of the state from civil society and of the national from the international. The aim is to protect individuals in civil society against external and internal threats and to free them from undue political interference by delimiting the legitimate use of political power (Held 1987: 41).

Most Western democracies are formally organised according to this negative and protective view of politics and democracy, where politics signifies power over others and where democracy amounts to freedom and protection from the omnipotent threat of political coercion. What has become increasingly problematic in this conventional representative view is the negative conception of the political that it builds upon, and the apolitical view of the economic and the social that it gives rise to. These create the expectation that power and freedom in their positive connotations as power and freedom to *do* something rest exclusively with the market of free exchange and with the voluntary forces in a civil society, which have the task of not only protecting and expanding spaces for negative liberty but also of enhancing positive freedom and of recreating egalitarian forms of solidarity without impairing economic self-regulation (Cohen and Arato 1994: 17–18).

However, governance, as we have seen, does precisely manifest a positive conception of power and freedom, which is neither reducible to that of the market nor to be identified with that of civil society. On the contrary, governance is becoming a common logic of all societal systems in a world where complexity means being forced to select, where selection implies contingency, and where contingency signifies risk (Luhmann 1995: 25). Politics cannot but creep into any high modern type of organising, where no decision can be finally determined, where all decisions are made from earlier decisions, and where only a decision can decide what is turning a decision into a decision (Andersen and Born 2001: 18–19). The constantly growing pressure for risky and, basically undecidable decisions introduces a new 'private politics' in the market place and a new 'community politics' in civil society.

Governance forges partnership, joint ventures and team building between elites and sub-elites from public, private and voluntary organisations. It situates in this way a Trojan horse, in the form of a political governing relation, at the very heart of autonomous market forces and voluntary solidarities. Of course, governance analysts and practictioners may be correct in claiming that this forging of partnerships across boundaries is necessary to success in our days of runaway change, as a public, private and voluntary organisation. However, governance does represent a problem for representative government, as to where and how the line has to be drawn in protecting and expanding human rights and to supervise and monitor that autonomous market forces and solidary civil society do not suffer undue governance interference.

Governance expresses a politicisation of the economic and the social which keeps all and every kind of activity under the spell of an autopoeitic reproduction, which depends on an adequate homogeneity of system operations to define the unity of a determinate type of system (Luhmann 1995: 40). Dean in chapter 7 obviously hits the nail on the head when asking:

> How is the diagram of a polycentric, individualising, enabling and network-ing form of governance laid upon a centric, totalising, commanding and hier-archical form of territorial power (and the international order made up of relations between such powers)? In other words, how is cultural governance connected with new figurations of disciplinary and sovereign forms of power?

The question of sovereignty is certainly becoming acute in a high modern society where 'the operational mode of self-referential systems change into forms of causality that to a large extent reliably prevent it from being steered from the outside' (Luhmann 1995: 41). Yet there are signs that new forms of sovereignty may be appearing even in autopoeitic systems of governance, which try to discipline people more communicatively, openly and indirectly. Like Dean, I call this tentative effort at forging new forms of sovereignty for coping with self-reference and complexity *culture governance*, though I expand the notion a bit further to cover not only the political regime but also the political community. Culture governance challenges people that, unless they are prepared to assume responsibility for and par-ticipate actively in solving their own everyday problems, the system stands little chance of being able to connect with them and deliver them the welfare goods they demand.

## The emergence of culture governance

Culture governance (CG) becomes visible as soon we ask ourselves how it happens that rule in hypermodern political society increasingly articulates itself as being addressed to expanding self-governance, empowerment, user influence, citizenship participation, private–public partnerships, human development, team building, and other culturally and normatively charged terms of deliberation and involvement? (March and Olsen 1995; Kooiman 1999; Scharpf 1999; Heffen et al. 2000; Pierre 2000; Pierre and Peters 2000; Bang et al. 2001; Behn 2001; Storey 2001.) A very simple answer, modelled after the notion of autopoeisis is that high modern society has grown so complex, dynamic and differentiated that no expert system can any longer rule itself solely by exercising hierarchical and bureaucratic control over people.

Today there is a growing awareness in systems that rule must be flattened out and exercised in a more dialogical and co-operative manner. The recognition is spreading that unless one's decision centres are willing to listen to and learn from members and environments, a system has little chance to acquire the power and knowledge that it needs in order for it to go on and evolve in the world as a relatively effective and coherent whole. High modern systems, public, private or voluntary, are shifting towards a code of governing in and through the exercise of self- and co-governance. A new systems rhetoric is emerging in public, private and voluntary organisations, which is *glocal* (local in the global) in its outlook, and which wants to empower people and engage them in rule across old boundaries. More and more high modern organisations are branding themselves as genuinely open systems. They communicate how flexibility, expansion and adaptation are increasingly based on flows of power and knowledge in networks, which express a commitment to new values of devolution, participation and sustainability.

Let me give three concrete examples of the new rhetoric, downloaded from the Web sites of two global organisations and one global network, namely the World Bank, Microsoft and the UN NGO Global Network:

## The World Bank's 'mission statement'

*Our dream is a world free of poverty*

To fight poverty with passion and professionalism for lasting results.

To help people help themselves and their environment by providing resources, sharing knowledge, building capacity, and forging partnerships in the public and private sectors.

To be an excellent institution able to attract, excite, and nurture diverse and committed staff with exceptional skills who know how to listen and learn.

*Our Principles*

Client centered, working in partnership, accountable for quality results, dedicated to financial integrity and cost-effectiveness, inspired and innovative.

*Our Values*

Personal honesty, integrity, commitment; working together in teams – with openness and trust; empowering others and respecting differences; encouraging risk-taking and responsibility; enjoying our work and our families. (http://web.worldbank.org/)

## Microsoft's mission statement

*Microsoft's Mission*

To enable people and businesses throughout the world to realize their full potential

*Microsoft's Vision*

Empowering people through great software – any time, any place and on any device

*Delivering on Our Mission*

The tenets central to accomplishing our mission include:

### Great People with Great Values

Delivering on our mission requires great people who are bright, creative and energetic, and who share the following values:

1 Integrity and honesty
2 Passion for customers, partners, and technology
3 Open and respectful with others and dedicated to making them better
4 Willingness to take on big challenges and see them through
5 Self critical, questioning and committed to personal excellence and self improvement
6 Accountable for commitments, results, and quality to customers, shareholders, partners and employees

### Excellence

In everything we do.

### Trustworthy Computing

Deepening customer trust through the quality of our products and services, our responsiveness and accountability, and our predictability in everything we do.

### Broad Customer Connection

Connecting with customers, understanding their needs and how they use technology, and providing value through information and support to help them realize their potential.

### Innovative and Responsible Platform Leadership

Expanding platform innovation, benefits, and opportunities for customers and partners; openness in discussing our future directions; getting feedback; and working with others to ensure that their products and our platforms work well together.

### Enabling People to Do New Things

Broadening choices for customers by identifying new areas of business; incubating new products; integrating new customer scenarios into existing businesses; exploring acquisitions of key talent and experience; and integrating more deeply with new and existing partners.

### A Global, Inclusive Approach

Thinking and acting globally, enabling a multicultural workforce that generates innovative decision-making for a diverse universe of customers and partners, innovating to lower the costs of technology, and showing leadership in supporting the communities in which we work and live. Last updated: Monday, July 01, 2002 – 9:45 a.m. Pacific Time. (www.microsoft.com/mscorp/)

### The UN NGO Global Network's Words of Welcome

*Welcome!*

This site is the home page for our global NGO community (Non-governmental organizations associated with the United Nations).

Its aim is to help promote collaborations between NGOs throughout the world, so that together we can more effectively partner with the United Nations and each other to create a more peaceful, just, equitable and sustainable world for this and future generations.

Please help make this site a valuable tool for connecting sharing, learning and growing, by participating. (www.ngo.org/)

The three statements above are indeed political, but not in the 'old' sense where politics is considered solely a feature of a legally circumscribed system of legitimate domination. They do not delimit the political to the sphere of the state, celebrating the role of parties, parliaments and politicians. Nor do they speak of politics and policy solely in the public language of organised interests, mass media, social movements and 'the people'. They speak directly to the individual and articulate themselves as global outlooks with local views on what it means to govern in specific sites or terrain's with and by people who perceive the situation differently, because they approach the world from different points of observation and with different concepts in mind. Furthermore, the principles adopted are not formally grounded in regulatory norms and procedures but in 'best practices' for producing effective results. Nor are the values articulated as abstract rights or liberties but as operative ones – such as connecting, learning, sharing and growing – for expanding the concrete practice of freedom in civil society.

The extent to which organisations act in accordance with this new rhetoric is, of course, open to question. But it would be out of place to approach the new systems rhetoric of culture governance by way of conventional concepts such as 'anarchy' (market), 'hierarchy' (state) and 'solidarity' (civil society). Culture governance obviously celebrates none of these logics, but rather tries to dissociate itself from any of them, focusing on identity more than 'economic man', networks as opposed to bureaucracy, and cultural difference before a common good. Rather, culture governance seems to cut across all old boundaries, theoretical, ideological and historical, between state, market and civil society. In this sense culture governance assumes the image of a new 'leviathan', which seeks to penetrate into every individual and group and to make all social systems or institutions to organise and programme themselves according to its rhetoric of 'good governance'. No matter whether the organising is public, private or voluntary the message is the same, namely that systems management and administration today are a matter of advocating, facilitating, guiding and moderating the spread of new forms of empowerment and involvement from below as well as of holding leadership and management more directly accountable to people (customers, consumers, users or citizens) so that their conventional wisdoms and self-governing capacities can be immediately expressed (cf. Etzioni-Halevy 1993; Scharpf 1999; Dekker and Uslaner 2001; Saward 2001).

## Culture governance as sovereignty

Culture governance shows how rule in any type of high modern organisation must increasingly operate through the capacity for self- and co-governance and thus needs to articulate, act upon, reform and utilise individual and collective identities so that their conduct can become amenable to such rule (Dean, p. 117). Culture governance is exactly addressed to ruling the waves in a rapidly changing world having no self-given or predetermined order, meaning or identity. Culture governance aims at empowering as many people as possible; not primarily for their own sake but to get them to help their organisations to get the minimal wholeness, coherence and effectiveness that they need, but which they can no longer supply by their old steering means (hierarchy, bureaucracy, corporatism, normative consensus, free exchange, solidarity or whatever).

In culture governance, rulers attempt to socialise and regulate people's conduct in an indirect manner by working on their identities and thereby their values, feelings, attitudes and beliefs via a variety of new interactive modes of dialogue and co-operation. The aim is to get them freely and willingly to employ their self-governing powers to help the system connect and deliver in an effective manner. I consider this new kind of rule a new feasible mode of sovereignty for controlling and establishing new, more communicative and co-operative relations between political authorities, the political regime and lay people in the political community.

Foucauldian governmentality analysis has long stressed this new mental rule as a mode of discipline and subjection (Dean 1999). In my view, however, there is more to culture governance than discipline and subjection. Furthermore, culture governance need not always be 'in the shadow' of government, that is, of how we conduct government and how government governs conduct (Dean 1999: 27). Dean considers culture governance as derivable from 'the intrinsic *logic* or strategy of a regime', meaning that it can be constructed only 'through understanding its operation as an intentional but non-subjective assemblage of all its elements' (1999: 22). Culture governance thus reflects the different ways in which a regime, as a set of institutional practices, 'can be thought of, made into objects of knowledge, and made subject to problematisations' (1999: 21).

I consider culture governance a feature not of the regime only but also of the *political community*, seen as 'that aspect of a group of persons as represented in those acts through which they contribute to a common political division of labor' (Easton 1965: 185). In culture governance political authorities work on the borderline between the regime and the political community in order to heighten the system's chances of acquiring at least some control not only over the programming and organising of political decisions within the regime but in particular over lay people's beliefs, use of conventions and consumption of culture. Culture governance expresses the view that rule today implies being able to steer indirectly in and through a political community, which links with political culture and reveals the endogenous relationship between beliefs and traditions in political interaction.

Culture governance in my model thus exhibits a concern with the ways in which we actively construct our experiences, whether we do it as rationally acting elites, organising and programming decisions and actions, or as ordinary self-reflexive members of a political community, who are able to invent new beliefs and traditions, which may be applied to construct a range of new tactics. Culture governance expresses the awareness that no political practice or institution can itself fix the ways in which its participants will act or how they will innovate in response to novel circumstances. Hence, in order to be effective, strategic communication must pay heed to the irreducibility of the 'small tactics' of lay people in the political community for making a difference. Otherwise rulers cannot utilise the capacities for self-governance to the full extent, namely to help the system in finding its future goals rather than merely subjecting them to attaining an already existing one.

Culture governance in political systems is mostly a feature of the steering activities of managers, administrators and other professionals, who try to cope both with the increase in self-reference and complexity and the growing mistrust in the ability of representative government to connect and deliver. Through their exercise of culture governance on the borderline they challenge the normative core of representative democracy, where, as Habermas puts it, 'the normative expectation of rational outcomes is grounded ultimately in the interplay between institutionally structured political will-formation and spontaneous, unsubverted circuits of communication in a public sphere that is not programmed to reach decisions and thus is not organized' (1996: 485). This normative ideal is consciously subverted by the culture governors in order for them to enhance the system's steering capacities. They not only attempt to assume control of more and more of the direct decision making in the regime, they also try to take over the old role of voluntary associations in the civic culture as nodal points for coupling formally and organisationally structured decision making with more spontaneously operating communicative and interactive networks of everyday knowledge and power.

In practice culture governance accomplishes this by entering into partnerships with civil society and citizens in a variety of connections, empowering voluntary organisations and lay people to participate both on the output side and in the broader public. Via culture governance systems managers and administrators try to give voice to people's grievances, making them interested in a certain issue, encouraging them to put pressure on politicians to force an issue on to the formal agenda, etc. Cobb *et al.* (1976:

132) call this 'the outside initiative model' of issue making. They consider it distinct from the 'inside' one of access and mobilisation, where initiative comes from office holders and political leaders – and today, I would add, also from big interest groups, the media and NGOs. In culture governance this distinction is dissolved by the politicisation of management and administration as a new political linking mechanism between authorities, regime and community which aims at facilitating and moderating both modes of issue articulation simultaneously for the sake of improving the system's overall governability. Through culture governance people and their publics are enabled and guided to 'discover' the 'correct' critical issues, value interpretations, sound reasons and possible solutions for the exercise of 'good governance'. To the extent that culture governance succeeds, this will improve the prospects of managers and administrators exercising indirect influence over bureaucracy and political leaders via the political community. Hence, as a result of such culture governance on the borderline, the image of the inside access model and the outside initiative model as presenting 'basic alternatives in how the public sphere and the political system influence each other' (Habermas 1996: 379) simply breaks down.

## Reassessing system and life world as political authority and community

Culture governance's message is that the political system must recognise the political community as a part of itself, since it needs the conventional power and knowledge of its members to secure its democratic effectiveness. No hypermodern expert system can any longer afford to approach ordinary people as either subordinated to its hierarchical authority or as mere objects of knowledge to be disciplined to do whatever they are required to do. Rather, expert systems must engage in dialogue and co-operate with ordinary people as reflexive subjects of power and knowledge.

Relations of culture governance articulate themselves primarily outside the formal framework of the state and its corporatist networks. The latter consist of those public institutions and interest organisations which, before parliaments and through the courts, give voice to social problems, aggregate and integrate broad demands, articulate abstract ideas about the public interest or good, and thus attempt to shape public issue and decision making through normative communication. Culture governance takes place more on the output side of political processes, and in particular as a result of practical administrative experience of how democratic government today can function successfully only through the managing of governance networks and practices that operate close to and in co-operation with civil society and citizens (Bang et al. 2000; Heffen et al. 2000).

Culture governance illuminates how the old image of administrative power and knowledge as the 'bureaucratic disempowering and desiccation of spontaneous processes of opinion- and will-formation' (Habermas 1989: 325) is hard to uphold in the new discursive modality of 'the system'. Here organisation, public or private, is 'defined simply in terms of non- or anti-bureaucratic qualities' (Salaman 2001: 191). The aim is therefore the opposite, namely to empower both the members of the system and ordinary citizens 'outside' in order to make them 'personally responsible for self-government – displaying the attributes the organisation requires' (2001: 204).

It follows that modern sociological approaches to the system's colonisation of the life world, as manifestations of 'a repressive integration emanating from an oligopolistic economy and an authoritarian state' (Habermas 1989: 391), no longer suffice as the foundation of a normative and democratic critique of systems colonisation. What ordinary people in their life worlds are up against today is not at all this old kind of repressive and disempowering system. Quite the contrary, really: what they have to guard the development of their own narratives and forms of life in the political community against is a much more benign and facilitating type of rule. This honours the ethical view 'that the most effective forms of connection between social research and policy-making are forged through an extended process of communication between researchers, policy-makers and those affected by whatever issues are under consideration' (Giddens 1987: 47). Yet it does, of course, still gain its autonomy as a mode of rational rule via its own specialised semantic, which, no matter how facilitating and caring it may be, necessarily (logically) has the consequence of ignoring those everyday narratives and forms of life that do not possess this kind and degree of specialisation (Habermas 1987, 1989, 1996; Mulhall 1994; Gunnell 1998; Geertz 2000).

According to Habermas, 'no more than Husserl (or later, Sartre) solved this problem of intersubjectivity has systems theory managed to explain how autopoeitically closed systems, could, inside the circuit of self-referential steering, be induced to go beyond pure self-reference and autopoeisis' (1996: 346). As we are forced to conclude by now, Habermas is in a way both right and wrong. Expert systems have become aware that they not only need the normative support but also the active power and knowledge of employees, civil society and individual citizens in securing their own effectiveness and relevance *as* expert systems. Connecting with employees (Marchington 2001; Salaman 2001) civil society (Hirst 1994; Pierre and Peters 2000) and citizens (Box 1998; Esselbrugge 2000; Klijn and Koppenjan 2000), enabling them to governing themselves, is simply becoming *the* new steering imperative.

Indeed, the very fact that rulers are beginning to admit that systems are dependent upon ordinary power and knowledge for their persistence and future specialisation 'does not escape the circle in which both external observation and self-observation are always a system's own observation; it does not penetrate the darkness of mutual opacity' (Habermas 1996: 347). But it does demonstrate that it would be wrong to state the problem of a political theory with a critical intent as: 'What resistance does the life world itself pose to such an instrumentalisation for imperatives either of an economy set loose in its own dynamic or of a bureaucracy rendered autonomous? Can the structures of the life-world – however warped, yet none the less tenacious in their own proper logic – stop processes of reification or politicisation?' (1982: 283). Obviously, no structure can 'stop' any kind of systems intervention in the life world; only human and political beings can do so. But, apart from being apolitical and socially deterministic in nature, these questions conceal how culture governance is a property neither of bureaucracy nor of the market but of a vast network of communicative and negotiable authority.

What civil society and ordinary citizens may have to 'stop' is neither reification nor a bureaucracy set loose in its internal dynamics. It is the culture governor, who does pay respect to lay people as subjects of knowledge, but who simply cannot see that there can be other logics relevant to democracy than the strategic one of success or influence. When, say, leaders and managers of voluntary organisations drop their old oppositional identity and enter into partnership with political systems on culture governance conditions, that is, for effectively producing outcomes, they become one more sub-elite in such systems. This need not be a problem for democracy, since it can help to expand pluralism further and establish new access points for ordinary people to the going regime. The problem emerges only if one forgets that voluntary association is not only, and not even primarily, the terrain of elite activists joining the organised programming of decision and action on the terrain of the political regime and political authorities. It also comprises all those individuals and collectivities in the political community who choose to try to exercise their political influence more indirectly, whether as oppositional movements fighting 'the system' or as everyday makers who rather want to create and enjoy their own small tactics, when they feel like it and can afford the time to do it (Bang and Sørensen, 2001). The point is that no political authority can *be* a political community in that the logic which applies to the making and implementing of strategic decisions does not cover the simple interactions and self-reflexive but non-rational activities which make up such a community. The integration of a hyper-complex political community, where one co-operates on the basis of the recognition of difference, cannot successfully be carried out in a systems rational-elitist fashion, that is, in a manner that bypasses the conventional knowledge and abilities localised inside a political community (Habermas 1987, 1989, 1996).

Hence once could say that culture governance's high modern kind of strategic action, as distinct from the 'old' objectivating or reifying one, is conducive to 'undistorted communication', because it springs from the insight that 'communication is realised if and to the extent that understanding comes about' (Luhmann 1995: 147). Strategic action has grown much more communicative as culture governance, realising that the system would collapse for want of power and knowledge unless it were able to connect communicatively, openly and meaningfully with people. In culture governance uncoupling means democratically ineffective rule, which is not merely a legitimation problem, which will always occur when the distance between rulers and ruled becomes too great, but which rather is a life-threatening steering problem. Any high modern political system needs to demonstrate that it can connect and deliver if it is to acquire legitimacy. But it cannot rule democratically and effectively unless it manages to empower people to take charge of more and more of this rule themselves.

Culture governance reflects the recognition that any kind of rule will eventually fail, and that the political system can no longer organise itself and rule society in an effective and relevant manner by its own means. To be a high modern sovereign means acknowledging that political authorities and the political regime are both anchored in the political community conventionally and not merely as artefacts that have to gain the support of civil society and ordinary citizens. Communicative political authority cannot be reduced to the executive part of a uniform social system, which can act for the whole and exercise its unilateral power and control over that whole as an administrative system of dominance (Habermas 1987: 357). But nor can it be fully comprehended by a concept of self-organising systems (autopoiesis), stating that 'there may be hierarchies, asymmetries, or differences in influence, but no part of the system can control others without itself being subject to control' (Luhmann 1995: 36; cf. Mingers 1995; Jervis 1997). Although this control is reciprocal and multi-causal, it still binds any and all individuals and collectives to a strategic commitment to seek control above all else when partaking in politics and policy.

Today, in the face of the globalisation, Europeanisation, regionalisation, localisation and individualisation of political power and knowledge, it is not enough 'that any control must be exercised in anticipation of counter-control' (Luhmann 1995). Rather, rulers must try to balance the need for diversity by the ability to communicate across systemic boundaries with individuals who do not need to perform according to a digital code of control and counter-control or articulate their everyday narratives into systematised differences when discussing their diversity and involvement in practices of freedom. Culture governance is on the threshold of recognising this in its attempt to rule on the borderline between authorities, regime and community. But it needs to be developed further and learn to set limits for its colonisation of the political community and to serve as a guarantor and facilitator that new tactics, ideas, images, values, etc., can occur outside the domain of the regime's 'valid' conception.

## Culture governance in the European Union

The EU Commission's White Paper on good governance (http://europa.eu.int/comm/governance/docs/index_en.htm) is a good example of how government and governance may play together in a hypermodern polity. The White Paper provides a programme for a new kind of sovereignty, implicating openness, participation, accountability, effectiveness and coherence on the part of the European Union as a political system (p. 10). The White Paper explicitly recognises that this new rule cannot take place through the distant, hierarchical rule of modern administrative systems. Rather, it articulates a new discursive, governmental modality of listening to and learning from civil society and citizens by coming closer to all regions, cities and localities.

The White Paper thus follows those who argue that 'getting the institutions right may not be enough to guarantee the viability of the democratic regime' (Lane and Ersson 1996: 175). But it goes far beyond the mainstream, where it is believed that this other side of government has to do only with developing 'a special political culture in and common understanding of the rules of the political game' (1996; cf. Putnam 1993; Pharr and Putnam 2000). Political culture is not merely a matter of having the right attitudes to the democratic regime but of co-operating in partnerships and networks in a democratic political community where people accept and recognise each other as capable and knowledgeable human beings (Benhabib 1996; Bang and Dyrberg 2001; Bang and Sørensen 2001; Bauman 2001). Political culture is as much about becoming and identity building as about the rules of the game. The EU White Paper is aware of this, which is why it presents an alternative community strategy for ruling by extensive consultation and dialogue, by including more and more citizens and voluntary organisations from civil society, by facilitating local and regional autonomy, by contributing to global governance, etc. The White Paper dissociates 'good governance', as ruling through consultation, partnership, team building, etc., from the uniform rule of the state as a normatively (or ideologically) integrated unity. The White Paper shows that government today is not just a matter of demonstrating the effectiveness of implementing a given programme, on the one hand, and guaranteeing the systemic acquisition of legitimacy by the organised extraction of mass loyalty on the other (Habermas 1996: 482–3). Government must act through governance by:

1 Limiting explicit social control from above.
2 Transforming corporatist 'iron triangles' into stakeholders in public–private partnerships.
3 Retraining public employees as self-responsible and service-minded public agents.
4 Attuning political institutions to a culture of consultation and dialogue.
5 Readdressing leadership towards new forms of public management, such as risk management and human resource management.
6 Involving civil society and citizens in politics and policy by committing them to demonstrate accountability and teamwork in relation to others.

The White Paper convincingly shows how the old dichotomisations of order and disorder, 'bottom up' and 'top down', centralisation and decentralisation, authority and democracy, etc., are becoming a hindrance to 'good governance' and to developing adequate analyses of governance networks as *connecting links* between central and local, ruling at the distance and ruling at close range, liberty and the practices of political freedom, etc. The White Paper wants less organisation and more co-operation in the system's operational coding to provide a more viable and democratic relation to its societal environments. It aims at a new form of government, which recognises that 'networks could make a more effective contribution to EU policies' (p. 18). This requires one to accept the limits of law and procedures, since 'Creating a culture of consultation cannot be achieved by legal rules which would create excessive rigidity and risk slowing the adoption of particular policies' (p. 17).

In a way the White Paper rhetoric echoes pre-modern, absolutist sovereignty, which did not distinguish between public and private or state and civil society either, and which regarded everything as potentially falling within the purview of the governable (cf. Bartelson 2001: 176). The resemblance is that the White Paper premises itself on the identity of the political authorities and the political community as a whole. Modern government and the state, it is recognised, not only enable but also hinder the full development of the art of governing. The White Paper identifies an actual and growing need for the political system to go beyond modern government and the state to gain new knowledge and power about how to persist in the face of self-reference and complexity. But, as distinct from absolutism, the White Paper has no intention of sustaining its rule by colonising the life world by force, outright manipulation or pervasive threats. It wants to recouple with civil society and citizens, as a new, more attentive, caring and facilitating form of rule that operates in relation to voluntary forces and close to the everyday life of ordinary individuals (cf. Barber 1998, Barker 1999; Wollebæk *et al.* 2000; Shawn 2001). This is not, of course, for the sake of the life world but for grasping the political consequences of what at first appears paradoxical: that civil society and citizens 'freely' take an active part in supplying the system with effectiveness, wholeness and coherence that it cannot provide itself (Bruijn and Heuvelhof 2000, Klijn and Teisman 2000).

## Culture governance as an issue manager

The EU White Paper is a good example of how administrators and managers at whatever level are attempting to use the rhetoric of culture governance to take over issue articulation from both representative government and civil society and the public sphere, both of which are considered insufficiently 'professional' to handle the articulation of complex issues in the face of increasing self-reference and complexity.

There are good reasons for the European Commission to engage actively in the managing of issues, since it is obvious that politicians (but also voluntary forces) have serious problems standing up to their conventional role as mediators between state and civil society. In Denmark, for example, a survey showed that whereas 95 per cent of the voters considered it from very important to important that politicians listened to them before they made decisions, only 26 per cent of them were confident to a higher or lower degree that they did so. In the same fashion 92 per cent of Danes considered it from very important to important to be informed about society's common concerns but only 29 per cent trusted to a higher or lower degree that they were provided with the relevant information for deciding on those problems (Bang 2000). The White Paper is directly targeted and segmented to cope with this gap between government and people, which has been constantly widening in a high modern society in which people crave for still more effective delivery, self-governance and information.

1 *Making the Union operate more openly.* 'Democracy depends on people being able to take part in public debate. To do this, they must have access to reliable information on European issues and be able to scrutinise the policy process in its various stages . . .' (p. 11).
2 *Reaching out to citizens through regional and local democracy.* 'The way in which the Union currently works does not allow for adequate interaction in a multi-level partnership . . . The process of EU policy-making . . . should allow Member States to listen and learn from regional and local experiences' (p. 12).
3 *Involving civil society.* 'Civil society plays an important role in giving voice to the concerns of citizens and delivering services that meet people's needs . . . It [provides] a chance to get citizens more actively involved in achieving the Union's objectives and to offer them a structured channel for feedback, criticism and protest' (pp. 14–15).
4 *Refocus the roles and responsibilities of each institution.* 'What is needed is a reinforced culture of consultation and dialogue' (p. 16). 'This should help citizens to hold their political leaders and the Institutions to account for the decisions that the Union takes' (p. 33).
5 *Build public confidence in the way policy makers use expert advice.* 'The European Union's multi-disciplinary expert system will be opened up to greater public scrutiny and debate. This is needed to manage the challenges, risks, and ethical questions thrown up by science and technology' (p. 33).
6 *Provide better policies, regulation and delivery.* The Union 'must find the right mix between imposing a uniform approach when and where it is needed and allowing greater flexibility in the way that rules are implemented on the ground. It must boost confidence in the way expert advice influences policy decisions' (p. 5).
7 *Contribute to global governance.* 'The White Paper looks beyond Europe and contributes to the debate on global governance. The Union should

seek to apply the principles of good governance to its global responsi-bilities. It should aim to boost the effectiveness and enforcement powers of international institutions' (p. 5).

The White Paper presents itself as a sovereign for mediating between states, regions, localities and citizens. The image it generates is that of a new pro-fessional, communicative, partnering, negotiating, co-operative, culturally oriented, etc., leadership and management with a 'glocal' outlook. The White Paper wants to take charge of the managing of issues with regard to both the old governmental and corporatist inside access and mobilisation model and the broader outside initiative model of the public sphere and civil society model (Cobb *et al.* 1976). The White Paper communicates that issue making in both dimensions is still more to be thought of as a busi-ness for communication experts, who know the twin management tech-nologies of segmentation and targeting and so are able to formulate political issues and public concerns into targeted appeals (cf. Gandy 2001). A good indication of this is the twelve working groups set up by the Commission in preparation for the White Paper:

1  Promoting dialogue, discussion and debate for a Citizens' Europe.
2  Democratising expertise and establishing scientific reference systems.
3  Consultation and participation of civil society.
4  Evaluation and transparency.
5  Better regulation.
6  A framework for decision-making regulatory agencies.
7  Decentralisation: better involvement of national, regional and local actors.
8  Involving experts in the process of national policy convergence.
9  Networking people for good governance in Europe.
10 Multi-level governance: linking and networking the various regional and local levels.
11 Strengthening Europe's contribution to world governance.
12 Policies for an enlarged Union. (http://europa.eu.int/comm/governance/areas/index_en.htm)

The preparation of the White Paper was organised into six work areas and twelve working groups in accordance with the method indicated in the working programme, which was affirmed by the Commission on 11 October 2000. The result of this work is presented in twelve reports. As the Commission stresses, 'Each working group, composed of European Commission officials from all Directorates General, has conducted external consultations presented in the report on the consultation. The reports are published in parallel with the White Paper. The contents of these reports do not reflect the official position of the Commission.'

## Everyday making as a new citizen tactic

It is tempting to follow the Commission's strategic communication and issue articulation still further but here I am more interested in figuring out what the new citizen to whom the White Paper is also addressed may look like? Who would be the ideal citizen in such an image, and who would be its 'natural opponent'?

Let us move from the 'big' European Union to a small town in Denmark with the name of Skanderborg. Here we found Eve, one of 171 persons interviewed in the research project 'Democracy from below' (Bang *et al.* 2000). Eve is a young woman, who would fail to live up to the modern image of the emancipated activist or citizen fighting against the system or struggling to hold it accountable to law and the democratic public, but who nevertheless has been able to find many loopholes for exercising her political freedom in co-operation with both public authorities and her fellow citizens in the political community. Eve simply *is* what Connolly defines as a *micropolitics of becoming*, which 'prizes the ineliminable plurality of contestable perspectives in public life and the recurrent need to form collective assemblages of common action from this diversity' (1999: 12; cf. Certeaux 1984, 1997). What have the democratic traditions of liberalism and socialism, communitarianism and a social democratic kind of welfare state to say about this kind of politics? Basically not very much, and they would probably agree that this woman is a downright case of the decay of citizenship values in Denmark (Andersen and Ulrich 2000).

Eve demonstrates great mistrust in political elites:

> The bosses and the politicians and the mayors and everyone else that has a lot of power in a municipality, city or state or that kind of thing – they are all so busy painting such a bright picture and putting themselves in such an incredibly glorious light, but they can never live up to any of it. Really, I think they are – excuse the expression – that they are a bunch of wimps.

Eve lacks tolerance of minorities:

> I mean, there are probably some Hell's Angels or something like that, but I would prefer to see them stick to the right path, right? If they think differently, then we can't really do anything about it, but, I mean, it can't come at the expense of the rest of us. Then [if they continue with their illegal activities] they have to hold their activities in a dark basement where there isn't anyone that is bothered by them, because I'm not going to accept having to watch riots in the High Street.

Eve shows no concern for party politics:

> As far as I can see there are a bunch of different men and women that have a bunch of different opinions and they can't quite agree about how they are supposed to make them work, and many of them bring up their arguments by just standing there and blabbering on about a lot of crap that they aren't going to be able to make into laws and regulations and rules and that kind of thing,

you know? And I mean – every year there is all kinds of stuff. Or when there is an election and that kind of thing, you know? Then all the politicians stand there and promise all kinds of things – lowering taxes, and that kind of thing – nothing happens anyway. So, the way I feel, since I turned eighteen I've never even voted. I voted last year by casting a blank ballot instead of not voting at all. Because, the way I look at it, if I don't have a decent feeling for any of the parties that are out there and I haven't properly oriented myself then I won't vote at all.

Eve admits to having only a little knowledge about national politics:

Yeah, but it was exactly because I don't know anything about any of the parties and I don't feel like taking the time to figure out what they are all about, because if I take the time to figure it out I'd do it for my own sake – then I'd do it because I feel like doing it or because that's what's expected of me.

Eve feels apathetic in relation to 'big' politics:

I mean – I don't feel as though I can change all that much myself. I know that there are a lot of young people that say, 'If everyone says that then we'll never be able to change anything,' and that if there is one person who says we have to change things then there are more that will follow along and then we'll ulti-mately be able to make a difference, but I just don't believe it.

Eve thus appears to represent a clear case of 'reification' and 'anomie' and in particular seems somewhat symptomatic of the younger generation's 'pathological' distrust of party politics, at least in Denmark (Andersen *et al.* 2000; Bang *et al.* 2000). However, if one listens to Eve's thoughts con-cerning her own daily life (Currie 1998; Czarniawska 1998) interesting reflections come to the fore. Her day-to-day life is nevertheless highly active. For example, she sings in a choir, is doing voluntary work for the music festival that the town is known for, and she is deeply 'radio-active' as a vol-untary disc jockey every Friday night at the local radio station. More than anything, if one shifts the point of observation to culture governance, Eve is not at all the 'distorted' and 'pathological' citizen that she is portrayed as in the democratic regime's authoritative conception of civic engagement in liberal democracy. For Eve is not satisfied with enjoying some universal rights and abstract liberties. She wants to practise her political freedom, right where she is, on her own conditions. Furthermore, Eve considers it natural that her local public authorities will facilitate and support her efforts to help herself out of the mess she is in.

Eve was thrown out of her home in the nearby city of Aarhus and given three weeks to find a place to stay. She chose Skanderborg because it was cheaper to live in, but she knew that if she did not do something to find herself a job immediately the state would give her the dole for a only very short period of time, after which she would be placed in an arbitrary acti-vation programme for young unemployed:

I knew that Welfare was just a temporary thing – I mean, I just went down to the municipality and said that I simply had to have a job right away because I couldn't take running around with nothing to do for another week.

Hence Eve does indeed show trust in public authorities after all, at least if they appear in the role of the culture governance administrator, manager or professional. But rather than having a relation to authorities in abstract terms, she regards them very concretely as a local resource for self-development in her everyday life. At this level Eve feels neither disempowered nor lacking in efficacy. Fortunately for her, she has come to a hyper-modern municipality, where the transition from government to governance has been explicitly designed and carried out as a new strategic and public management for empowering, communicating and co-operating with civil society and citizens. It comes as no surprise, then, that she actually managed to get the municipality to give her a job with a social aspect in the community centre, which functions as a kind of 'warming centre' for 'weaker elements', while she pursues other job opportunities. She can accept to enter into relations of culture governance with other local actors, but only in so far as her involvement in culture governance is compatible with her everyday maker lifestyle.

In fact, Eve is living proof of the difference between pluralism and a kind of pluralisation, which, as Strong says, works 'to the effect that there is no single thing that I am, or rather than I am *in potentia* everything and everyone'. Eve simply *is* becoming the claim that whatever anyone is, has been and might be in her political community has to do with *her*, and not just with what public authorities (formal or informal) judge to be rational and reasonable. She shows the possibility of a way of being human and of acknowledging others as human in the life world which, beyond all its systematised differences, is simple, interactive and ethical (Certeau 1984, 1997).

## Everyday making as a critique of representation

The EU White Paper and Eve both identify a need for a renewal of representative politics. When Eve appears blank with regard to the functioning of party politics, it is not because she is the unknowing victim of a new populism which holds undemocratic values, emotionalises the public sphere, appeals to the beast in everybody – and all the other negative characteristics that are associated with the kind of distrust of politicians to which she subscribes. In the language of political correctness of both left and right discourses, the successes of the radical and extreme right are explained by its ability to exploit the situation by appealing to the most irrational and emotionally laden sections of the masses with their fundamentalist love of the nation and their common hate of foreigners and distrust of all expertise. No doubt the New Right may be accused of these things. But they do not tell the whole story of how the current distrust in party politics arises. As the case of Eve indicates, distrust is also generated

by the 'old' parties, precisely because they tend to dismiss lay critique, such
as that of Eve, as emotional, irrational, etc.

However, the practical self-reflexivity required for acting and finding
one's way about in an ever more dynamic, complex and differentiated
society is indeed remarkable. Between the domains of the rational and the
irrational, this book has argued, a rapidly expanding discursive field
appears where the ability to make and exercise a difference is highly appreciated. In this field the quest for self- and co-governance is probably the
main reason why people like Eve grow increasingly sceptical when it comes
to all-encompassing ideologies, unified bureaucracy and concerted elite rule.
A main problem is that representative institutions are not at all designed
to deal with a social world in which the capacity to 'make a difference' is
considered as intrinsic to democracy as are values and norms. They are
constructed to appeal to rational actors and to masses, not to 'ordinary'
reflexive individuals. Their *modus vivendi* is predominantly *for* the people
– elitist, bureaucratic, emancipatory, procedural and calculative – not *by*
and *with* the people, as reflexive individuals would demand it to be today.

If political parties could find time to listen to narratives like Eve's, and
even exercise some requisite irony, as Jessop suggests in chapter 6, they
would soon discover that there is more to the distrust and apathy in which
they are held than can be told in the logic of political correctness.

First of all, Eve's apparent lack of tolerance in effect carries a distinction
between mere toleration, giving people access to the democratic regime, and
deep toleration that rests on the reciprocal recognition of difference in a
democratic political community (Connolly 1999; Philips 1999):

> I've thought a lot about that, because I can't take Nazis and racists and that
> kind of thing, you know? I mean – real racists and neo-Nazis. But on the other
> hand everyone has the right to . . . I mean, there's freedom of speech; if you
> say that you can't express your opinion about black people because – what's
> it called? – then you don't respect other people, but that is also freedom of
> speech, right? . . . so for them it's also – for them you can say that there isn't
> freedom of speech if the blacks can't express themselves and their opinions
> without the Nazis coming after them, you know.

Although Eve would prefer it if the Hell's Angels could be made to dis-
appear from her life world, she certainly does not lack a sense of justice or
common responsibility. Her point is only that, although rights or liberties
are intrinsic to living a proper life in a political community, they do not in
and of themselves guarantee the free exercise of one's political freedoms:

> I'm also a little hypocritical, because I want to do the right thing, you know?
> I want to be reasonable and support freedom of speech for everyone, but I also
> have to admit that I think it's terrible that it damages society. It isn't healthy
> to hate someone that way, is it?

What really seems to be the 'problem' with Eve is that she feels, and does
also appear, as if she were being 'beamed down' from a foreign planet when
it comes to party politics:

when there's an election and that kind of thing, then the newspapers are totally full of what everyone is saying, and the one thing and the other, you know? And then I usually kind of sit and look over it all. That's probably what I did last year in the event that I should vote for a party, but I just don't think that there was a party that had all the stuff that I would like to see. There were some who kind of offered some of the stuff that I am interested in, but then there were other things that I absolutely wasn't interested in – that's why I cast a blank ballot.

Eve really wants to have a reflected opinion about party politics, but she cannot relate to the old interest politics and strategic games of parties, and she also lacks their collective memory of what security, order and economic growth might mean after two world wars and, in particular, the Holocaust. She takes her liberties for granted and instead demands more room for exercising her practice of freedom (Foucault 1994a, b). 'I think that my everyday life is too predictable. I hate predictability. I like it when something is going on all the time.'

However, although Eve is sceptical of representative democracy in its present form, she is not sceptical of being represented as such. Eve is like Nora portrayed in chapter 10: she does not oppose herself to another as long as it can be recognised as *her* other:

I mean, there are times when you want to be able to take care of things yourself. The way I look at it, I would prefer to be able to do everything myself, right? That's the way I would like it to be, and I would like to be the master of my own destiny, you know? But I often find that I can't quite take care of things on my own – everything I want to be able to do – then I just want someone to be able to do it for me. But there isn't. I can only do it myself. And that's why I sometimes wish that there was someone or another that would smile down on me and give me some more strength or come and figure things out for me. Because I can kind of become really stressed out if I can't stay on top of everything. I have so many balls in the air, which means that I can easily get pretty confused.

Eve does want to be represented, but by politicians who show tact and respect for the fact that, as she herself puts is, 'just because you don't become engaged with the country and the municipality and politics and everything else and you don't watch that much news on television – that doesn't just mean that you aren't thinking about anything'. The new political and public management, as discussed here, is explicitly aware of this and would do its utmost to empower and 'domesticate' Eve still further, so that she could become an active contributor to providing the system with the necessary degree of effectiveness, coherence and wholeness that it needs to 'go on' as a differentiated unity.

The question, however, is whether Eve would want to do so. She is in a way also the natural opponent of culture governance, because she loathes the ongoing 'mechanisation' and professionalisation of the political, the public and the everyday. Eve wants to be a 'glocal' citizen. Distinct from those on the extreme and radical right, Eve thinks in terms of a local and cosmopolitan politics and democracy (Taylor and Gutmann 1994), which she wants to see layered into national political institutions. As she says:

> I am just a Dane who happens to live in Denmark – I could just as easily have been Spanish and lived in Spain. That's kind of the way I look at it . . . It doesn't matter where I live. I mean, I think it's sometimes sad that some Danes have – I mean, those real archetypal Danes – it's kind of 'Yes, we are Danes, we represent this and that, and we can't have all of them in our country, and they destroy our morale and our values, and blah, blah, blah,' you know? I think that kind of thing is pathetic.

Eve is growing up in a globalised locality, where 'you meet many different kinds of styles, I mean styles in music and clothes and everything else, you know? And there are also more new religions and cultures that are "in" and then "out" the next day. Everything's changing all the time.' She has, for instance, drawn dots over her eyebrows as modelled after an oriental culture. But as she emphasises:

> I mean, everyone is so busy trying to find their own style and discovering a way of expressing themselves. This is my freedom of speech [she connects her 'dots'] with a fine culture – but it's not because I'm the supporter of that culture or religion or I'm trying to imitate people that way or trying to make fun of people. I just think it's lovely and complements my eyes, don't you?

Eve simply cannot identify with the nationalism and mistrust of foreigners which today characterises certain parties and segments of the population in the European Union. She likes to stick out, but not at the expense of others in her political community:

> No, I like the word 'community', but when it comes to my personality I love to share my personality in community – with the community. If I'm standing in a crowd of fifty people I like it if it's me you take note of. That's the way I like it. I can't always make it that way, but I mean – that's what I like. [Cf. Strong 1994]

When everyday makers like Eve are not heard by their politicians it may be because they do not subscribe to an 'old' left-wing philosophy according to which it is necessary to constantly provoke and exert opposition to 'the system'. They have an alternative 'ideology' which says:

> Do it yourself.
> Do it where you are.
> Do it *ad hoc* or part-time.
> Do it for a concrete reason.
> Do it alone or in joint action with others.
> Do it for fun but also because it is a worthy cause.
> Do it preferably together with other lay people but draw on experts if need be.

Everyday makers cannot make sense of the 'old' left-wing activist line of thinking, because they do not see the state as only an instrument of power or capital – the evil forces that are to be fought and kept at a distance at any price. Nor do they have anything against working closely together with public authorities concerning the solution of their daily life problems – *but* only as long as it contributes to their own practices of freedom. What everyday makers do in politics has to be experienced as fun and not just as a dour plight. Furthermore, they want to be able to jump on and off various projects and engagements, and not get the feeling that the co-operation is 'for life'.

Thus everyday makers are in a way the ideal subjects for the exercise of culture governance, because they have all the individual, co-operative and output-oriented traits that the system needs to function successfully. But at the same time everyday makers could also be the nightmare of culture governance, exactly because they want to pursue their own possibilities, exploit political and public spaces for their own 'small' tactical reasons, loathe being enveloped and nursed by 'professionals', etc. Actually, everyday makers share some of the same democratic deficiencies as culture governors. They both shy away from discussing normative contents, ideologies, broad welfare programmes, the public reason, etc., and all other such 'big issues' which have been hallmarks of representative democracy and the public sphere, and which have also been basic to protecting and expanding our rights and liberties. On the other hand, they also point out the weaknesses of representative government – its negative views of political power and freedom, its lack of a conception of politics and policy as communication, and, most of all, its tendency to forget that just as essential to democracy as are rights and liberties are the empowering and self-governance which are required for each and all to practise their freedom to make a difference.

## References

Andersen, J., and Ulrich, J. (2000), 'Men jeg er glad for at bo i Skanderborg', in H. P. Bang, A. D. Hansen and J. Hoff (eds), *Demokrati fra neden. Casestudier fra en dansk kommune* (Copenhagen: Jurist- &Økonomforbundets Forlag).

Andersen, J. G., Torpe, L., and Andersen, J. (2000), *Hvad folket magter* (Copenhagen: Jurist- & Økonomforbundets Forlag).

Andersen, N. Å., and Born, A. W. (2001), *Kærlighed og omstilling* (Copenhagen: Nyt fra Samfundsvidenskaberne).

Bang, H. P. (2000), 'Dansk republikanisme på en skillevej' in H. P. Bang, A. D. Hansen and J. Hoff (eds), *Demokrati fra neden. Casestudier fra en dansk kommune* (Copenhagen: Jurist- & Økonomforbundets Forlag).

Bang, H. P., and Dyrberg, T. B. (2001), 'Governance, self-representation and the democratic imagination', in M. Saward (ed.), *Democratic Innovations* (London: Routledge).

Bang, H. P., and Sørensen, E. (2001), 'The everyday maker: building political rather than social capital', in P. Dekker and E. M. Uslaner (eds), *Social Capital and Participation in Everyday Life* (London: Routledge), pp. 148–62.

Bang, H. P., Hansen, A. D., and Hoff, J., eds (2000), *Demokrati fra neden. Cases-tudier fra en dansk kommune* (Copenhagen: Jurist- & Økonomforbundets Forlag).

Barber, B. R. (1998), *A Place for Us: How to Make Society Civil and Democracy Strong* (New York: Hill & Wang).

Barker, J. (1999), *Street-level Democracy* (West Hartford CT: Kumarian Press).

Bartelson, J. (2001), *The Critique of the State* (Cambridge: Cambridge University Press).

Bauman, Z. (2001), *Community: Seeking Safety in an Insecure World* (Cambridge: Polity Press).

Behn, R. D. (2001), *Rethinking Democratic Accountability* (Washington DC: Brookings Institution).

Benhabib, S., ed. (1996), *Democracy and Difference* (Princeton NJ: Princeton University Press).

Bennett, W. L., and Entman, R. E. (2001), *Mediated Politics: Communication in the Future of Democracy* (Cambridge: Cambridge University Press).

Box, R. C. (1998), *Citizen Governance* (London: Sage).

Bruijn, H. de, and Heuvelhof, E. ten (2000), 'Process management', in O. van Heffen, W. J. M. Kickert and J. J. A. Thomassen (eds), *Governance in Modern Societies* (Dordrecht: Kluwer), pp. 313–28.

Connolly, W. E. (1999), *Why I am not a Secularist* (Minneapolis MN: University of Minnesota Press).

Currie, M. (1998), *Postmodern Narrative Theory* (London: Macmillan).

Czarniawska, B. (1998), *A Narrative Approach to Organization Studies* (London: Sage).

Certeau, M. de (1984), *The Practice of Everyday Life* (Berkeley CA: University of California Press).

Certeau, M. de (1997), *The Capture of Speech and other Political Writings* (Minneapolis MN: University of Minnesota Press).

Cobb, R., Rosee, J. K., and Ross, M. H. (1976), 'Agenda building as a comparative political process', *American Political Science Review* 70: 126–38.

Cohen, J. L., and Arato, A. (1994), *Civil Society and Political Theory* (Cambridge MA: MIT Press).

Dean, M. (1999), *Governmentality: Power and Rule in Modern Society* (London: Sage).

Dekker, P., and Uslaner, E. M., eds (2001), *Social Capital and Participation in Everyday Life* (London: Routledge).

Easton, D. (1965), *A Systems Analysis of Political Life* (New York: Wiley).

Esselbrugge, M. (2000), 'Interactive policy making as a serious alternative' in O. van Heffen, W. J. M. Kickert and J. J. A. Thomassen (eds), *Governance in Modern Societies* (Dordrecht: Kluwer), pp. 299–312.

Etzioni-Halevy, E. (1993), *The Elite Connection* (Cambridge: Polity Press).

European Commission (2001) *European Governance: A White Paper* (Brussels: Commission of the European Communities).

Foucault, M. (1994a), *Power*, ed. J. D. Faubion (New York: Free Press).

Foucault, M. (1994b), *Ethics*, ed. P. Rabinow (New York: Penguin Books).

Gandy, Oscar H., Jr (2001), 'Dividing practices', in W. L. Bennett and R. E. Entman (eds), *Mediated Politics: Communication in the Future of Democracy* (Cambridge: Cambridge University Press), pp. 141–81.

Geertz, C. (1983, 2000), *Local Knowledge* (New York: Basic Books).

Giddens, A. (1987), *Social Theory and Modern Sociology* (Cambridge: Polity Press).

Gunnell, J. G. (1998), *The Orders of Discourse: Philosophy, Social Science, and Politics* (Lanham MD: Rowman & Littlefield).

Habermas, J. (1982), 'A reply to my critics' in J. B. Thompson and D. Held (eds), *Habermas Critical Debates* (London: Macmillan), pp. 219–83.

Habermas, J. (1987), *The Philosophical Discourse of Modernity* (Cambridge: Polity Press).

Habermas, J. (1989), *The Theory of Communicative Action* II (Cambridge: Polity Press).

Habermas, J. (1996), *Between Facts and Norms* (Cambridge MA: MIT Press).

Heffen, O. van, Kickert, W. J. M., and Thomassen, J. J. A., eds (2000), *Governance in Modern Societies* (Dordrecht: Kluwer).

Held, D. (1987), *Models of Democracy* (Cambridge: Polity Press).

Held, D. (1996), *Models of Democracy*, 2nd edn (Cambridge: Polity Press).

Hirst, P. (1994), *Associative Democracy* (Cambridge: Polity Press).

Jervis, R. (1997), *System Effects: Complexity in Political and Social Life* (Princeton NJ: Princeton University Press).

Klijn, E.-H., and Koppenjan, J. F. M. (2000), 'Interactive decision making and representative democracy: institutional collisions and solutions', in O. van Heffen, W. J. M. Kickert and J. J. A. Thomassen (eds), *Governance in Modern Societies* (Dordrecht: Kluwer), pp. 109–33.

Klijn, E.-H., and Teisman, G. R. (2000), 'Managing public–private partnerships', in O. van Heffen, W. J. M. Kickert and J. J. A. Thomassen (eds), *Governance in Modern Societies* (Dordrecht: Kluwer), pp. 329–48.

Kooiman, J. (1999), 'Social-political governance: overview, reflections and design', *Public Management (Review)*, 1: 67–92.

Lane, J.-E., and Ersson, S. O. (1996), *European Politics* (London: Sage).

Luhmann, N. (1984/1995), *Social Systems* (Stanford CA: Stanford University Press).

March, J. G., and Olsen, J. P. (1995), *Democratic Governance* (New York: Free Press).

Marchington, M. (2001), 'Employee involvement at work', in John Shotter (ed.), *Cultural Politics of Everyday Life* (Buckingham: Open University Press), pp. 232–53.

Mingers, J. (1995), *Self-producing Systems* (New York: Plenum Press).

Mulhall, S., and Cavell, S. (1994), *Philosophy's Recounting of the Ordinary* (Oxford: Oxford University Press), pp. 258–82.

Pharr, S. J., and Putnam, R. D. (2000), *Disaffected Democracies* (Princeton NJ: Princeton University Press).

Philips, A. (1999), *Which Equalities Matter?* (Cambridge: Polity Press).

Pierre, J., and Peters, B. G. (2000), *Governance, Politics and the State* (London: Sage).

Pierre, J., ed. (2000), *Debating Governance: Authority, Steering and Democracy* (Oxford: Oxford University Press).

Putnam, R. D. (1993), *Making Democracy Work* (Princeton NJ: Princeton University Press).

Salaman, G. (2001), 'The management of corporate culture change', in J. Storey (ed.), *Human Resource management: A Critical Text* (London: Thomson), pp. 190–206.

Saward, M., ed. (2001), *Democratic Innovations* (London: Routledge).

Scharpf, F. W. (1999), *Governing in Europe: Effective and Democratic?* (Oxford: Oxford University Press).

Shawn, S. (2001), *Public Dialogue and Participatory Democracy* (New York: Hampton Press).

Shotter, J. (1993), *Cultural Politics of Everyday Life* (Buckingham: Open University Press).

Storey, J., ed. (2001), *Human Resource Management: A Critical Text* (London: Thomson).

Strong, T. B. (1994), *Jean-Jacques Rouseau: The Politics of the Ordinary* (London: Sage).

Taylor, C., and Gutmann, A., eds (1994), *Multiculturalism* (Princeton NJ: Princeton University Press).

Thompson, J. B., and Held, D. (1982), *Habermas: Critical Debates* (London: Macmillan).

Wollebæk, D., Selle, P., and Lorentzen, H. (2000), *Frivillig innsats* (Bergen: Fakbokforlaget).

# Index